MILITARY VETERAN PSYCHOLOGICAL HEALTH AND SOCIAL CARE

When servicewomen and men leave the Armed Forces, their care transfers to the statutory and third sector where the quality and provision of services can vary enormously. This edited book, encompassing a range of perspectives, from service user to professional, provides a comprehensive overview of services available. Each chapter, in turn, examines the policy underpinnings of systems and services covering the psychological health and social care of military veterans and then focuses on the needs of a discrete number of types of military veterans. These include early service leavers, veterans in the criminal justice system and older veterans and reservists, together with the needs of the children of veterans' families.

This is the first UK book to examine the whole spectrum of contemporary approaches to the psychological health and social care of military veterans both in the United Kingdom and overseas. The book is edited by Professor Jamie Hacker Hughes, a former head of healthcare psychology within the UK Ministry of Defence and all contributors are experts in policy, service provision and academic research in this area. It will be of special interest to those designing and planning, commissioning, managing and delivering mental health and social care to military veterans and their families.

Jamie Hacker Hughes is Visiting Professor and The Founder Director of the Veterans and Families Institute at Anglia Ruskin University, past President of the British Psychological Society and former head of the Ministry of Defence's healthcare psychology services. A clinical psychologist, neuropsychologist and psychotraumatologist, Jamie was the author, with Mark Neville, of *Battle Against Stigma* and before his career in psychology, Jamie was a Short Service Army Officer.

MILITARY VETERAN PSYCHOLOGICAL HEALTH AND SOCIAL CARE

Contemporary Issues

Edited by Jamie Hacker Hughes

Routledge
Taylor & Francis Group

LONDON AND NEW YORK

First published 2017
by Routledge
2 Park Square, Milton Park, Abingdon, Oxon OX14 4RN

and by Routledge
711 Third Avenue, New York, NY 10017

Routledge is an imprint of the Taylor & Francis Group, an informa business

British Library Cataloguing in Publication Data
A catalogue record for this book is available from the British Library

Library of Congress Cataloging in Publication Data
Names: Hacker Hughes, Jamie, editor.
Title: Military and veteran psychological health and social care: contemporary approaches / [edited by] Jamie Hacker Hughes.
Description: Abingdon, Oxon; New York, NY: Routledge, 2017. |
Includes bibliographical references.
Identifiers: LCCN 2016050974 | ISBN 9781138949485 (hardback) |
ISBN 9781138949492 (pbk.) | ISBN 9781315195117 (e-book)
Subjects: | MESH: Mental Health Services | Veterans Health |
Veterans–psychology | Health Policy | Great Britain
Classification: LCC RC455.4.E8 | NLM WA 305 FA1 |
DDC 362.196/89008697–dc23
LC record available at https://lccn.loc.gov/2016050974

ISBN: 978-1-138-94948-5 (hbk)
ISBN: 978-1-138-94949-2 (pbk)
ISBN: 978-1-315-19511-7 (ebk)

Typeset in Bembo
by Deanta Global Publishing Services, Chennai, India

Printed in the United Kingdom
by Henry Ling Limited

To all British ex-military personnel and veterans and their families, and to all those working with them.

CONTENTS

FIGURES

TABLES

PREFACE

The United Kingdom's veteran or ex-Service community, including dependents, is currently some 6 million strong, derived from a current military establishment of approximately 160,000 personnel, with some additional 35,000 reserves and an annual 'churn' (those joining or leaving) of around 10,000. It is a very diverse community, which, in the main, is ageing and shrinking year by year. Thus, while the current ex-Service community forms just under 10 per cent of the UK population, just 10 years ago the community was nearly twice that size and comprised over 15 per cent of the population. Similarly, whereas in 2005 30 per cent of the military veteran community were aged 65 to 74, in 2014 35 per cent were aged between 75 and 84 and now 40 per cent are aged over 75. At one end of the spectrum, there are no longer any World War I veterans left alive and the bulk of the veteran population is now made up of World War II and Northern Ireland veterans. At the other end of the spectrum, it is possible to be termed as a veteran after only one day's service, so many of our military veterans are young women and men who have not even finished their basic and military training, let alone deployed into conflict zones.

Many military veterans or ex-military personnel go on to do well in 'civvy street', making a good 'transition' and many going on to gain and hold down employment in a civilian world. Others are less fortunate. Some cannot find jobs, some become unemployed and some suffer physical and psychological problems related to their service. Some have difficulties with alcohol and drugs of addiction and some become involved with the criminal justice system.

This book is about all of these military veterans and ex-Service personnel, with a focus on their psychological health and social care. We look at government policy surrounding military veterans and their needs and then, in the remainder of Part 1, consider the psychological and social needs of various groupings of military veterans and ex-military personnel: early service leavers, military veterans in the criminal justice systems and older veterans and reservists, together with the children of veterans' families.

In Part 2, we look at a variety of models of service for providing for these psychological and social care needs, one from England, one from Wales, one from Scotland and an example of a national third sector service, together with services provided to military veterans abroad, in Australia, Canada, the Netherlands and the United States.

Overall, the book provides a comprehensive overview of the character, makeup and needs of British military veterans and ex-Service personnel today, together with their families and of the variety of models of service provision that have evolved to meet those needs, both in the United Kingdom and overseas.

It is hoped that the reader of this book, veteran, staff member, manager, director, trustee, commissioner, politician or policy maker, researcher or academic, may find material here which informs their studies and research, their decision making and their appreciation and understanding of this unique and complex group of the population to whom we refer as the ex-military, ex-Service or military veteran community.

Jamie Hacker Hughes
London, September 2016

ABBREVIATIONS

ADF	Australian Defence Force
AFC	Armed Forces Covenant
AMHP	Approved Mental Health Practitioner
ASAP	Armed Services Advice Project
BPS	British Psychological Society
BWW	Big White Wall (An online early intervention, peer support, wellbeing and counselling service)
CAB	Citizens Advice Bureau(x)
CBUK	Child Bereavement, UK
CCG	Clinical Commissioning Group(s)
CEAS	Children's Education and Advisory Service
CJS	Criminal Justice System
COBSEO	Confederation of Service Charities
CBT	Cognitive Behavioural Therapy
CQC	Care Quality Commission
CS	Combat Stress
CTP	Career Transition Partnership
CYP	Children and Young People
DAOR	Discharge as of Right
DASA	Defence Analytical Services and Advice
DCMH	Department(s) of Community Mental Health
DCSF	Department of Children, School and Families
DCYP	Department of Children and Young People
DfE	Department for Education
DMRC	Defence Medical Rehabilitation Centre (Headley Court)
DNA	Did Not Attend
DSM	Diagnostic and Statistical Manual

DWP	Department for Work and Pensions
EMDR	Eye Movement Desensitisation and Reprocessing
ESL/s	Early Service Leaver/s
FF	Fighting Fit
FHP	Future Horizons Programme
FiMT	Forces in Mind Trust
GHQ	General Health Questionnaire
GP	General Practitioner
GVMAP	Gulf Veterans Medical Assessment Programme
HCDC	House of Commons Defence Committee
HIT	High Intensity Therapist(s)
HM	Her Majesty('s)
HMP	Her Majesty's Prisons
HMSO	Her Majesty's Stationery Office
IAPT	Improving Access to Psychological Therapies
ICP	Integrated Care Pathway
IED	Improvised Explosive Device
IPS	Individual Placement Support
ITP	Intensive Treatment Programme
JSA	Job Seeker's Allowance
JSP	Joint Service Publication
KCL	King's College, London
KCMHR	King's Centre for Military Health Research
L&D	Liaison and Diversion
LHB	Local Health Board
LIBOR	London Interbank Offered Rate
MAP	Medical Assessment Programme
MCEC	Military Child Education Coalition
MCTC	Military Corrective Training Centre
MD	Doctor of Medicine
MDS	Minimum Data Set
MDHU	Ministry of Defence Hospital Unit(s)
MFRCs	Military and Veteran Family Resource Centres
MHAC	Mental Health Act Commission
MHT	Mental Health Trust(s)
MoD/MOD	Ministry of Defence
MoJ	Ministry of Justice
MP	Member of Parliament/Military Police
MVS	Military Veterans Service
NAPO	National Association of Probation Officers
NATO	North Atlantic Treaty Organisation
NICE	National Institute for Clinical and Health Excellence
NHS	National Health Service
NOMS	National Offender Management Service

OASYS	Offender Assessment System
OMCCS	Offender Management Community Cohort
OMNHE	Operational Mental Health Needs Evaluations
ONS	Office of National Statistics
OP	Observation Post
OP-HERRICK	The deployment to Afghanistan 2001 onwards
OP-TELIC	The deployment to Iraq 2003 onwards
PAC	Parent Adult Child Ego States
PC	Principal Clinician
PCFT	Pennine Care NHS Foundation Trust
PIR	Prison in Reach
PRU	Personnel Recovery Unit
PSSU	Personal Social Service Research Unit
PTSD	Post-Traumatic Stress Disorder
PTSS	Post-Traumatic Stress Symptoms
PWP	Psychological Wellbeing Practitioner
QC	Queen's Counsel
RBL	Royal British Legion
RCT	Randomised Controlled Trials
RFEA	Regular Forces Employment Association
RBLI	Royal British Legion Industries
RMN	Registered Mental Nurse
SAMH	Scottish Association for Mental Health
SCAN	Second Career Assistance Network
SCE	Service Children's Education
SHA	Strategic Health Authority
SIBAM	Sensation, Image, Behaviour, Affect, Meaning
SL/s	Service Leaver/s
SMS	Short Message Service
SPVA	Service Personnel and Veterans Agency
SSAFA	Sailors', Soldiers' and Airman's Families Association
SVR	Scottish Veterans Residencies
TA	Territorial Army/Transactional Analysis
TCK	Third Culture Kids
TRiM	Trauma Risk Management
UHB	University Health Board
UK	United Kingdom
US	United States
VA	Department of Veterans Affairs
VFI	Veterans and Families Institute (VFI)
VICS	Veterans in Custody Support
VIP	Veterans in Prison
VNHSW	Veterans' NHS Wales
VRMHP	Veterans and Reserves Mental Health Programme

VSO   Veterans Support Officer
VT   Veterans Therapist
VVCS   Veterans and Veterans' Families Counselling Service
WHO   World Health Organisation
WIS   Wounded, Injured and Sick
WWI   World War One
WWII   World War Two

CONTRIBUTORS

Dr Lucy Abraham, MA, DClinPsychol, is Consultant Clinical Psychologist and the Veterans F1rst Point Scotland Lead. Dr Abraham joined Veterans F1rst Point (Lothian) as Service Lead in 2011. In 2013, she was appointed clinical lead for Veterans F1rst Point Scotland and awarded 'Civilian of the Year' for her contribution to veteran healthcare. She works with veterans who suffer from a wide range of mental health conditions and is trained in the use of various treatment approaches including cognitive behavioural therapy, cognitive analytic therapy, compassionate mind training and eye movement desensitisation and reprocessing therapy. She holds an MA in Psychology (Aberdeen), a doctorate in Clinical Psychology (Edinburgh) and a postgraduate diploma in Cognitive Analytic Therapy (Sheffield Hallam).

Dr Alice Aiken, PhD, Dean of the Faculty of Health Professions at Dalhousie University, Canada, is a Canadian Armed Forces Veteran who served for 14 years in the Royal Canadian Navy. She was the co-founder and Scientific Director of the Canadian Institute for Military and Veteran Health Research (CIMVHR) comprised of more than 35 universities and 550 researchers.

Charlie Allanson-Oddy, MSc, Consultant Psychological Therapist and Service Lead Veterans F1rst Point Lothian, has been the Service lead at Veterans F1rst Point Lothian since June 2014 and was previously at The Rivers Centre for Traumatic Stress. He studied cognitive behavioural psychotherapy to Masters level at Dundee University and is particularly interested in the treatment of psychological trauma.

Andy Bacon, BA (Hons) psc, leads the central team at NHS England with responsibility for the Armed Forces. He has been a senior health leader for over 20 years in England and overseas. He has worked in the public and the charitable/not for profit sectors. He served for over ten years as an infantry officer and holds several voluntary non-executive posts concerned with the Armed Forces and international health in low income countries.

Dr Jeya Balakrishna, MBBS, FRCPsych, LLM, is a Consultant Psychiatrist in Defence Primary Healthcare in the UK Ministry of Defence and an Honorary Consultant Forensic Psychiatrist with the mental welfare charity, Combat Stress. He is national clinical lead for the Veterans and Reserves Mental Health Programme. He was an infantry medical officer in Singapore before his psychiatric training in London. His career in forensic and adult services spans public, independent and voluntary sectors. His experience in psychological trauma includes helping refugees and emergency services personnel at the Institute of Psychotrauma, St Bart's Hospital, London, victims of domestic violence in south England and detainees in Immigration Removal Centres.

Dr Alan Barrett, BSc (Hons), MSc, ClinPsyD, CPsychol, AFBPsS, is a Clinical Psychologist and is the Clinical Lead for the North West based Military Veterans Service. As an active member of the North West Armed Forces Network, Alan additionally represents the region in national forums and is a member of the National Armed Forces Clinical Reference Sub-Group for Mental Health at NHS England. Alan is also a visiting lecturer to several universities in the region in addition to remaining a clinical and professional advisor to the CQC. With 20 years of clinical experience, Alan has supported numerous individuals in their journeys towards recovery.

Dr Karen Burnell, BSc (Hons), MSc, PhD, MBPsS, CPsychol, read Psychology at the University of Southampton and was then awarded a 1+3 ESRC postgraduate award to complete an MSc Research Methods in Psychology. Her PhD, completed in 2007, concerned the reconciliation of traumatic war memories throughout the adult lifespan. Karen joined University College London in 2008 and the University of Portsmouth in 2011. Karen's research focuses on the impact of war experience of formerly serving military personnel throughout the lifespan.

Dr Walter Busuttil, MBChB MPhil MRCGP FRCPsych, is a Consultant Psychiatrist and Director of Medical Services at the veterans' charity, Combat Stress. He qualified in Medicine in Manchester in 1983, joining the RAF as a medical student cadet. Serving for 16 years, he qualified first as a general practitioner and then as consultant psychiatrist. He was in the team that rehabilitated the British Beirut hostages and was instrumental in setting up rehabilitation services for Gulf War I combatants suffering from PTSD. On retirement from the RAF in 1997, he set up tertiary general adult and forensic psychiatric services for adult survivors of sexual abuse suffering from Complex PTSD. He was appointed Director of Medical Services to Combat Stress in 2007 and has led the development of clinical services including residential programmes, outreach and community, expanding clinical capability nationally and attaining National Specialist Commissioning for an

Intensive Treatment Programme in 2011. He is active in the media, campaigning and encouraging statutory NHS services to be set up for veterans' mental health. He has published and lectured internationally about rehabilitation of chronic and complex presentations of PTSD.

Dr Nick Caddick, BSc (Hons), MSc, PhD, is a research fellow in the Veterans and Families Institute at Anglia Ruskin University. He was awarded his PhD from Loughborough University in 2014. Nick's research explores several interrelated topics including mental health, employment, transition and social issues with regard to veterans and their families.

Dr Carl Castro, BA, MA, PhD, has been an Assistant Professor and Director of the Center for Innovation and Research on Veterans & Military Families, University of Southern California, since 2013, after serving 33 years in the US Army, where he obtained the rank of Colonel and served in a variety of research and leadership positions, including as director of the Military Operational Medicine Research Program, Headquarters, US Army Medical Research and Materiel Command, Fort Detrick, Maryland. Castro has completed two tours in Iraq, as well as peacekeeping missions to Saudi Arabia, Bosnia and Kosovo. He is currently chair of a NATO research group on military veteran transitions, a Fulbright Scholar and member of several Department of Defense research advisory panels focused on psychological health. He is the current editor of *Military Behavioral Health*, the flagship academic journal about the biopsychosocial health and wellbeing of service members, veterans and military families. Castro has authored more than 150 scientific articles and reports in numerous research areas. His current research efforts focus on assessing the effects of combat and operations tempo (OPTEMPO) on soldier, family and unit readiness and evaluating the process of service members' transitions from military to civilian life.

Dr John Crossland, DSW, MA, PGDip, PGCert, BA (Hons), Cert Rehab, FHEA, worked in both front line and management positions in several local authority adult social care departments for over two decades, before moving into an academic role whilst completing his professional doctorate in social work (DSW). John's professional and research interests focus on older people, sensory impairment, comparative adult social care policy and how the specific health and social care needs of older people who identify as lesbian, gay or bisexual are being addressed.

Dr Jacco Duel, PhD, is a senior researcher at the Netherlands Veterans Institute. He served in the Royal Netherlands Army from 1981 until 2013 and ended his military career as a Lieutenant-Colonel. During the last period of his career, he was a military psychologist studying the morale of troops on missions and the wellbeing of military personnel after deployment. His current research focuses on the effects of deployments for veterans from a life-course perspective. He obtained his PhD on teamwork in the military from Tilburg University in 2010.

Martin Elands, MA, is a military historian. In the years 1992 to 2000 he worked for the military history branch of the Netherlands Armed Forces and published about Dutch military experiences during the Korean War, the War of Indonesian Decolonisation and Peace Missions. In 2000, he joined the Netherlands Veterans Institute as a senior researcher, focusing on veterans' issues, veterans policy, public opinion and oral history. Currently, Martin Elands is Head of the Centre of Research and Expertise of the Veterans Institute.

Matt Fossey, BSc (Hons), MSocSc, DipSW, DipMHStud, FRSA, is the director of the Veterans and Families Institute at Anglia Ruskin University. He originally trained as a mental health social worker and his career has taken him through practice to developing national policy at the Department of Health. He has a specific interest in the development of evidence-based services for groups marginalised by society. Matt has written and published widely on issues relating to the health and social care needs of veterans and their families.

Dr Lauren Godier, BSc (Hons), MSc, DPhil (Oxon), is a postdoctoral research assistant at the Veterans and Families Institute at Anglia Ruskin University. Lauren was awarded a DPhil in Psychiatry from the University of Oxford in 2015. Her research interests centre on using translational research to inform the development of strategies promoting mental health and wellbeing.

Professor Neil Greenberg, BM, BSc, MMedSc, FHEA, MFMLM, DOccMed, MInstLM, MEWI, MFFLM, MD, FRCPsych, is an academic psychiatrist and served in the United Kingdom Armed Forces for more than 23 years. He has deployed, as a psychiatrist and researcher, to a number of hostile environments including Afghanistan and Iraq. At King's College London, Neil is one of the senior members of the military mental health research team. He is the President of the UK Psychological Trauma Society and the Royal College of Psychiatrists' Lead for Military and Veterans Health.

Professor Jamie Hacker Hughes, BSc (Hons), DipClinPsychol, MPhil (Cantab), MSc, PsychD, CPsychol, CSci, FBPsS, FRSM, FAcSS, is a clinical psychologist, clinical neuropsychologist, psychotherapist and academic who has worked in the field of psychological trauma throughout his career. After serving as a Short Service Army Officer and several years in business, Jamie retrained as a psychologist and went on to become senior clinical lecturer at King's College London, Head of Defence Clinical Psychology and Defence Consultant Advisor to the Surgeon General and later co-founded the Veterans and Families Institute and Veterans Research Hub at Anglia Ruskin University. He is the immediate Past President of the British Psychological Society and its current Vice President.

Dr Stephanie Hodson, CSC, PhD, BPsych (Hons) MAPS, is the National Manager of the Veteran and Veteran Families Counselling Service in Australia. She served for 21 years in the Australian Army as a psychologist, is currently a reserve Colonel and has extensive experience working with serving and ex-serving military personnel and their families both in Australia and on operational deployment. She completed her doctoral studies investigating the mental health impact of deployment to Rwanda and was awarded the Conspicuous Service Cross for the work she did supporting Australian military personnel in operations.

Dr Neil Kitchiner, RMN, ENB 650, BA (Hons), MSc, PhD, is employed by Cardiff and Vale University Health Board as the Principal Clinician of the Veterans' NHS Wales service. He was a Captain in the Army Reserve with 203 (Welsh) Field Hospital, between 2011 and 2014 where he deployed to Afghanistan from October 2013 to January 2014, as part of a MOD two-person Field Mental Health Team, delivering a peripatetic mental health service to UK service personnel.

Helen Lambert, BA (Hons), MA, is the Military Veterans' Service Coordinator. She is an experienced public sector manager whose career has spanned Local Authority, Audit Commission and the NHS in both commissioning and provider roles. Her particular expertise is in partnership working across a range of sectors with the aim of providing effective services to those most in need of them.

Claire Maguire, BA (Hons), MSc, DipPsych CPsychol, is a Consultant Clinical Psychologist and Psychodynamic Psychotherapist and is the Clinical and Professional lead for Psychological Therapies at Pennine Care NHS Foundation Trust. She has worked in a number of commissioning roles including acting as a Clinical Advisor to the CCG on veterans' issues. Between 2013 and 2015, Claire was the Chair of the North West Armed Forces Network. She was involved in the National development of the Improving Access to Psychological Therapies (IAPT) programme for Children and Young People, and is also a member of the local regional Clinical Senate Council.

Dr Deirdre MacManus, BSc(Hons), MB, ChB, MRCPsych, MSc, PhD, is a Consultant Forensic Psychiatrist in a London prison as well as clinical lead for the London Veteran Service, which provides community mental healthcare for veterans in the Greater London area including a specialist veterans' prison in-reach service. She is also a Senior Clinical Lecturer at King's College London and has carried out research into mental health and offending behaviour among military personnel.

Mrs Joy O'Neill, FRSA, FHEA, MSc Oxon, PGCE London, PGCHE London, Adv Dip Ed SEN, BSc, BA, BA EY, is an educator, researcher, author and National Governance Leader with over 14 years' experience. She is also wife of a veteran and has experienced first-hand bringing up children while moving around the UK and overseas. Joy is Head of Education for a national charity with a focus on disadvantaged children and young people. Her current research focuses on early intervention strategies.

Dave Rutter led the Department of Health Armed Forces and Veterans Team for ten years to the end of 2016. During this time, he was responsible for developing policies and commissioning services for veterans with physical and mental health issues resulting from their time in the Armed Forces. He also brought together working partnerships across this whole sector ensuring that MoD, NHS, service charities and others were able to work in a more co-ordinated way, making best use of all resources available. Dave is a career civil servant with a wide range of experience across government over the past 38 years.

Lieutenant-Colonel Dr C. van den Berg, PhD, joined the Royal Netherlands Army in 1983. Since 1994, he has worked as a military psychologist in a wide range of functions, such as teaching cadets and officers, behavioural sciences research and advice. His work has concerned, among other themes, leadership, stress, psychological support, military ethics and intercultural communication and negotiation. Currently, Lieutenant-Colonel Van den Berg is a staff officer for the Inspector General of the Netherlands Armed Forces. He obtained his PhD on the effect of real threat on soldiers' perceptions, attitudes and morale from Radboud University Nijmegen in 2009.

Nick Wood, FHEA, served in the Royal Navy and is the Education and Development Lead (Military Culture and Transition) delivering the 'Understanding Military Culture and Transition' continuing professional development to health and social care professionals. He has recently introduced Military Culture into student lectures to reflect the Armed Forces Covenant's inclusion into the NHS Constitution Handbook. Nick created the Veterans in Custody support model for National Offender Management Services and is a member of the COBSEO Veterans in the CJS cluster and SSAFA Prison in Reach focus groups. Nick is currently studying MSc Global Veterans and Families Studies at Anglia Ruskin University.

PART I

The British Veteran

1

INTRODUCTION

*Walter Busuttil, Jamie Hacker Hughes
and Neil Kitchiner*

The British military in the twentieth century

Following the Second World War, the North Atlantic Treaty Organisation (NATO) was formed in 1949, with its remit of collective defence in response to an attack by an outside aggressor (Isby and Kamps, 1985). Britain and its military capability has been involved in various NATO missions including defending its territories from attack, peace-keeping duties and, more recently, as a member of the multi-national coalition forces in Iraq (NATO Training Assistance Implementation Mission) and Afghanistan (International Security Assistance Force).

It could be argued that Britain has been at peace since the end of the Second World War in 1945, yet between then and the time of writing, only in 1968 has a serviceman or woman not been killed in action somewhere in the world (Higham, 1972). Serving in the Armed Forces was a common occurrence for men of conscription age, particularly following the end of the Second World War in 1945, despite compulsory National Service ending briefly. In 1947, National Service was re-imposed by the UK Government in an attempt to boost Armed Forces numbers. National Service had a duration of 18 months initially but this was later extended to 2 years. This policy finally ceased in 1960, with the last National Serviceman demobilised in May 1963 (Ruhl, 2003).

On 1 November 2011, the manning levels for the whole of the three British armed services were officially set at 176,680 (the actual number in post was 173,830) providing a deficit of 2,850 individuals (Ministry of Defence, 2010). These numbers represented a dramatic decline in the number of individuals exposed to a period of military service since the end of National Service. This, in turn, has resulted in the vast majority of the UK population having no experience of serving in the military.

Current aims and strategic objectives of the MOD

The following will briefly describe the role, function and current focus of the Ministry of Defence (MOD) in its deployment of equipment and personnel.

Defence aim

The defence aim is 'to deliver security to people in the UK and the Overseas Territories by defending them, including against terrorism; and to act as a force for good strengthening international peace and stability'.

This ambitious aim is a challenge to deliver in a world in which security threats are less ambiguous and more rapidly changing than in previous decades. To achieve this aim requires the Armed Forces to be able to undertake expeditionary operations around the world, in a flexible and operationally agile manner (Ministry of Defence, 2011). In 2009 to 2010, defence was estimated to be the fourth highest area of government expenditure behind education, health, work and pensions. In addition, Britain was the fourth highest-spending country on military expenditure in the world, spending 58.3 billion US dollars (Ministry of Defence, 2010).

Life in the modern British Armed Forces

Choosing to follow a career in the Armed Forces has many positive and negative aspects. For instance, many recruits join as young adults when they are beginning to shape their own values, beliefs and attitudes about themselves, the world and others. The Armed Forces' powerful culture laden with its own values and standards socialises these young adults, leading them to adopt military values and ideals as their own, which they may well carry with them for the rest of their lives (SAMH, 2009).

Military life has been described as a great leveller (Humber Foundation NHS Trust, 2010), particularly for those from disadvantaged backgrounds, often allowing them to enjoy a more productive and fulfilling life. Many service personnel and veterans develop close relationships and bonds with colleagues, in order that they can rely on each other in times of crisis. Military basic training also promotes strict conformity to high standards of behaviour, in terms of discipline, punctuality, orderliness, cleanliness and obedience. Other social and economic reasons for joining the Armed Forces include personal improvement through learning new skills. This may include a trade, for example, electrical engineering, with job security and full-time employment. It also allows for extensive travel opportunities to experience life in different parts of the world and the opportunity to do something different with their life (SAMH, 2009).

There is, however, a downside to the military lifestyle which brings with it many unique concerns challenges and pitfalls. Major issues include the adjustment to an often highly mobile lifestyle in foreign lands where there may be considerable differences in language and culture, as well as isolation from the civilian community and extended family support. In addition, there is likely to be adjustment to military rules, regulations and frequent family separations. Other factors may compound these stressors such as the difficulties experienced by the spouses or partners and children of service personnel. Spouses may have difficulty gaining employment in the area local to the military placement. They may also be responsible for bringing up children single handed for extended periods during deployments as well as managing the varied household duties (Black, 1993).

The British Government in a recent cross-party agreement entitled 'The Nation's Commitment to the Armed Forces Community', aimed to stop any disadvantage that being in the Armed Forces might bring to serving personnel and their families (HMSO, 2008). For instance, service personnel have often complained about barriers to obtaining services and facilities that most people take for granted, such as obtaining a mortgage, opening a bank account, finding a dentist, accessing benefits, applying for social housing or applying for residency or citizenship for themselves or their dependents.

These issues have now been highlighted and policies are being developed to minimise the likelihood of future disadvantage for service personnel (Ministry of Defence, 2010) with a pledge from the previous British Prime Minister, David Cameron, that the mutual obligations between the nation and its Armed Forces, named the military covenant, will be enshrined in UK law (Ministry of Defence, 2010).

Who makes up the military?

There is a lack of demographic data and official statistics to definitively describe where recruits to the Armed Forces hail from originally, although many army regiments have historically recruited more often from specific regions. These are often situated within areas of economic and social deprivation such as the north east of England and Scotland, as well as the larger UK cities, Northern Ireland and the South Wales Valleys. The Armed Forces offer potential recruits many prospects such as a large variety of highly to semi-skilled trades and the opportunity of foreign travel that may not have been available to them if they were to remain in their local communities (Fossey, 2010).

Childhood factors and early adversity

In general, the Armed Forces recruits individuals who are young and physically fit and from a wide variety of backgrounds, regardless of marital status, race, ethnic origin, religious belief or sexual orientation (Ministry of Defence, 2009). Individuals with poor health are largely excluded from joining the Armed Forces following a comprehensive medical assessment, meaning serving personnel are on the whole physically healthier than the rest of the population. At present, there are no policies and practices in place to detect potentially vulnerable individuals who may develop mental health problems in the future, although this may change following further research into its effectiveness.

There is a commonly held view that some new recruits to the Armed Forces, particularly the army, may come from dysfunctional family backgrounds and/or poor employment opportunities, and use the Armed Forces as a means of escape from such social environments (Johnstone, 1978). Weich et al.'s (2009) systematic review of family relationships in childhood and their association with anxiety and depressive disorders in adult life, demonstrated that abusive relationships predicted these disorders and post-traumatic stress disorder (PTSD). Maternal emotional unavailability in early life also predicted suicide attempts in adolescence.

Woodhead et al. (2011) compared the health outcomes and treatment seeking of 257 post-National Service veterans aged 16 to 64 years and 504 matched non-veterans living in the community in England. Male veterans reported more childhood adversity and were more likely to have experienced a major trauma in adulthood than non-veterans. Those veterans who had left service early (less than four years' service) were more likely to be heavy drinkers, experience suicidal thoughts and to have self-harmed than longer serving veterans.

A recent UK study of 4,762 (61 per cent) randomly selected Armed Forces personnel who had been deployed to Iraq since 2003, investigated the relative contribution of demographic variables (including: the nature of exposure to traumatic events during deployment; appraisal of these experiences; homecoming experiences; and childhood adversity) in relation to the prevalence of PTSD. The presence of PTSD symptoms was associated with lower rank, being unmarried, lower educational attainment and a history of childhood adversity (Iversen et al., 2008).

Data from a US Marines cohort of 8,391 individuals, who completed a survey during initial training, identified several risk factors for the subsequent development of PTSD, including adverse childhood experiences prior to being deployed to either Iraq or Afghanistan 2001–2004. A review of patient medical records several years later highlighted that that those who reported physical neglect in childhood were more likely to be diagnosed with post-deployment PTSD (Leardmann et al., 2010).

Iversen et al. (2007) examined the association between self-reported childhood vulnerability and later health outcomes in a large randomly selected British male military cohort. Data was collected from the first stage of an ongoing cohort study comparing Iraq veterans and non-deployed British military personnel. Male regular Armed Forces participants (n = 7,937) completed a detailed questionnaire. The results highlighted pre-enlistment vulnerability was associated with being in the army, a low educational achievement, coming from the lower ranks and being unmarried. Pre-enlistment vulnerability such as a 'family relationships' factor reflecting the home environment and an 'externalising behaviour' factor reflecting behavioural disturbance, was associated with a variety of negative health outcomes (Iversen et al., 2007).

Brewin et al. (2012) compared a cross-sectional sample of UK veterans; 43 had developed PTSD after discharge from service, 35 controls were receiving war pensions for a physical disorder and 48 had developed PTSD in service. The delayed

PTSD group described significantly more disciplinary offences, including absence without leave, disobedience and dishonesty compared with the no-PTSD group; these differences were present before any exposure to trauma. These data supports the link for externalising disorder and vulnerability to PTSD.

A study by Andrews *et al.* (2009) compared 142 British veterans (from the same cohort as Brewin) awarded a war pension for either PTSD or physical disability. The aim was to investigate who developed immediate-onset versus delayed-onset PTSD compared with those with no PTSD. Veterans with PTSD were similar with regard to the number and type of symptoms reported at onset. The delayed PTSD group described a gradual accumulation of symptoms that started early in their military career and continued throughout. They were more likely to report major depressive disorder and alcohol abuse prior to PTSD onset and to have experienced a severe life stressor in the year before onset. The authors suggest that delayed onset involves more general stress sensitivity and a progressive failure to adapt to continued stress.

In summary, these studies appear to support the claim that early dysfunctional relationships and childhood adversity are associated with mental health problems in civilians and veterans post exposure to a combat theatre. Although the link is likely to be multi-factorial, there is now evidence that some veterans enter the military service with pre-existing vulnerability factors, which are displayed in various disciplinary offences pre-exposure to traumatic events. These data may be useful for the Armed Forces and NHS veteran services to consider when designing appropriate detection and treatment pathways (Kitchiner and Bisson, 2015).

Military service: Health and wellbeing

The potential adverse impact of active military service on health and wellbeing has long been recognised with physical and psychological symptoms being commonly reported by veterans (Jones *et al.*, 2002). Concerns regarding impaired health and wellbeing amongst veterans have achieved a high profile because of the current service demands made of military personnel (Unwin *et al.*, 1999).

The prevalence of mental health problems amongst United Kingdom veterans and their needs are not accurately known. It is recognised that the majority of veterans do not develop mental health problems and appear to adjust well to civilian life (Dasa, 2010). Some veterans do, however, develop difficulties and have significant needs as a result. It is important not to view mental health problems in isolation from social and physical issues, nor to over-medicalise them. It is, however, important to consider research into their prevalence in veterans. Iversen *et al.* (2005) conducted a cross-sectional telephone survey of 496 vulnerable UK veterans who had scored as cases on the General Health Questionnaire when previously interviewed; 315 (64 per cent) responded of whom 138 (44 per cent) had a psychiatric diagnosis with high levels of co-morbidity. Fifty-three per cent of those diagnosed were on the depressive spectrum, 18 per cent anxiety disorders, 16 per cent post-traumatic stress disorder and 12 per cent probable alcohol dependence. Just over half with self-reported problems were currently seeking help, mainly from their general practitioners. Most received treatment, mainly medication; 28 per cent were in contact with a service charity, 9 per cent under a psychiatrist and 4 per cent were receiving cognitive behavioural therapy (IAPT, 2009).

US soldiers and marines returning from deployment to Afghanistan, Iraq and other destinations in 2003 and 2004 also reported significant mental health problems. Problems were reported by 19 per cent of those returning from Iraq, 11 per cent from Afghanistan and 9 per cent from other locations (Hoge *et al.*, 2007). Recent research into suicide rates amongst UK veterans found that young male veterans who served in the army for a short period and were of low rank were two to three times more likely to commit suicide than the general population or serving personnel. Risk was highest in the first two years after leaving service and rates of contact with any mental health services prior to suicide was low (Kapur, 2009).

British veterans

In Britain, a veteran is defined as someone who has served in the Armed Forces for at least one day and who has now left the military. While there are approximately 4.2 million veterans, and more than as many family dependents in Britain, the majority of the veterans represent those who completed National Service. In most other Western countries, a veteran is defined as someone who has served in the military on operations or a mission – combat or humanitarian.

Since 1948, the NHS has been responsible for looking after the health of veterans. However, until recently, specific NHS provision for veterans' mental health services was non-existent.

A pilot study conducted in six NHS clinics between 2007 and 2010 funded by the MOD appraised the acceptability and uptake of dedicated NHS veterans' clinics. This study demonstrated that veteran-orientated and specific services would be well received and well attended by veterans even if they were run by the NHS (Dent-Brown *et al.*, 2010). Following this, in 2010, Dr Andrew Murrison MP wrote a paper named 'Fighting Fit', directing that regional veterans' mental health networks were to be set up in collaboration with Combat Stress by the then NHS strategic health authorities in England (Murrison, 2010). Similar services were to be established in the other devolved British countries. Up to four of these veterans' network services delivered outpatient clinical services, and the others emphasised better staff education and improving access to generic services for veterans. Funding was restricted to £150,000 per service. One service, however, managed to secure significant additional funding. So far, the clinical services which were set up have been shown to be effective in engaging significant numbers of veterans. Many have worked in close collaboration and partnership with Combat Stress. Positive treatment outcomes have been published by one NHS service, Pennine NHS Trust (Clarkson *et al.*, 2013).

The MOD continues to offer a mental health assessment service to veterans. This service moved to Chilwell in Nottingham from St Thomas' Hospital in London and has now moved again, this time to Colchester, Essex, where assessments are coordinated. (The actual assessments now take place in all MOD Departments of Community Mental Health [DCMH] by military psychiatrists). This provides an assessment service by an experienced consultant psychiatrist. Treatment recommendations are made but no actual treatment is delivered.

Increasing clinical need

Veterans from all conflicts and wars, including the Second World War up until the present may present with mental health illness. Unfortunately, there are no cross-sectional studies assessing the British veteran population as a whole or identifying the bio-psychosocial and spiritual needs of all veterans irrespective of their military service or combat era. This ideal study would aid service planning, investment and target care.

Some studies have provided indications as to the mental health needs of veterans. The service personnel and veterans' mental health studies relating to the wars in Iraq and Afghanistan (OPTELIC/OPHERRICK) have been reported longitudinally until 2010 by the King's Centre for Military Health Research (KCMHR) (Fear *et al.*, 2010). These studies demonstrated, in a representative sample of 25,000 who were deployed to Iraq and Afghanistan, that the overall rate for those deployed for PTSD was 4 per cent, no different to those who were not deployed; and that the PTSD rate increased to 6.9 per cent in front line combatants. Alcohol-related problems were high – reported at 13 per cent – and common mental health disorders were 19.7 per cent. Reservist personnel were more vulnerable to developing PTSD with a rate of 5 per cent versus 1 per cent base line rate. This longitudinal study is still ongoing and further reporting is expected soon.

While previous studies have demonstrated that the rates of mental illness in serving personnel were thought to be relatively low, a more recent study which evaluated this same cohort demonstrated that common mental disorders were twice as common in serving personnel if this was compared with an equivalent employed civilian population, as opposed to a general civilian population which included the unemployed and the employed (Goodwin *et al.*, 2014).

A separate study demonstrated that delayed-onset PTSD was much more common in veterans than in civilians, and more likely to present in the first year after discharge from the military, where it was postulated that loss of support structures and adjustment to civilian life increased vulnerability (Andrews *et al.*, 2009).

An independent telephone survey study conducted in 2007 on veterans living in Wales assessed three different groups randomly selected from Combat Stress, the Service Personnel and Veterans Agency (SPVA) and the King's Centre for Military Health Research (KCMHR) (Welsh Affairs Committee, 2011; Wood *et al.*, 2011). Significant differences in their psychiatric presentations are highlighted (Table 1.1). Other findings showed that, of 63 veterans diagnosed with PTSD, only one did not

TABLE 1.1 Welsh Affairs Committee written evidence from all Wales veterans'

	Combat Stress	SPVA	KCMHR
Mean age	49	67	38
Major depression	62%	13%	4%
Lifetime suicide attempts	44%	6%	1%
Hazardous drinking	20%	17%	37%
Probable alcohol dependence	27%	2%	6%
Post-traumatic stress disorder	73%	10%	3%

SPVA, Service Personnel and Veterans Agency; KCMHR, King's Centre for Military Health Research.
Source: Welsh Affairs Committee (2011).

have another psychiatric diagnosis. Only 46.9 per cent with a diagnosis of a mental disorder had sought professional help. The main reason not to seek help was the perception that help was not needed. Informal sources of help were more likely to be used than professional ones. It should be noted that the KCMHR population is an epidemiological population, whereas the Combat Stress population is a help-seeking population. The SPVA population are people applying for war pensions generally, and not necessarily for mental health issues.

A study conducted in Afghanistan and Iraq on UK war veterans demonstrated that violent behaviour post-deployment is high, with a 12.6 per cent prevalence. This is strongly associated with pre-enlistment antisocial behaviour, holding a combat role and being exposed to multiple traumatic events on deployment as well as with mental health problems such as PTSD and alcohol misuse (MacManus et al., 2012). A further study showed that violent offending in UK personnel deployed to Iraq and Afghanistan is three times higher in the under thirty-year-olds, compared with a similar non-military population. It also demonstrated that men of lower rank and with a history of pre-service violence are the most at risk of violent offending, whilst being deployed in a combat role and witnessing traumatic events also increases the risk. Men with direct combat exposure are 53 per cent more likely to commit a violent offence than those who are not exposed to combat. The frequency of traumatic events was also a risk factor in increasing the risk of violence. PTSD, high levels of self-reported aggressive behaviour on return from deployment and alcohol misuse were found to be strong predictors of subsequent violent offending (MacManus et al., 2013).

A separate scoping study conducted in Scotland identified huge areas requiring research, for example: vulnerable groups including early service leavers and those who were held at Colchester Military Correction and Training Centre (MCTC), issues regarding stigma, barriers to care, problems leaving the military, women, reservists, families, partners and carers. This study concluded that a cross-sectional population study of all veteran groups is badly needed (Klein et al., 2013).

Summary

The British military, although much reduced from previous conflicts, is a complex machine and those that serve in it have a unique and distinctive experience. But within the ranks of those who have served in it, that experience will vary vastly. Some will have fought in World War II, on the beaches of Normandy, in the skies above Britain and the continent or further afield, in Italy, North Africa or Burma, while some will have been at sea. Some will never have left these shores at all. Some, a little younger, may have been in Aden, or Cyprus or Kenya, and some will have been conscripted into National Service. A large number, the largest still living, will have been in Northern Ireland, one of this country's longest campaigns in recent memory and may have served one, two or numerous tours. Some will have been in the South Atlantic, at sea under frequent enemy attack or on the ground, possibly engaged in bayonet and hand-to-hand fighting. And the younger ones will have been in Iraq and Afghanistan.

Some will have served full careers, some will only have been in training for a day. Some will have been prematurely discharged on disciplinary or medical grounds. Some will have been invalided out on a pension having suffered often terrible injuries.

There is no such thing as a typical veteran, nor are the reasons why people join or leave the Forces similar. But this is a population with unique qualities and specific needs.

The remainder of this book will examine the variety of groups that constitute not only the veteran population but the military community and will then consider how services, psychological and social might be provided, drawing on several examples from home and abroad.

References

Andrews, B., Brewin, C.R., Philpott, R., Hejdenberg, J. (2009). Comparison of immediate-onset and delayed-onset posttraumatic stress disorder in military veterans. *Journal of Abnormal Psychology*, 118, 767–77.

Black, W.G. (1993). Military-induced family separation: A stress reduction intervention. *Social Work*, 38, 273–80.

Brewin, C.R., Andrews, B., Hejdenberg, J., Stewart, L. (2012). Objective predictors of delayed-onset post-traumatic stress disorder occurring after military discharge. *Psychological Medicine*, 42, 2119–26.

Clarkson, P., Giebal, C.M., Challis, D. (2013). *Military Veterans Improving Access to Psychological Therapies (MV IAPT) Services*. Final Report of an Independent Evaluation to Pennine Care NHS. Manchester: PSSRU.

Dent-Brown, K., Ashworth, A., Barkham, M., Connell, J., Gilbody, S., Hardy, G. (2010). *An Evaluation of Six Community Mental Health Pilots for Veterans of the Armed Forces: A Case Study Series*. A Report for the Ministry of Defence. Sheffield: University of Sheffield. Available online at www.sheffield.ac.uk/polopoly_fs/1.120472!/file/Sheffield-evaluation-published-version-15-Dec-2010.pdf (accessed 20 January 2017).

Fear, N.T., Jones, M., Murphy, D., Hull, L., Iversen, A.C., Coker, B., Machell, L., Sundin, J., Woodhead, C., Jones, N., Greenberg, N., Landau, S., Dandeker, C., Rona, R.J., Hotopf, M., Wessely, S. (2010). What are the consequences of deployment to Iraq and Afghanistan on the mental health of the UK armed forces? A cohort study. *The Lancet*, 375, 1783–97.

Fossey, M. (2010). *Across the Wire: Veterans, Mental Health and Vulnerability*. London: Centre for Mental Health.

Goodwin, L., Wessely, S., Hotopf, M., Jones, N., Greenberg, N., Rona, R.J., Hull, L., Fear, N.T. (2014). Are common mental disorders more prevalent in the UK serving military compared to the general working population? *Psychological Medicine*, 45, 1881–91.

Higham, R. (1972). *A Guide to the Sources of British Military History*. London: Routledge and Kegan Paul Ltd.

HMSO (2008). *The Nation's Commitment: Cross-Government Support to Our Armed Forces, Their Families and Veterans*. ID5856691. London: HMSO.

Hoge, C.W., Terhakopian, A., Castro, C.A., Messer, S.C., Engel, C.C. (2007). Association of posttraumatic stress disorder with somatic symptoms, health care visits, and absenteeism among Iraq war veterans. *The American Journal of Psychiatry*, 164, 150–3.

Humber Foundation NHS Trust (2010). *Life Force: A Practical Guide for Working with Military Veterans*. Hull: SAMH.

IAPT (2009). *Improving Access to Psychological Therapies. Veterans Positive Practice Guide*. London: Department of Health.

Isby, D.C., Kamps, C. (1985). *Armies of NATO's Central Front*. London: Jane's Publishing Company Ltd.

Iversen, A., Nikolaou, V., Greenberg, N., Unwin, C., Hull, L., Hotopf, M., Dandeker, C., Ross, J., Wessely, S. (2005). What happens to British veterans when they leave the armed forces? *European Journal of Public Health*, 15, 175–84.

Iversen, A., Fear, N., Simonoff, E., Hull, L., Horn, O., Greenberg, N., Hotopf, M., Rona, R., Wessely, S. (2007). Influence of childhood adversity on health among male UK military personnel. *The British Journal of Psychiatry*, 191, 506–11.

Iversen, A., Fear, N.T, Ehlers, A., Hacker Hughes, J., Hull, L., Earnshaw, M., Greenberg, N., Rona, R., Wessely, S., Hotopf, M. (2008). Risk factors for post-traumatic stress disorder among UK Armed Forces personnel. *Psychol Med*, 38, 511–22.

Johnstone, J. (1978). Social class, social areas and delinquency. *Sociology and Social Research*, 63, 49–72.

Jones, E., Hodgins-Vermaas, R., McCartney, H., Everitt, B. (2002). Post-combat syndromes from the Boer war to the Gulf war: a cluster analysis of their nature and attribution. *British Medical Journal*, 324, 1–7.

Kapur, N. (2009). *Suicide After Leaving the Armed Forces – A Cohort Study. From Warzone to Wythenshawe*. Manchester Conference Centre: Combat Stress.

Kitchiner, N.J., Bisson, J. (2015). Phase I development of an optimal integrated care pathway for veterans discharged from the armed forces. *Military Medicine*, 180, 766–73.

Klein, S., Alexander, D., Busuttil, W. (2013). *Scoping Review: A Needs-Based Assessment and Epidemiological Community-Based Survey of Ex-Service Personnel and their Families in Scotland*. Aberdeen: Robert Gordon University. Available online at www.scotland.gov.uk/Resource/0041/00417172.pdf (accessed 17 January 2017).

Leardmann, C.A., Smith, B., Ryan, M.A.K. (2010). Do adverse childhood experiences increase the risk of post deployment posttraumatic stress disorder in US Marines? *BMC Public Health*, 10, 437.

MacManus, D., Dean, K., Al Bakir, M., Iversen, A. C., Hull. L., Fahy, T., Wessely, S., Fear, N.T. (2012). Violent behaviour in UK military personnel returning home after deployment *Psychological Medicine*, 42, 1663–73.

MacManus, D., Dean, K., Jones, M., Rona, R.J., Greenberg, N., Hull, L., Fahy, T., Wessely, S., Fear, N.T. (2013). Violent offending by UK military personnel deployed to Iraq and Afghanistan: A data linkage cohort study. *Lancet*, 381, 907–17.

Ministry of Defence (2009). *Your Guide to Army Life*. London: Ministry of Defence. Available online at www.army.mod.uk/join/25652.aspx (accessed 17 January 2017).

Ministry of Defence (2010). *Military Covenant to be Enshrined in Law*. London: Ministry of Defence. Available online at www.gov.uk/government/news/military-covenant-to-be-enshrined-in-law (accessed17 January 2017).

Ministry of Defence (2011). *Secretary of State for Defence*. London: Ministry of Defence. Available online at www.MOD.uk/DefenceInternet/AboutDefence/People/Ministers/SecretaryOfStateForDefence.htm (accessed17 January 2017).

Murrison, A. (2010). *Fighting Fit: A Mental Health Plan for Servicemen and Veterans*. London: Ministry of Defence. Available online at www.gov.uk/government/uploads/system/uploads/attachment_data/file/27375/20101006_mental_health_Report.pdf (accessed 8 May 2013).

Ruhl, T. (2003). National Service – History. British Armed Forces and National Service – Website. Available online at http://www.britisharmedforces.org/ns/nat_history.htm (accessed 17 January 2017).

SAMH (2009). *Life Force: A Practical Guide for Working with Scotland's Veterans*. Glasgow: SAMH.

Unwin, C., Blatchley, N., Coker, W., Ferry, S., Hotopf, M., Hull, L., Ismail, K., Palmer, I., David, A., Wessely, S. (1999). Health of UK servicemen who served in Persian Gulf War. *Lancet*, 353, 169–78.

Weich, S., Patterson, J., Shaw, R., Stewart-Brown, S. (2009). Family relationships in childhood and common psychiatric disorders in later life: Systematic review of prospective studies. *British Journal of Psychiatry*, 194, 392–8.

Welsh Affairs Committee (2011). *Written Evidence from All Wales Veterans' Health and Wellbeing Service*. London: Welsh Affairs Committee. Available online at www.publications.parliament.uk/pa/cm201213/cmselect/cmwelaf/131/131we03.htm (accessed 17 January 2017).

Wood, S., Jones, C., Morrison, S., Kitchiner, N., Dustan, F., Fear, N.T., Bisson, J. (2011). *Mental Health, Social Adjustment, Perception of Health and Service Utilisation of Three Groups of Military Veterans Living in Wales: A Cross-Sectional Survey*. Unpublished study. Cardiff: Cardiff University.

Woodhead, C., Rona, R.J., Iversen, A., MacManus, D., Hotopf, M., Dean, K., McManus, S., Meltzer, H., Brugha, T., Jenkins, R., Wessely, S., Fear, N.T. (2011). Mental health and health service use among post-national service veterans: Results from the 2007 Adult Psychiatric Morbidity Survey of England. *Psychological Medicine*, 41, 363–72.

2

THE POLICY

Andy Bacon and Dave Rutter

Introduction

The policy framework for meeting the health and social care needs of the Armed Forces, their families and veterans has developed over many years, reflecting the changing face of conflicts over this past century (and more) and the way in which health services are delivered to the population of the UK. The establishment of many of the service charities that are part and parcel of meeting the needs of the Armed Forces community have their roots in the First World War. The formation of the National Health Service (NHS) in the immediate post-war years of the Second World War, creating the basis of the services we have today, is built on the overriding principle of free healthcare to all at the point of delivery.

The large military infrastructure, including the military hospitals that were provided, could provide health services to serving personnel, veterans and families of serving personnel. However, it was recognised by the Ministry of Defence (MOD) that a better use of resource and training for military clinicians and health professionals was better placed within mainstream NHS hospitals. Following the closure of the military hospitals in the 1990s, a number of MOD Hospital Units within NHS facilities were established, namely: MDHU Portsmouth (Queen Alexandra Hospital, Portsmouth Hospitals NHS Trust); MDHU Derriford (Derriford Hospital, Plymouth Hospitals NHS Trust); MDHU Frimley Park (Frimley Park Hospital NHS Foundation Trust); MDHU Northallerton (Friarage Hospital, South Tees Hospitals NHS Trust); and MDHU Peterborough (Peterborough and Stamford Hospitals NHS Foundation Trust).

The mental health needs of serving personnel are now met through MOD Community Mental Health Services with further support from an external contract, currently held by a chain of NHS providers. Veterans and reservists have limited access to MOD mental health services through the veterans and reserves mental health programme – as well as being able to access general or veteran focused mental health services from the NHS and service charities.

Recent conflicts in the Balkans, Gulf Wars and Afghanistan have re-focused the attention of the public, politicians, the media and government on the way in which the healthcare of the Armed Forces community is delivered, and particularly the mental health of those who serve in the Armed Forces and their subsequent lives as veterans. For this contemporary perspective, the starting point is the 2008 Government Command Paper – *The Nation's Commitment: Cross-Government Support to our Armed Forces, their Families and Veterans* (Ministry of Defence, 2008). The publication of this paper reflected a rapidly changing public perception of UK involvement in international conflicts with the de-coupling of the negative views of UK involvement from an overriding desire to ensure that the Armed Forces were nonetheless deserving of the very best health care having put themselves on the battlefield to defend the UK.

The essential starting point for the Command Paper was the concept of 'no disadvantage' for the Armed Forces, their families and veterans by virtue of what they do. This principle of no disadvantage being captured under the broad themes of:

- As much lifestyle choice as any other citizen
- Continuity of public services
- Proper return for sacrifice
- The Armed Forces constituency matters

Of the health commitments in relation to veterans' health, two specified in the Command Paper (Ministry of Defence, 2008) laid the foundation for the policies and services that have been developed and delivered for veterans' mental health over the following seven years, namely:

2.11 Veterans' Health Needs. We need to improve our information about how veterans' health needs differ from those of the population generally. Most healthcare professionals do not have direct knowledge of the Armed Forces and may not be sensitive to their particular needs. We will look at whether more needs to be done to assess the healthcare needs of veterans. We will raise awareness among healthcare professionals about the needs of veterans so that these needs are met.

2.12 Roll-out of Community Mental Health Following Pilots. Mental health services do not always fully address the needs of veterans. We are establishing pilot schemes to provide community mental health services for veterans in 6 locations across Great Britain. These pilots concentrate on improving veterans' access to mental health services. Community Mental Health Services will be provided across Great Britain, taking into account the lessons learned from these pilots. In addition, meeting the needs of veterans will be an important element in the selection of the next round of psychological therapies sites in England for 2009/10. In Northern Ireland, this commitment is met by the Royal Irish Aftercare service.

These commitments were further prioritised as government policy through:

- The Coalition Government's commitment to rebuild the Military Covenant by providing extra support for veterans' mental health needs (HM Government, 2010);
- The Coalition Government's agreement of the recommendations of the 'Fighting Fit' report by Dr Andrew Murrison, MD, MP (Murrison, 2010); and
- The creation of the Armed Forces Covenant in November 2011 (Ministry of Defence, 2011).

Who is a veteran?

Before discussing the policy and services that have been put in place to address the mental health and other needs of veterans, it is important to understand what is meant by a 'veteran' and the boundaries in which NHS services are provided. This is important as the expectations of the roles of those providing mental health services are influenced by the requirements of legislation on the NHS and charitable articles of association.

The Armed Forces Covenant defines veterans as those who have served for at least a day in HM Armed Forces, whether as a regular or as a reservist. Professor Sir Hew Strachan's *Report of the Task Force on the Military Covenant* (Ministry of Defence, 2010) noted that one of the reasons why policy for veterans was confused was as a result of this definition. He noted that other countries expect that veterans should have at least completed basic training. As a result of the broader UK definition of a veteran, the Task Force report noted that many did not know they were considered to be veterans or, if they did, did not want to be so identified as such.

This broad definition of veteran therefore applies to all who have served from the Second World War and thereafter – including those required to do National Service (ending in 1960), those joining up 'to learn a trade and see the world', and those who simply leave the Armed Forces within weeks of joining up.

The definition of veteran therefore covers a wide age range and a wide range of experiences. The 2014 annual population survey of UK Armed Forces veterans residing in Great Britain (Ministry of Defence, 2016) noted that there are approximately 2.6 million veterans in the Great Britain, of whom 50 per cent are over the age of 75. This reflects the large numbers of men and women who served during the Second World War, or who undertook post-war National Service. At the time of the 'Fighting Fit' report in 2010, it was estimated that there were approximately 4.5 million veterans in the UK. The sharp decline in numbers of veterans will continue over the next 15 years reflecting this higher age bias in the veteran population. The Royal British Legion's Household survey of 2014 (The Royal British Legion, 2014) also recognised that many of the problems faced by elderly veterans are little different to those faced by the UK's elderly as a whole: isolation, physical health problems and difficulties with mobility and care.

Around one in four of the population are likely to experience a mental health problem each year. Anxiety and depression are common issues; other serious issues such as post-traumatic stress disorder (generally referred to as PTSD) are a lot lower at approximately 4 per cent of the population. The rate of mental health problems amongst veterans appears to be similar to that of the population as a whole – including rates of PTSD. The work that has been undertaken to meet the mental health needs of veterans therefore needs to be seen against this context of a very broad definition of veteran and the wider prevalence of mental health issues in the wider population.

NHS Mental Health Services for veterans

The NHS England Constitution (2015) underlines the abiding principles of the NHS and in particular:

> The NHS provides a comprehensive service, available to all irrespective of gender, race, disability, age, sexual orientation, religion, belief, gender reassignment, pregnancy and maternity or marital or civil partnership status.
>
> (*NHS England, 2015*)

Commissioning of NHS services should be governed, as far as practicable, by the principle of equal access for equal clinical need. Individual patients or groups should not be unjustifiably advantaged or disadvantaged on the basis of age, gender, sexuality, race, religion, lifestyle, occupation, social position, financial status, family status (including responsibility for dependants), intellectual/cognitive function or physical functions. There are proven links between social inequalities and inequalities in health, health needs and access to healthcare.

In making commissioning decisions, priority may be given to health services targeting the needs of subgroups of the population who currently have poorer than average health outcomes (including morbidity and mortality) or poorer access to services.

NHS services are therefore not provided based on occupation (or previous occupation). In designing services that are veteran focused, it is therefore important that these core principles of the NHS are met. The need to make best use of services that are not provided by the NHS – mainly those provided by the MOD and service charities – becomes important in designing the framework in order to get the best possible range of services and good outcomes for veterans. It is this that central government through the Department of Health, working with the MOD, service charities and others, have sought to achieve. In the work to achieve this, the importance of eliminating overlap in services and having a clear understanding of what can be provided is important.

The Armed Forces Covenant

The Armed Forces Covenant (the Covenant) was put in place by the Coalition Government, and enshrined within the Armed Forces Act in 2011 (HM Government, 2011). The Armed Forces Covenant is the expression of the moral obligation that the government and the nation owe to the Armed Forces community. The Covenant

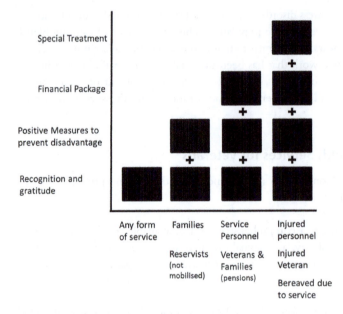

FIGURE 2.1   Benefits accruing for different categories.
Source: From the Armed Forces Covenant (Ministry of Defence, 2011).

acknowledges that members of the Armed Forces sacrifice some freedoms and often face dangerous situations. It recognises that families play a vital role in supporting the operational effectiveness of the Armed Forces (Figure 2.1).

There are two key principles in the Armed Forces Covenant. First, that the Armed Forces community faces no disadvantage in the provision of public and commercial services – reflecting the key message of the earlier Command Paper. Second, that special consideration should be given when required, such as to the injured or the bereaved. The Armed Forces community is defined as serving personnel, reservists, veterans and families.

As noted previously, when discussing veterans and veterans with mental health problems, it is important to keep the very wide definition of a veteran in mind and within the context of those (lesser numbers of veterans) identified by the Covenant as requiring special provision.

In relation to healthcare, the Covenant states:

> The Armed Forces Community should enjoy the same standard of, and access to, healthcare as that received by any other UK citizen in the area they live. For serving personnel, including mobilised Reservists, primary healthcare is provided by the MOD, whilst secondary care is provided by the local healthcare provider. Personnel injured on operations should be treated in conditions which recognise the specific needs of Service personnel, normally involving a dedicated military ward, where this is appropriate for them, and medical rehabilitation in MOD facilities. For family members,

primary healthcare may be provided by the MOD in some cases (e.g. when accompanying Service personnel posted overseas). They should retain their relative position on any NHS waiting list, if moved around the UK due to the Service person being posted. Veterans receive their healthcare from the NHS, and should receive priority treatment where it relates to a condition which results from their service in the Armed Forces, subject to clinical need. Those injured in Service, whether physically or mentally, should be cared for in a way which reflects the Nation's moral obligation to them whilst respecting the individual's wishes. For those with concerns about their mental health, where symptoms may not present for some time after leaving Service, they should be able to access services with health professionals who have an understanding of Armed Forces culture.

This reference within the Covenant to veterans being able to access mental health services with health professionals who understand Armed Forces culture reflects the recommendations made by Dr Andrew Murrison MP's report to the Coalition Government, '*Fighting Fit: A Mental Health Plan for Servicemen and Veterans*' (Murrison, 2010).

Fighting Fit: A Mental Health Plan for Servicemen and Veterans

The Coalition programme for government issued in May 2010 committed that: 'We will work to rebuild the Military Covenant by providing extra support for veterans' mental health needs'.

The Coalition Government asked Dr Andrew Murrison, an MP, GP and both regular and reservist Royal Naval medical officer, to undertake a review of mental health services to serving personnel and veterans. Dr Murrison identified the following propositions in making his recommendations:

- Established models of care should be used in designing the programme.
- Any provider that can deliver against National Institute for Health and Clinical Excellence (NICE) guidelines and Care Quality Commission (CQC) standards should be considered in accordance with the precepts of 'The Big Society'.
- Follow-up and management should be as close to home as possible.
- Stigma deters Servicemen from engaging with conventional mental health provision.

The key recommendations relating to mental health services for veterans were as follows:

- It is recommended that a serviceman whose requirement for a specialist opinion is identified at the time of his discharge should be able to obtain it and any follow-on treatment from a military Department of Community Mental Health (DCMH) for the next six months.

- It is recommended that regulars and reserves are followed-up approximately 12 months after they leave.
- It is recommended that the cadre of 15 new mental health professionals announced in April 2010 is doubled.
- Mental Health Trusts (MHTs) will be required to formulate a plan for managing cases referred by embedded mental health professionals, general practitioners (GPs) or other agencies.
- The Medical Assessment Programme at St Thomas' Hospital and the Reserves Mental Health Programme will continue in their assessment role accepting referrals and self-referrals.
- The MHT embedded mental health professionals established under Fighting Fit (FF) will undertake community outreach work in order to discover cases and refer appropriately to other professionals and ex-Services organisations.
- The e-learning veterans' health package being designed for GPs should introduce FF and highlight the availability of MHT embedded outreach professionals and the 'Big White Wall' (BWW) type service.
- The BBW type online mental wellbeing website will be available to existing veterans together with, subject to the agreement of local healthcare commissioners, membership of the online support network.

The response by the Department of Health, working with the NHS, Combat Stress and others was to put in place a number of services aimed at meeting the thrust of the recommendations made by Dr Murrison. These included the following services.

Increased number of healthcare professionals – although Dr Murrison argued for a doubling of veteran mental healthcare professionals to 30, it was decided to put in place 10 veterans' mental health teams across England. By doing this, not only did this more than double the number of healthcare professionals (overall, more than a 100 across the 10 teams – with many more being trained in veterans' mental health), it also meant that case managing and related issues raised by Dr Murrison were also being addressed. Each of the ten teams provides a service using a different model reflecting their local veterans' population needs and requirements – although many are very similar. A National Veterans' Mental Health Network has been put in place with the aim of identifying good practice across the veterans' mental health teams and elsewhere.

A Veterans' Information Service is provided by the MOD, which contacts those who have been discharged from the Armed Forces one year after they have left, linking to the Royal British Legion knowledge database where advice can be provided either online or, if more complex, on a one-to-one basis. In parallel, the MOD has been improving the information/connectivity with NHS GPs to ensure that on discharge, the GP is provided with a summary of healthcare and fully informed of the veterans' status of the new patient. In future, this transfer of summary care will be made electronically.

A 24-hour veterans' mental health helpline was commissioned through Combat Stress and Rethink, the Mental Health Charity. The Helpline receives over 800 calls per month.

BWW (an on-line early intervention, peer support, wellbeing and counselling service) was commissioned to provide services for members of the Armed Forces, their families and veterans. This has proved very successful with approx. 7,000 members from the Armed Forces community (43 per cent veterans, 31 per cent serving personnel and 26 per cent family members) taking up the opportunity to make use of BWW services. The Department of Health worked with BWW to develop a mobile phone app access to its services. One of the most encouraging aspects of the service has been the high number of users accessing mental health counselling services for the first time.

An e-learning package for GPs, providing an 'entry level' package of advice/guidance on the health needs of the Armed Forces, their families and veterans, focusing on relevant aspects of both physical and mental health has been put in place. The package is facilitated by the Royal College of GPs who are now working with Health Education England to ensure that the training continues to be up to date and more accessible for all health professionals. This package has since been updated for all clinical professionals by Health Education England and NHS England.

The focus on veterans' mental health and the work described previously has led to other innovative measures at local and national level. These have been provided by service charities, NHS and others. An example is the NHS in England funding of up to £3.2 million per annum through Specialist Commissioning, arrangements with Combat Stress to provide acute PTSD services for veterans. Other initiatives have been funded through the London Interbank Offered Rate (LIBOR) fine. The Coalition Government identified an initial £35 million of the fines levied on banks for attempting to manipulate LIBOR for Armed Forces related causes. Several million pounds have been allocated by the government for veterans' mental health including funds to Combat Stress to help those veterans seek help for alcohol related issues and to Help for Heroes to provide low-level mental health support at its rehabilitation centres. Other examples of LIBOR fines being used to support veterans' mental health work included:

- Big White Wall – To offer ten evidence-based self-management 'Guided Support' programmes for the Armed Forces community.
- North Somerset Citizens Advice Bureau – To pilot an information, advice and mentoring service offering practical help to veterans, reservists and serving personnel and their families to fully integrate into civilian society. With a particular focus on mental health.
- Gardening Leave – To provide horticultural therapy for serving and ex-service Armed Forces personnel.
- North Yorkshire County Council – To offer specific group sessions in coping with stress, anger management and dealing/tackling domestic abuse.
- Oxfordshire Mind – To pilot an innovative and bespoke eight-week group programme, which will help improve the mental health, wellbeing and social integration of spouses and partners of Service personnel.

- Royal British Legion Scotland – To assist and promote and to insure quality of care to veterans in Scotland.
- Riverside ECHG – To employ a baker who will concentrate on the therapeutic value of baking bread, by introducing relevant training to single homeless ex-Forces veterans in temporary accommodation.
- Royal Navy & Royal Marines Children's Fund – To produce a booklet for Service families on PTSD.
- SSAFA Forces Help – To train 200 volunteers in mental health first aid who will then be tasked to train others.
- The Bridge for Heroes – To provide face-to-face mental health support to serving personnel, veterans and their families in Norfolk.
- Veterans Aid – To improve the delivery of their 'Homeless ex-Servicemen's mental health treatment and care programme'.
- Veterans Council – To establish a dedicated 'one stop shop' that provides a single, easily accessible pathway into bespoke mental health, health/social care and transitional services.
- Veterans F1rst Point – To establish a number of mental health support centres in Scotland for veterans.

There are many others. What these examples show, when looked at in the context of the services put in place following Dr Murrison's report, is that almost from a standing start, the focus on veterans mental and the wide variety of services relating to it have expanded significantly over a very short period of time. But with this comes challenges from a wider policy perspective as well as at a service delivery level where there can be overlap or duplication in services leading to wasted resources. In some cases, mental healthcare may be provided that is not evidence based or meeting CQC or NICE standards.

Challenges

This chapter has noted the declining number of veterans and identified that not all of these veterans will have been in combat situations, indeed, given the wide definition of a veteran, many will not even have completed basic training. We have also seen that there has been a tremendous amount of effort and resources put into providing the right mental health services for veterans. Nonetheless, there continues to be a constant backdrop of media and other commentators criticising NHS services and, in some cases, services provided by long-established service charities as not meeting the mental health needs of veterans – particularly those with PTSD. It is worth reflecting on some of the myths/misunderstandings that have grown in parallel with the services that are actually being provided to veterans.

The following is myth-busting advice provided by the charity, Combat Stress:

> We often hear that people struggle to understand mental health and trauma because the injuries that Veterans come to Combat Stress with cannot be seen. We have developed this quick 'Myth Buster' guide to answer some

questions we hear regularly. We want people to know more about Veterans' mental health and the symptoms of trauma so that they can have the conversations that tackle stigma and make it easier for people to seek help.

Post-Traumatic Stress Disorder (PTSD) is the only mental illness caused by military service.

PTSD is one of the mental illnesses most associated with military service but there are a range of other more common mental illnesses which might affect Service and ex-Service personnel. These include depression, feelings of anxiety, panic attacks and substance misuse, most commonly alcohol misuse.

Mental illnesses only occur amongst junior ranks, senior ranks don't get them.

This is incorrect. Mental illness as a result of the traumatic experiences witnessed during Armed Forces service can affect any member of the Armed Forces regardless of rank. We have treated Veterans of various ranks suffering from PTSD and other mental ill-health – from Privates up to Brigadiers.

You can only get mental illness if you have seen combat.

Far from it, there are many traumatic experiences that sailors, soldiers and airmen could witness during their military careers which take place outside of live combat situations. Whether it is training incidents, administering medical treatment, or other activities in war zones, these traumatic experiences can stay with personnel and lead to mental ill-health in later life.

PTSD is the biggest mental health problem facing the UK Veteran community.

PTSD is a problem for a minority of Veterans. Around one in 25 Veterans of the Iraq and Afghanistan wars are likely to develop PTSD, similar to that in the general public. However, while the rate of occurrence is similar, the complexity of the disorder tends to be much greater in Veterans. Furthermore, it often occurs alongside other medical problems such as pain, disability and substance misuse, particularly alcohol misuse.

You cannot cure PTSD.

PTSD that is been left untreated for a number of years or decades will require more intensive treatment. There are still positive health outcomes for sufferers, and the potential for a life beyond symptoms, but seeking suitable, timely treatment is key to maximising the chances of recovery. If PTSD is diagnosed early and the sufferer receives the right treatment in the right environment, rates of recovery are very positive. Veterans can live normal fulfilling lives, able to work with the condition and generally become symptom free for long periods.

There is a risk of delayed-onset of PTSD, where symptoms do not occur for years or decades after the traumatic event. Veterans who present with delayed-onset PTSD have often been exposed to the effects of multiple traumas over a longer period of time. This suggests that those who serve multiple tours are more at risk of developing PTSD several years after leaving the Military.

Most UK Armed Forces personnel who have served in Iraq and Afghanistan return with psychological injuries.

The majority of Armed Forces personnel deployed do not experience lasting mental wounds as a result of their service. However, around one in 25 Regulars and one in 20 Reservists will report symptoms of PTSD following deployment in Iraq or Afghanistan. This is very similar to the rate in the general population.

Furthermore, one in five Veterans are likely to suffer from a common mental illness – such as depression, anxiety or substance (generally alcohol) misuse – which has been caused or aggravated by their Armed Forces experiences.

The suicide rate amongst Veterans is higher than the general population.

Suicide remains a rare occurrence in both UK Regulars and Veterans. In fact, the suicide rate is not significantly different to the rate amongst the UK general population, and for most age groups is actually lower. Seeking help for suicidal thoughts remains crucial and there is extensive mental health support available to both serving and ex-Service personnel.

There is a bow wave of Veterans' mental health problems building up.

As the UK's leading veterans' mental health charity, Combat Stress has experienced an increase in the number of referrals year on year. However, recent studies suggest this is due to an increased awareness of the symptoms and where to seek help.

(*Combat Stress, 2016*)

This advice, produced by the Service charity, Combat Stress, is important. Resources have to be used to best possible effect to meet the mental health needs of veterans. It is arguable that the proliferation of veterans' mental health services and charities providing mental health or wellbeing services have been created off the back of the myths that have mushroomed over the past five to ten years. Are all these services adding value? Is the fact that many veterans (not necessarily recognised as veterans within the NHS system) can access mainstream NHS mental health services with good results being lost within the noise and hubris around veterans' mental health being 'special' and dominated by PTSD?

Lord Ashcroft, in his review of veterans' transition to civilian life (Lord Ashcroft, 2014), makes clear that it is a myth that veterans are plagued by problems such as PTSD, homelessness and alcoholism when they leave the forces. Lord Ashcroft commented that these myths are damaging, as they imply that the Armed Forces did not do enough to look after their personnel and it creates an extra hurdle for Service leavers when looking for a job.

Successive governments have been fully committed to continual improvement in the treatment of mental health conditions for veterans and the general public alike. But the focus remains on improving mental health services for all. Wider improvements in accessing mental health services have been put in place, such as the standard for waiting times, which places the treatment of mental health problems on a par with physical health and ends years of discrimination between mental and physical health services. Since April 2015, patients needing talking therapies – for conditions such as depression – can now expect to start their treatment within six weeks. The commitment to improve mental health services across England can also be seen with the launch of the national Crisis Care Concordat in February 2014 (HM Government, 2014) and the *Mental Health Task Force's Five Year Forward View for Mental Health* in 2016 (NHS England, 2016a). Every local area now has detailed action plans aimed at ensuring no-one is turned away by crisis services and improving access to quality support before, during and after crisis. All these improvements to mental health services will benefit those veterans who, like others in our society, face the challenges of a mental illness.

Over time, services will continue to evolve in response to government policy, resource priority, improved knowledge and a better understand of patients' needs. NHS England has published the findings from a national engagement on NHS veterans' mental health services that took place earlier in 2016 (NHS England, 2016b). The report sets out key feedback following views received from over 1,270 veterans, families, service charities, commissioners and providers. Whilst many of the improvements mentioned previously were noted, it suggested that further changes are needed. These includes the need to improve awareness of these services and where to go for help, and to increase understanding amongst health professionals of the issues faced by those who have served in the Armed Forces. It was also felt that more should be done to support a smoother transition from armed forces healthcare to the NHS. This is further evidenced in the 'Gate to Gate' report (Community Innovations Enterprise, 2016) that calls for an integrated approach between health and criminal justice, the continuing involvement and participation of veterans and family members and a mental health strategy to take account of veterans with complex mental health and related problems. NHS England has undertaken a procurement process to expand and enhance mental health services that reflect these clarified needs with a new model of care.

Conclusion

As a nation, we are rightly proud of the courage and dedication of our Armed Forces and for the vast majority their experience of serving is positive. However, for those who have been injured either physically or mentally, there is commitment throughout government and the NHS to ensure they continue to receive the very best possible care. Veterans face the same mental health issues as we all do and can access the same core mental health NHS services as the general population. For some veterans, their mental health issues may originate from a time before or during service in the Armed Forces and evidence suggests that the stigma surrounding mental illness is still the greatest barrier for individuals seeking help, both while serving and after leaving the service. However, research also shows that whilst the incidence of mental health issues has remained relatively constant, Service personnel and veterans are now seeking help far earlier than they did previously, both through Defence Medical Services, the NHS and service charities, reflecting changes in society and also the impact of many anti-stigma campaigns.

It is important that the veterans' mental health services that have been put in place following the Fighting Fit Report are both sustainable and fully embedded within the mainstream of the NHS, so that veterans can move to other mental health services if necessary and at the right time. Best use must be made of the right support that is available from service charities and others that now also provide mental health and wider support to veterans. Perhaps the key challenge now for government, the NHS, service charities and others is to identify all services now being provided, refine these and create a holistic approach to ensuring that veterans with mental health problems can access the right services in the right place at the right time.

References

Combat Stress (2016). *Combat Stress – Myth Busters*. Available online at www.combatstress. org.uk/veterans/myth-busters/ (accessed 16 July 2016).

Community Innovations Enterprise (2016). *Gate to Gate: Improving the Mental Health and Criminal Justice Care Pathways for Veterans and Family Members*. Available online at http:// www.ciellp.com/wpress/gate-to-gate/ (accessed 8 September 2016).

HM Government (2010). *The Coalition: Our Programme for Government*. London: HM Government.

HM Government (2011). *The Armed Forces Act 2011*. London: HMSO.

HM Government (2014). *Mental Health Crisis Care Concordat: Improving Outcomes for People Experiencing Mental Health Crisis*. London: HM Government.

Lord Ashcroft (2014). T*he Veterans' Transition Review*. London: Lord Ashcroft KCMG PC. Available online at www.veteranstransition.co.uk/vtrreport.pdf (accessed 29 January 2016).

Ministry of Defence (2008). *The Nation's Commitment: Cross-Government Support to Our Armed Forces, Their Families and Veterans*, July 2008 CM7424. London: Ministry of Defence.

Ministry of Defence (2010). *Report of the Task Force on the Military Covenant* – Professor Sir Hew Strachan. London: Ministry of Defence.

Ministry of Defence (2011). *The Armed Forces Covenant*. London: Ministry of Defence.

Ministry of Defence (2016). *The 2014 Annual Population Survey: UK Armed Forces Veterans Residing in Great Britain*. London: Ministry of Defence.

Murrison, A. (2010). *Fighting Fit: A Mental Health Plan for Servicemen and Veterans*. London: Ministry of Defence. Available online at www.gov.uk/government/uploads/system/ uploads/attachment_data/file/27375/20101006_mental_health_Report.pdf (accessed 8 May 2013).

NHS England (2015). *The NHS England Constitution (revised July 2015)*. London: NHS England.

NHS England (2016a). *The Five-Year Forward Plan for Mental Health: A Report from the Independent Mental Health Taskforce to the NHS in England*. London: NHS England.

NHS England (2016b). *Armed Forces and Veterans Mental Health*. London: NHS England. Available online at www.england.nhs.uk/2016/09/armed-forces-veterans-mh/ (accessed 1 September 2016).

The Royal British Legion (2014). *The Royal British Legion Household Survey*. London: The Royal British Legion.

3

EARLY SERVICE LEAVERS

History, Vulnerability and Future Research

Nick Caddick, Lauren Godier and Matt Fossey

Introduction

Providing help for personnel whose time in the military is cut short due to disciplinary, administrative or early separation reasons, is an area that has generated considerable debate. Recent changes[1] in the UK military's approach to the provision of transition support for its personnel have helped to stimulate this debate. The traditional approach to the provision of support has been based on longevity of service as opposed to need. Whilst this has its obvious benefits in encouraging retention and providing assistance for those that may have been institutionalised by many years within the military system, it is a response that may not consider the broader challenging social issues faced by the more vulnerable individuals who leave the military. Under the new approach, early service leavers (ESLs) are entitled to some support to help them deal with the challenges they may face during their transition.

Despite the identification of ESLs as vulnerable, very little is known about how they experience the process of transition (defined as the period of reintegration into civilian life from the Armed Forces; Forces in Mind Trust, 2013). Indeed, as Fossey (2013) stated, 'In effect nobody knows what happens to ESLs once they have left the Armed Forces' (Fossey, 2013: 6). Furthermore, there is a need to understand in much greater detail the reasons behind ESLs' early separation from military life (Buckman *et al.*, 2013). A better understanding of ESLs and their experiences of transition into civilian life is therefore required (Buckman *et al.*, 2013; Fossey, 2013; Woodhead *et al.*, 2011).

In this chapter, we explore the current debate around the care and support that is afforded to ESLs and draw upon telephone interview research in which the views of national opinion formers were sought. As Lord Ashcroft (2014) explained in his review of veterans' transition, improving outcomes for ESLs is essential to improving transition overall and creates additional incentives for recruitment to the military. In addition to academic researchers, this chapter will therefore be of practical relevance to a range of organisations including the Ministry of Defence (MOD), the National Health Service (NHS) and government departments (e.g. Department for Work and Pensions).

Definitions, history and vulnerability

Up until 2002, discharge planning and assistance with transition was the responsibility of single services. For those discharged for disciplinary reasons, or terminating their contract early, assistance was the responsibility of the individual's unit and often was little more than cursory provision, such as a travel warrant.

It was not until the MOD introduced an external contract for transition support provision that there was greater uniformity of approach across the three branches (Royal Navy, Army and Royal Air Force). To inform all units of this change and what this meant operationally, the MOD issued a Joint Service Publication setting out the eligibility criteria for support and the processes that were to be followed (JSP 534 Issue 1). This revoked the extant single service policies.

The first time that the term 'early service leavers' was defined and used in policy was in the second issue of JSP 534, which was published in April 2004. This was released alongside JSP 575 Issue 1, a publication specifically aimed at providing unit level staff with a set of procedures to help them in discharging ESLs. At this time, ESLs were defined as:

1. Personnel discharged compulsorily from the trained strength who lose eligibility/entitlement which they otherwise would have because of the circumstances surrounding, and the category of, discharge.
2. Personnel discharged from the untrained strength, either compulsorily or at their own request.

This definition has been further refined over subsequent issues of both the resettlement manual (JSP 534) and the specific ESL publication (JSP 575) until the amalgamation of these two publications and the most recent definition contained within Issue14 of JSP 534, as of 1 October 2015:

Early Service Leavers (ESLs) are defined as Service Leavers (SL) who are discharged:

1. Compulsorily[2] from the trained strength or untrained strength and who lose entitlement to resettlement provision in accordance with JSP 534 that they would otherwise have because of the circumstances of their discharge.
2. At their own request from the trained or untrained strength, having completed less than 4 years' service (Para 0302 *et seq.*).

What are the practice implications of these definitions? With the advent, in 2002, of a contract to streamline transition support provision for service leavers, certain

TABLE 3.1 Entitlement to transition support

Years' Service	Normal discharge				Medical discharge*			
	CTP	GRT	IRTC	Travel warrants	CTP	GRT	IRTC	Travel warrants
<1	CTP Future Horizons	0	No	0	CRP	10	Yes	4
1+	CTP Future Horizons	0	No	0	CRP	30	Yes	6
4+	ESP	0	No	0	CRP	30	Yes	6
6+	CRP	20	Yes	4	CRP	30	Yes	6
8+	CRP	25	Yes	5	CRP	30	Yes	6
12+	CRP	30	Yes	6	CRP	30	Yes	6
16+	CRP	35	Yes	7	CRP	35	Yes	7

CTP, Career Transition Partnership; GRT, graduated resettlement time (working days); IRTC, individual resettlement training costs; ESP, Employment Support Programme; CRP, Core Resettlement Programme.

*This includes reservists who have been medically discharged due to injuries sustained during operational commitments.

Reproduced and modified from JSP 534 Issue 14, October 2015, Para. 0313.

categories of provision were mandated for the first time in an overarching tri-service policy. For service leavers who have entitlement to support, this is detailed within all the iterations of the tri-service resettlement manual (JSP 534). The entitlement to support is complex and it is summarised in Table 3.1.

Of the different categories of ESL, by far the largest majority are those that leave during phase 1 basic training, which is within the first 26 or so weeks of entering the military. In the UK military, there are certain contractual break points when new recruits can make a decision to self-discharge, this is known as 'discharge as of right' (DAOR) and in the Infantry, this accounts for nearly 30 per cent of all recruits (Fossey, 2013). Of the 1,249 ESLs who participated in the Future Horizons ESL Programme Pilot at the Infantry Training Centre, Catterick Garrison, 1,156 were discharged during basic training, 69 left between basic training and their 4-year entitlement window and 24 were entitled to support, having served more than 4 years, but had lost this benefit due to the nature of their discharge (Fossey and Hacker Hughes, 2014).

For ESLs, the processes as detailed in JSP 575 were not associated with supporting the individual to transition through a graduated system of employment support rewards. Rather, the procedure was focused on the most efficient way of processing the individual out of the military so that equipment is returned, necessary medical checks undertaken and the requisite paperwork completed. The efficiency of this process means that it was completed in as little as a couple of weeks.[3]

There are obvious implications. For personnel who are determined that they want to get out of the military and do so before they have any entitlement to support, they are not expecting any assistance with transition. However, for those who have served more than four years and have accrued an entitlement, being summarily discharged may have profound implications for themselves and their families: loss of immediate prospects, accommodation and supportive environment being but three.

To date, the research has tended to focus on those ESLs who have served for less than four years (Buckman *et al.*, 2013), who represent by far the largest number of ESLs. However, we know nothing about the vulnerability or outcomes for the proportion of ESLs who have lost entitlement to formal transition support. Analysis of recently obtained data (unpublished) from the MOD suggests that, across all branches, the proportion of ESLs who would have been entitled to support might be as high as 20 per cent (Godier *et al.*, forthcoming).

Literature review

Little is known about ESLs in the UK. However, the research that has been conducted suggests that this group are more vulnerable to problems in transitioning back to civilian life. This may be related to pre-service vulnerabilities, such as social circumstances or educational attainment, or may be associated with their service history. In demographic terms, ESLs are more likely to be male,[4] single, younger, in the Army and of lower rank (Iversen *et al.*, 2005; Woodhead *et al.*, 2011; Buckman *et al.*, 2013; Giebel *et al.*, 2014), compared with non-ESLs. However, this research has used the definition of those who have served for four years or fewer, meaning that we know little about those who have been discharged early for disciplinary reasons.

Leaving the Armed Forces early means that many ESLs will not have had the chance to develop transferable skills and gain qualifications that would help them in finding civilian employment. In addition, they are not entitled to the same level of employment support that other service leavers are provided with. A survey carried out by the National Audit Office suggested that 16 per cent of ESLs who left the service in the 2 years prior to October 2006 were unemployed, compared with just 6 per cent of non-ESLs (National Audit Office, 2007). Furthermore, post-discharge employment statistics for ESLs in this period showed that 61 per cent were registered with the Department for Work and Pensions and 34 per cent were claiming Job Seekers Allowance (National Audit Office, 2007). This datum suggests that a number of ESLs struggle to find employment on separation from the military.

Being an ESL has been associated with poorer mental health outcomes compared with non-ESLs. Research commissioned by the Royal British Legion (RBL) suggested that 25 per cent of young ESLs experience depression, anxiety or PTSD (Rhodes *et al.*, 2006). Higher levels of common mental health disorders and PTSD, as well as fatigue and multiple physical symptoms, have been reported in ESLs (Buckman *et al.*, 2013; Iversen *et al.*, 2005). Furthermore, a cross-sectional analysis of adults responding to a national survey further suggested that ESLs were more likely to be heavy drinkers, have suicidal thoughts and self-harm (Woodhead *et al.*, 2011).

Whilst these studies suggest that being an ESL is associated with increased risks of mental health problems, the cross-sectional nature of the studies means that it is not possible to determine the direction of this association. It may be that pre-existing mental health problems and/or adversity increases vulnerability to leaving the service early. For example, Buckman *et al.* (2013) reported that higher levels of childhood adversity were associated with being an ESL. This is consistent with literature from the US which points to a significant relationship between childhood abuse and early separation from the military (Patrick *et al.*, 2011). Furthermore, pre-existing mental health problems have been associated with greater disadvantage (two or more of the following: debt, temporary accommodation, mental health problem, unemployment) in individuals leaving the Armed Forces early via military prison (Van Staden *et al.*, 2007). This suggests that pre-existing problems may be associated with both being an ESL and poorer outcomes on leaving the military.

It is also possible that early separation itself leads to an increased risk of developing a mental health problem. Indeed, scores on measures of general mental health and PTSD have been found to increase over time in ESLs, in comparison to non-ESLs, whose scores decreased over time (Iversen *et al.*, 2005). ESLs are entitled to a reduced resettlement provision, making it less likely that they will get help after leaving the services (Ashcroft, 2014). Indeed, Woodhead *et al.* (2011) reported that ESLs with a mental health disorder were less likely to seek help for an emotional or mental health problem compared with non-ESLs, making it more likely these problems will persist or worsen.

Compared with the UK, significantly more research has been carried out in the US, most commonly focusing on those who leave the military during basic training or in their first contracted term (Knapik *et al.*, 2004). Leaving early is associated with several mental-health related risk factors, such as pre-service sexual/physical abuse, depression and suicidal ideation/self-harm (Booth-Kewley *et al.*, 2002; Staal *et al.*, 2000). However, in contrast to UK research, a number of studies suggest that being married is associated with early separation from the US military (Fishl and Blackwell, 2000; Pollack *et al.*, 2009). This difference may be related to differences in lengths of deployment, which tend to be longer in the US military, and may be less conducive to family life. In addition, whilst ESLs tend to be younger in the UK, early separation is reported to show a bimodal relationship with attrition in the US, with 17 to 18 year olds and those over 23 at greatest risk of early attrition (Knapik *et al.*, 2004; Pollack *et al.*, 2009; Reis *et al.*, 2007). Both these disparities need to be further investigated in the UK, considering the paucity of research on ESLs. Additional factors associated with leaving the military early in the US include lower educational attainment, white ethnicity, lower physical activity and higher body mass index prior to service (Knapik *et al.*, 2001; Pollack *et al.*, 2009; Packnett *et al.*, 2011; Reis *et al.*, 2007).

Despite the vulnerabilities associated with being an ESL, there are few services available to ESLs in the UK to help in the transition back to civilian life, and they are not entitled to the same resettlement provision as non-ESLs. In an effort to further improve the transition pathway for ESLs, the MOD commissioned the Future Horizons Programme (FHP) in 2011 to consider how the employment and transitional needs of ESLs could be met. This programme aims to help ESLs with their transition, and importantly, to help ESLs find appropriate employment. ESLs were given access to a range of different forms of employment and welfare provision. FHP engaged with 777 ESLs at Catterick Garrison during this trial, and 63.4 per cent of the individuals were in education or training within 6 months, comparing very favourably with previous governmental employability schemes (Fossey, 2013).

The factors associated with difficulties in transition are likely to be interrelated, for example, mental health problems may make it difficult for ESLs to gain employment, and conversely, unemployment is associated with mental health problems. As such, programmes such as the FHP may have a wider impact on successful transition. Further research is required to better understand the factors associated with being an ESL in the UK in order to develop successful interventions and services that will help with successful transition.

Current thinking and research priorities

Given the lack of prior research with ESLs in the UK, the Veterans and Families Institute at Anglia Ruskin University conducted a scoping study with key industry figures and stakeholders to understand what the priorities for future research with this cohort should be. The aim of this scoping study was to identify what topics need to be addressed, and what questions asked, in order to enhance understandings of ESLs and to ascertain what information about ESLs would be of benefit to the various stakeholders and agencies responsible for their care.

Several agencies and organisations were identified as key industry stakeholders with an interest in, or responsibility for, the fate (across several broad domains including health, employment and social needs) of ESLs in civilian society. These included the NHS, MOD, Forces in Mind Trust (FiMT), Career Transition Partnership (CTP), FHP, RBL, Royal British Legion Industries (RBLI), Combat Stress (CS) and the Kings Centre for Military Health Research (KCMHR) at King's College London (KCL). Through our own contacts, we identified ten individuals who we considered to be high-level or experienced personnel within these organisations and who would be knowledgeable about their organisation's role or interest regarding ESLs. All of them were senior managers or executives, or held specialist research and/or policy-focused positions within these organisations and had a specified or previously avowed interest in ESLs.

Each of the ten identified representatives volunteered to take part in the scoping study and gave informed consent to participate in a telephone interview. Interviews were organised around the central question 'What do you think the priorities for research with early service leavers should be, and why?'. Follow-up questions included what studies or methodologies may be appropriate to investigate the key identified research topics, and what were the interviewees' perceptions of the way in which ESLs have been defined as a group. The interviews took place between February and March 2016 and lasted 23 minutes on average. They were conducted and transcribed by the same researcher (Nick Caddick). Each interview was then content analysed by two of the study authors (Nick Caddick and Lauren Godier). A thematic analysis (Braun and Clarke, 2006) was then conducted to identify key emerging themes from the interview transcripts. Ethical approval for the scoping study was granted by Anglia Ruskin University's Research Ethics Committee.

Priorities for future research

Four key themes reflect the most commonly identified priorities for future research from the perspective of key industry stakeholders with an interest in ESLs. These are broad themes which encapsulated several more specific questions which will also be identified in the following discussion. A fifth theme, 'proposed studies and methodologies' described the kinds of studies suggested by the consulted representatives that would help to answer some of the key research questions.

Understanding the different 'types' of ESL encapsulated by the definition

There was agreement across the board from our consulted representatives regarding the need to understand key differences within the category of 'early service leaver'. Differences between ESLs discharged during basic training, from the trained strength but before four years, and those receiving a compulsory discharge were repeatedly cited as a priority for further investigation. As one representative from the Forces in Mind Trust commented on the category of 'ESLs':

> [It] brackets a huge range of Service Leavers, each of which warrants their own little bit of work and attention. And to mix them all up as a homogenous cohort entitled ESLs can be very misleading to people who don't understand what is in it. When you include somebody who's done a day's basic training in the same cohort as somebody who does his very first tour in Afghanistan and returns home having done a tour of duty, you can see the nonsense. But it causes huge difficulties in understanding pathways into failure and into success. And also when it comes to supporting ESLs, it brings huge issues around where and how that support is delivered.

It was therefore suggested by several of the interviewees that the needs and vulnerabilities of ESLs may vary considerably depending on factors such as the length of their service and the nature of their discharge. For instance, the representative from King's College London commented that compulsorily discharged ESLs may harbour additional vulnerabilities due to the enforced nature of their discharge. This was echoed by the representatives from the RBL and RBLI, and the representative from CS, who shared the following insight from a clinical practice perspective:

> I think clinically when I work with those people, they're very angry at the military and they're very angry at how they left the military. It may be that they have a whole host of post-service transition problems which I suspect – that

anger at the military is part of those transition problems, but also it's difficult for them to transition because maybe they left because they were experiencing mental health difficulties or they were experiencing social problems. And so they didn't leave in a way that was conducive to a good transition.

There is, however, no existing research relating to compulsorily discharged ESLs, given that the limited research on ESLs to date has focused on those who leave before four years of service (Buckman *et al.*, 2013). One priority for future research is thus to develop a better understanding of the different reasons why an individual may end up as an ESL and the implications of the route to discharge on the transition experiences and outcomes of ESLs. As part of this, research should consider what factors may lead to a service member being compulsorily discharged via the Military Corrective Training Centre (MCTC; Van Staden *et al.*, 2007), and whether – as suggested by a representative from the NHS – there may be underlying mental health or social problems that could have contributed in some cases. Overall, the interviewees were unanimous in their suggestions that future research with ESLs should not treat them as a homogenous group, and should look to tease apart important differences between the various 'types' of ESL. Furthermore, teasing out differences between ESLs from different services (Army, Royal Navy and RAF) was also considered important by our interviewees.

Understanding where the vulnerabilities arise from

Linked to the previous theme, another prominent suggestion from our interviewees was that future research should seek to understand where the 'vulnerabilities' that ESLs present with arise from. In particular, the consulted representatives were concerned with whether ESLs were considered vulnerable due to pre-service influences, such as poverty and lack of opportunity, or whether experiences in-service had negatively influenced the life and careers of ESLs and caused them to leave the military early. As the representative from KCL asked:

> Are these people that have come in with vulnerabilities, they've left and they're still vulnerable – that they're the ones that actually aren't doing very well, and are struggling to make their way further into the future?

Once again, the question of vulnerability was linked to the purported differences between different 'types' of ESL. For instance, several of our interviewees speculated that for ESLs exiting very early or during basic training, pre-service factors may explain the 'failure' to adapt to military life. By contrast, for those choosing to leave before four years, experiences in service (e.g. on operational tours) may have contributed vulnerabilities (e.g. mental or physical health problems), which, in turn, may complicate transition.

Understanding the causes of vulnerability was therefore cited as a priority for research with ESLs. The rationale for this focus on causality was articulated by a representative from the NHS as follows:

One thing that I'd like to get to the bottom of is those things which are peculiar to service, and those things which are due to social background factors … not because it would make us treat them differently, but it would allow us to be able to identify those things that we can change in service and those things that we can't. So how we solve the problem depends on if the aetiology of the circumstances is different, it may require a different course of treatment.

Understanding the causality of vulnerability would thereby enable key stakeholders – such as the MOD and NHS – to better target resources and interventions to support ESLs either in-service or pre/post transition. As part of understanding the causes of vulnerabilities, representatives from the NHS, FiMT, RBLI and FHP all spoke of the need to understand the backgrounds of ESLs as well as their motivations for joining the Forces. For example, is it the case (as was commonly suggested) that high numbers of ESLs from the Infantry carried pre-existing vulnerabilities, routed in social disadvantage, into military life which caused them to fail? If so, what about their disadvantaged backgrounds, specifically, caused some to fail whilst other recruits from deprived areas succeeded in military life and achieved upward social mobility as a result? In addition, rather than focusing purely on the notion of 'vulnerability' – as indeed any service leaver might potentially be 'vulnerable' in some way – a representative from the MOD questioned whether brief periods of military service might have equipped people to deal better with poor circumstances. Looking beyond sensationalised media accounts of ESLs 'crashing and burning' in civilian life, this interviewee therefore stated that research might also consider potential positive influences of military life upon ESLs:

> I would suggest research in that area, looking at the raw material coming in, and the baggage that they bring, and comparing that to when they exit. And, yes they've still got baggage, but actually their life in the military may have actually removed some of that baggage that they leave with, and better coping skills than they would otherwise have had, had they not had the military intervention.

Related to this, our interviewees wanted to know what motivating factors were leading ESLs to sign up to a military career in the first place. As our representative from the RBLI queried: 'whether it was always their aspiration, or whether it was for example a means of escape?' And as this interviewee further explained:

> If it wasn't a genuine vocational goal then perhaps their mind wasn't in it, perhaps the level of the support network that they had either before or during Service just simply hasn't been there. So trying to understand the causal piece because I think if we understood the causal piece we might have a better understanding of how better to support them.

Finally, one further question about vulnerability and causality was related to the effects of military training and understanding how the transition into military life may complicate the later transition back into civilian society:

> We talk about the transition from military to civilian life, and I wondered whether there is any sense of when you can perhaps be considered to have transitioned into military life. Is that the day that you join? That you are then military? So if you join for a week and then leave, how much of a military person have you become in that time?
>
> (*FiMT*)

As our representative from FiMT implies, understanding the temporal nature of transition into military life has potential implications for ESLs leaving at different points in the training cycle (after one week, one month, three months, etc.). Understanding to what extent a person may become 'militarised' by different lengths of exposure to military training may therefore help to unpack the influence of training during the transition back to civilian life. Following on from this, the point at which an ESL is discharged could then be considered in terms of an individual's strength of identification with the military and how much this may need to be 'undone' through their transition.

What are the actual transition experiences of ESLs?

Another priority for research focuses on understanding how ESLs themselves experience the process of transition back into civilian life. There were several aspects of the transition experience that our interviewees felt it was important to focus on. First, there was the question of what the issues are for ESLs themselves. In the words of our representative from the RBL:

> We think we know what the issues are but sometimes it's really good just to go back to basics and say, for ESLs now living in the world that we live in at this moment, what are their biggest barriers, what are their biggest problems?

Beyond familiar and instrumentalised categories, such as homelessness, crime, drugs, alcohol and mental health, our interviews therefore advocated talking to ESLs and finding out, from their perspective, what are the major issues and difficulties associated with the experience of transition.

A second subtheme arose around understanding ESLs' experience of the resettlement process; that is, 'the formal processes and procedures by which transition is managed, and the formal support provided to Service leavers during transition' (Forces in Mind Trust, 2013: 16). In this regard, representatives from the RBL and CTP both commented on the need to understand the reasons why ESLs might engage with, or disengage from, the resettlement process during their transition. For the CTP – the organisation in charge of delivering employment and resettlement support to ESLs – there was a particular challenge regarding 'engagement' which called for further exploration through research:

One challenge we have is with the delivery model. We get hold of ESLs at the very 11th hour, in fact at the 11th and a half, because of the way in which they are discharged from the military. And a lot of these guys – guys and girls but principally guys, it's very much – at the point at which they're dealing with us – all they want to know is 'how do I get home'. And someone likened it to me in the past, and I think this analogy works – it's like going to a party, having a stinking hangover, and just wanting to get home. You don't want to think about what comes afterwards until you've got over the hangover. So often we're trying to give people information and it's the only time we've got, but in terms of them listening to us and engaging with us, it's very difficult to get the engagement. And a lot of work has gone into how we can best engage with these guys behind the wire prior to discharge … What is the stuff that works – we don't know. And the other thing is, of course – what caused them to disengage?

It was therefore suggested that understanding ESLs' experiences of engaging (or not) with transition and resettlement support would help to enhance the transition pathway for ESLs. Linked to this was a need to understand the 'tools' used within the resettlement process and whether these tools were useful to the ESLs undergoing transition. The value of such tools (e.g. job-finding service, career planning applications, resettlement briefings) to ESLs' own transition experiences is not well known, and consequently, 'what works' in supporting successful transitions for ESLs is not yet fully understood. Furthermore, the RBLI representative asked whether ESLs were engaging with the broader notion of 'transition'; whether they accepted the circumstances of their discharge or whether it constituted a 'head-in-the-sand' moment for them. Given that, anecdotally, 'a significant majority have this feeling of wanting to get back in' (RBLI), it would be useful for research to consider what effect the circumstances of an ESL's discharge has on his or her experience of, and engagement with, transition.

What are the various transition 'outcomes' and how do ESLs fare in civilian life?

Understanding what 'outcomes' are achieved by ESLs – across several domains including health, housing, education, employment and welfare – and how these differ from non-ESLs, was identified by our consulted representatives as another important priority for research. As Fossey (2013) identified, very little is known about what happens to ESLs after they leave the military. Tracking their 'outcomes' in civilian life thus constitutes a key priority:

We actually don't know that much about these outcomes amongst ESLs. So one piece of work, I would say, is before you can say 'how does it need to be improved', you need to actually get a robust idea of what are the rates of these adverse outcomes and how do they compare with what we would expect based on those that have served for longer, and how do they compare with the general population as a whole?

(KCL)

One outcome of particular interest to our interviewees was employment. For the CTP representative, finding suitable civilian employment was seen as a key pillar (albeit not the only one) of successful transition. Given that only 52 per cent of ESLs are reported to be in employment 6 months after leaving (compared with 85 per cent of longer-serving veterans), employment outcomes for ESLs do indeed seem worthy of consideration (Ashcroft, 2014). Understanding how ESLs fare in the long-term in the civilian labour market was considered an important priority by interviewees from the MOD, KCL, CTP, RBLI and Future Horizons. Furthermore, according to our CTP representative, an important part of understanding employment outcomes is considering the outcomes that ESLs actually want:

> One of the challenges that comes with that [understanding employment outcomes] is the recognition that a number of them go into things that statisticians and the government don't like, in terms of the grey economy – you know, they're very much hand-to-mouth a lot of these guys, it's what they want, it's what suits them given their age and where they're at. And in stats terms, people want them to have a proper meaningful resilient job – so there's a bit of a conflict there I think.

Considering the types of work sought out by ESLs, therefore, seems to be an important component of understanding what successful, sustainable employment means in the context of transition for ESLs. Likewise, identifying the pathways into employment (i.e. *how* ESLs find and secure civilian jobs) would help to explain the process of a 'successful' transition.

Beyond a focus on employment, transition outcomes such as health, housing and social integration remain largely unexplored for ESLs. Aside from the Buckman *et al.* (2013) finding that ESLs experienced a higher degree of mental health problems, no research has explored long-term health outcomes in ESLs. Understanding health outcomes, help-seeking behaviours and service utilisation by ESLs was therefore identified as another priority for research. In addition, our representative from Combat Stress added the issue of social exclusion to the list of considerations. As this interviewee suggested:

> Something about whether veterans are able to form an identity which is not just as a veteran, whether it's also as a civilian – and whether they're able to hold both. I don't know whether that would make a good transition or not, but one suspects that if you were able to feel part of the wider general public, that might support you.

Certainly, research would suggest that strong identification as a veteran may be linked to a lack of integration among some ex-service personnel (e.g. Demers, 2011).

Exploring the extent to which a 'legacy' of military life (Cooper *et al.*, 2017) may complicate transition and contribute to social exclusion thus seems worthwhile.

Finally, an issue raised by our FiMT representative was the duration of the resettlement process for ESLs. According to the Transition Mapping Study conducted by the Forces in Mind Trust (2013), one of the foremost factors contributing to successful transition to civilian life is time for preparation 'behind the wire'. Given that the discharge process of ESLs is typically very rapid (often no more than two weeks; see Fossey, 2013), research may also wish to consider what preparations ESLs are able to undertake during their discharge and resettlement process, and whether these are sufficient to enable them to make a successful initial transition.

Proposed studies and methodologies

Many of the identified research priorities seem to call for longitudinal, prospective follow-up studies to track the development of ESLs' trajectories through service life, during discharge and following the process of transition. For instance, understanding transition 'outcomes' and identifying causal factors related to vulnerability would both require the tracking of ESLs at numerous time points. As our representative from KCL explained:

> So I think you almost need a recruit study – you need to get people the minute they walk through the door to be able to start to follow them up from that point and just kind of see what happens to them as they go through their career … The data that is out there is cross-sectional. We do need longitudinal data and until we've got that, it's difficult to have a strong evidence base and to know where the problems really are and where we could and should intervene.

Such a 'recruit study' would thereby facilitate an understanding of the life course and trajectories of ESLs post-discharge, and would help to address a number of the research priorities. As representatives from KCL, Combat Stress and the RBL also noted, however, such large scale prospective follow-up studies are typically expensive and logistically difficult to conduct.

Qualitative research was also highlighted as particularly relevant for understanding ESLs' actual experiences of transition. Indeed, exploring the issues from ESLs' own perspectives and developing a more in-depth understanding of their backgrounds and motivations for joining the military are topics that would seemingly lend themselves to qualitative exploration. In addition, understanding the reasons why ESLs either engage or disengage from the resettlement process – and the process of transition more broadly – also call for a qualitative approach. Representatives from the NHS and KCL both commented generally on the need for qualitative and/or mixed methods research:

> I think there's something about the qualitative issues that go behind it that actually enable you to understand what's going on.

> (NHS)

> Being able to triangulate 'quant' and 'qual' data. To maybe do some focus groups or interviews with recruits, asking them some of the more qualitative questions that would match the quantitative data that you're trying to drill down to get at.
>
> (KCL)

Discussion

Little is currently known about the experiences and vulnerabilities of ESLs in the UK, and why this group appear to fare worse post-transition. Interviews with key industry stakeholders suggested that future research with ESLs should focus on where vulnerabilities arise from and how this differs with regard to length of service and type of discharge. It was further suggested that mapping the transition experience and the health and social 'outcomes' of transition in ESLs should be priorities for research in this group.

Whilst the literature reviewed in this chapter suggests that ESLs fare worse after service in terms of employment and general and mental health than their regular peers (Buckman et al., 2013; Iversen et al., 2005; National Audit Office, 2007; Woodhead et al., 2011), it is not clear why this group appears to be particularly vulnerable to problems in transition. As identified by the interviewees, the cross-sectional nature of the research that has been carried out means that conclusions cannot yet be drawn in regard to where these vulnerabilities arise from. For example, both pre-existing mental health problems, and childhood adversity are associated with being an ESL (Buckman et al., 2013; Woodhead et al., 2011). However, mental health problems are also shown to increase post-service in ESLs compared with non-ESLs (Iversen et al., 2005). Further research into the transition 'outcomes' of ESLs and untangling the causality of poor post-transition outcomes in ESLs were therefore seen as important research priorities.

The limited research that has been carried out has used the definition of those who have served for four years or fewer, excluding those ESLs who have been discharged early for disciplinary reasons and those discharged during basic training (Buckman et al., 2013; Iversen et al., 2005). As such, a recurring priority identified for future research was to understand how different 'types' of ESLs differ in their vulnerability to poor post-transition outcomes and in their need for support. Interviewees felt that those discharged for disciplinary reasons may be a particularly vulnerable group in this context. The enforced nature of discharge may mean that separation from the military is against the individual's wishes, potentially making transition a more challenging process. Indeed, administrative discharge has been associated with greater disadvantage post discharge (in terms of debt, temporary accommodation, mental health problems and unemployment) in those leaving via military prison (Van Staden et al., 2007). Furthermore, differentiation by type of service was also highlighted as important due to the potential impact of differences in discharge procedures between services. Previous research suggests that the Army is proportionally overrepresented in ESLs compared with non-ESLs (Buckman et al., 2013). Thus, differentiating between different subgroups of ESLs may help identify those most vulnerable to experiencing problems in transition.

A better understanding of the actual experience of transition from the perspective of ESLs was also seen as an important priority for future research. Very little is currently known about the transition experiences of ESLs, how they view the current resettlement support and why they may engage/disengage with support. Interviewees felt that 'getting back to basics' and asking the ESLs themselves what problems they experienced during transition would be important in identifying where to target support services. Furthermore, whilst previous research has focused on traditional transition outcomes, such as employment and mental health, interviewees highlighted that a number of other factors such as housing and social support required more investigation in ESLs. Using research to create a wider picture of ESLs transition experiences and outcomes was therefore seen by interviewees as necessary to aid the improvement of, and engagement with, support services.

We also find it useful to reflect critically on the methods and methodologies that may begin to shape emerging areas of research with ESLs. Undoubtedly, large-scale epidemiological studies and statistical analyses will need to play a role in understanding the general cohort of ESLs. Such studies will be necessary in order to identify key differences between the various 'types' of ESL and to ascertain from where particular vulnerabilities arise.

In addition, there are other potentially less expensive or complex methodologies that may yield fruitful insights into the nature of transition for ESLs. One example – suggested by a representative from the NHS – is that of ethnography (an approach to studying people and the cultures they inhabit, typically relying on the researcher immersing him- or herself in that culture and conducting extensive observations and interviews with its 'inhabitants'). With regard to ESLs, ethnography may constitute a primary means of exploring the cultural transition that ESLs necessarily undertake when leaving the forces. In particular, an ethnographic angle could help to explore the sense of 'reverse culture shock', which Bergman *et al.* (2014) posited may be acutely experienced by ESLs. As these authors suggest for ESLs, 'already culturally disorientated from commencing the process of becoming a soldier, they now have to face returning to a civilian world which already regards them as "different"' (2014: 65). An ethnographic study could, for example, involve a study of 'Hook Company' within the British Army; the primary purpose of which is to ensure smooth transition of ESLs and medically discharged soldiers back into civilian life (Fossey, 2013).

Alternatively, researchers could utilise narrative inquiry to explore the identity stories of ESLs in connection with their military and post-military experiences (Smith and Sparkes, 2008). Following the suggestions of our consulted representatives, a narrative approach would help to illuminate the transition journeys undertaken by ESLs, examine the extent to which they identify with the character of 'soldier' or 'veteran' and explore the effect this has upon their integration back into civilian society. The inclusion of the previous methodological examples is not meant to circumscribe the type of research that might be conducted with ESLs, or even to suggest that these studies must be done in order to advance the state of research on ESLs. Rather, we aim to stimulate possibilities and to encourage a broad perspective on the kinds of studies that may yield important insights about ESLs, and lead to further improvements in policy and practice.

It is intended that this chapter will help to maximise the impact of future research with ESLs by ensuring that such research is driven by, and designed according to, the knowledge needs of the key stakeholders. This chapter has provided a list of key research priorities and a series of questions that may be asked to enable future studies to exploit the most significant knowledge gaps and to address the most pertinent needs for evidence. In order to move the research on ESLs forward, funding commitments are likely to be needed to enable the type of longitudinal, prospective follow-up studies that are also required. Funding might also be prioritised for research that will yield important insights into the transition experiences of ESLs and lead to improvements in policy and service provision.

Conclusion

To address the knowledge needs outlined by key industry stakeholders, the long-term priority for research should be to build a picture of ESLs through their military career and transition. The aim of this research should be to identify where support should be targeted – and how the existing pathways can be built upon – to have the biggest impact in improving transition for ESLs. Indeed, in the *Veteran's Transition Review*, Ashcroft (2014) suggested that 'Improving outcomes for these Service Leavers is essential to improving transition overall, and will be to the benefit of the Armed Forces and the country as a whole' (Ashcroft, 2014: 14). At present, transition support for ESLs is limited to a basic package provided by the FHP, via the CTP, going some way to meet the recommendation set out by Lord Ashcroft:

> All Service Leavers who have completed basic training should be eligible for the full transition support package … offered by the Career Transition Partnership. Early Service Leavers, who have served up to four years, are the most likely to experience unemployment and other problems and get only the most basic transition support.
>
> (*Ashcroft, 2014: 15*)

Programmes such as the FHP have been shown to be successful in improving transition outcomes for ESLs (Fossey, 2011), and this programme has become standard provision for ESLs under the new CTP contract. It is hoped that the research priorities identified in this chapter will stimulate research that will aid in the development and improvement of evidence-based interventions to improve transition experience and outcomes for ESLs.

Notes

1 All military personnel, regardless of length of service, are now eligible for a certain amount of support under the new contract with the Career Transition Partnership (the UK military's contracted suppliers for transition support).

2   Conditions under which personnel are categorised as Compulsorily Discharged from the trained strength may be found in Single Service regulations.
3   For those discharging as of right (DAOR), there is a contractual requirement that discharge is completed within two weeks.
4   In terms of proportion, females are more likely than males to leave early, whereas in the overall cohort of ESLs, males vastly outnumber females due to the much greater numbers of male recruits.

References

Ashcroft, M. (2014). *The Veterans Transition Review*. London: Lord Ashcroft KCMG PC. Available online at www.veteranstransition.co.uk/vtrreport.pdf (accessed29 January 2016).

Bergman, B., Burdett, H., Greenberg, N. (2014). Service life and beyond – institution or culture? *The RUSI Journal*, 159, 60–8.

Booth-Kewley, S., Larson, G.E., Ryan, M.A.K. (2002). Predictors of naval attrition. I. Analysis of 1 year attrition. *Military Medicine*, 167, 760–9.

Braun, V., Clarke, V. (2006). Using thematic analysis in psychology. *Qualitative Research in Psychology*, 3, 77–101.

Buckman, J.E.J., Forbes, H.J., Clayton, T., Jones, M., Jones, N., Greenberg, N., Sundin, J., Hull, L., Wessely, S., Fear, N. T. (2013). Early service leavers: A study of the factors associated with premature separation for the UK Armed Forces and the mental health of those that leave early. *European Journal of Public Health*, 23, 410–14.

Cooper, L., Caddick, N., Godier, L., Cooper, A., Fossey, M. (2017). Transition from the military into civilian life: An exploration of cultural competence. *Armed Forces & Society*. DOI: 10.1177/0095327X16675965.

Demers, A. (2011). When veterans return: The role of community in reintegration. *Journal of Loss and Trauma*, 16, 160–79.

Fishl, M.A., Blackwell, D.L. (2000). *Attrition in the Army from Signing of the Enlistment Contract Through 180 Days of Service*. Alexandria: US Army Research Institute for the Behavioral and Social Sciences. Available online at www.dtic.mil/cgi-bin/GetTRDoc?AD=ADA372717 (accessed 1 February 2016).

Forces in Mind Trust (2013). *The Transition Mapping Study*. London: Forces in Mind Trust. Available online at http://www.fim-trust.org/wp-content/uploads/2015/01/20130810-TMS-Report.pdf (accessed 19 January 2017).

Fossey, M. (2011). *Unsung Heroes: Developing a better understanding of the emotional support needs of Service families*. London: Centre for Mental Health.

Fossey, M. (2013). *Transition Support for British Army Early Service Leavers: An Evaluation of the Future Horizons Programme*. Catterick: Future Horizons Programme. Available online at www.rfea.org.uk/wp-content/uploads/2015/08/An-Evaluation-of-the-Future-Horizons-Programme-Infantry-Training-Centre-Catterick.pdf (accessed 29 January 2016).

Fossey, M. and Hacker Hughes, J. (2014). *Future Horizons Programme: Final Report*. London: RFEA.

Giebel, C. M., Clarkson, P., Challis, D. (2014). Demographic and clinical characteristics of UK military veterans attending a psychological therapies service. *Psychiatric Bulletin*, 38, 170–5.

Godier, L., Caddick, N., Fossey, M. (forthcoming). Transition support for vulnerable service leavers: Providing care for early service leavers.

Iversen, A., Nikolaou, V., Greenberg, N., Unwin, C., Hull, L., Hotopf, M., Dandeker, C., Ross, J, Wessely, S. (2005). What happens to British veterans when they leave the armed forces? *European Journal of Public Health*, 15, 175–84.

Knapik, J.J., Canham-Chervak, M., Hauret, K., Hoedebecke, E., Jones, B.H. (2001). Discharges during US Army basic combat training: Injury rates and risk factors. *Military Medicine*, 166, 641–7.

Knapik, J.J., Jones, B. H., Hauret, K., Darakjy, S., Piskator, E. (2004). *A Review of the Literature on Attrition from the Military Services: Risk Factors for Attrition and Strategies to Reduce Attrition*. Ft Knox: Center for Accessions Research. Available online at http://oai.dtic.mil/oai/oai?verb=getRecord&metadataPrefix=html&identifier=ADA427744 (accessed 1 February 2016).

National Audit Office. (2007). *Ministry of Defence: Leaving the Services*. (HC 618 Session 2006–2007, 27 July 2007.) London: The Stationery Office Limited. Available online at www.publications.parliament.uk/pa/cm200708/cmselect/cmpubacc/351/351.pdf (accessed 29 January 2016).

Packnett, E.R., Niebuhr, D.W., Bedno, S.A., Cowan, D.N. (2011). Body mass index, medical qualification status, and discharge during the first year of US Army service. *American Journal of Clinical Nutrition*, 93, 608–14.

Patrick, V., Critchfield, E., Vaccaro, T., Campbell, J. (2011). The relationship of childhood abuse and early separation from the military among army advanced individual trainees. *Military Medicine*, 176, 182–5.

Pollack, L.M., Boyer, C.B., Betsinger, K., Shafer, M.-A. (2009). Predictors of one-year attrition in female Marine Corps recruits. *Military Medicine*, 174, 382–91.

Reis, J.P., Trone, D.W., Macera, C.A., Rauh, M.J. (2007). Factors associated with discharge during Marine Corps basic training. *Military Medicine*, 172, 936–41.

Rhodes, D., Pleace, N., Fitzpatrick, S. (2006). *The Experience of Homeless Ex-service Personnel in London*. York: Centre for Housing Policy. Available online at https://www.york.ac.uk/media/chp/documents/2008/HomelessExServiceinLondon.pdf (accessed 29 January 2016).

Smith, B., Sparkes, A. (2008). Contrasting perspectives on narrating selves and identities: An invitation to dialogue. *Qualitative Research*, 8, 5–35.

Staal, M.A., Cigrang, J.A., Fiedler, E. (2000). Disposition decisions in U.S. Air Force basic trainees assessed during mental health evaluations. *Military Psychology*, 12, 187–203.

Van Staden, L., Fear, N.T., Iversen, A. C., French, C.E., Dandeker, C., Wessely, S. (2007). Transition back to civilian life: A study of Personnel leaving the UK Armed Forces via 'Military Prison'. *Military Medicine*, 172, 925–30.

Woodhead, C., Rona, R. J., Iversen, A., MacManus, D., Hotopf, M., Dean, K., MacManus, S., Meltzer, H., Brugha, T., Jenkins, R., Wessely, S., Fear, N.T. (2011). Mental health and health service use among post-national service veterans: results from the 2007 Adult Psychiatric Morbidity Survey of England. *Psychological Medicine*, 41, 363–72.

4

VETERANS' CHILDREN

Joy O'Neill

Being a military child never ends.

(Musil, 2013)

Introduction

This chapter is for practitioners, researchers, parents or indeed anyone who is interested in veterans' children. My purpose is to shine a light on this often-invisible group of children and, additionally, to offer some insights and suggestions based on both wider research and evidence-based interventions that were developed and used with service and veterans' children in the UK since 2009.

My background is in early years and primary education with a focus on disadvantaged children and young people and I am also a veterans' wife, having lived within the service community for over 20 years. I have approached this chapter through the lens of an early years' educator, placing the child's voice at the heart of the piece and considering the multi-layered issues and how they impact on children and young people.

Specifically, we will explore:

- Who are veterans' children?
- What is so different about veterans' children?
- The context in which they live
- Case studies
- Current research
- The potential impacts on this group of children
- Recommendations for future research, practice and policy

Before we begin let us first consider some definitions that will be used throughout the chapter.

Service child or military child

A service child is a child who has one or both parents currently serving in HM Forces or the military forces of other countries.

Veteran

A person who has served for any length of time in any branch of the military.

Veterans' child

The child of a veteran. It is important to note that some and perhaps most veterans' children will have lived the life of a service child prior to their parent leaving the military. However, some children will have been born after their parent has already become a veteran.

This chapter will focus on the needs of veterans' children who have experienced life as a service child so it is important to understand the context in which service children live and use that as a base for our discussion.

What is so different about service children?

'Most people have a place they call home all their lives but for some home is not a place but a state of mind' (Brats without Borders, 2016).

In many ways, service life is unique and the experiences that service families face will be quite different from those of their civilian counterparts. Service life presents both benefits and challenges, which the majority of service families take in their stride. However, it should be noted that service families often face a combination of these stressors simultaneously, and at these times, they may become vulnerable.

The main stressors that have been identified (Coe, 2007) are:

- Moving home – (mobility and transition)
- Parental deployment
- Special educational needs and additional educational needs provision
- Bereavement and trauma
- Continuity of education

Although it is widely accepted that the experiences of service children will often be very different from that of their non-service peers, it should also be noted that there might be significant differences between service children as a group. Some children will cope well with the challenges they face and continue to thrive and flourish. The opportunities to travel as they move with their parents due to postings, particularly overseas postings, will expose them to new cultures and experiences. For some children, these experiences will broaden their horizons and foster and develop their self-confidence and understanding of their place in the world. However, for other children these experiences are not positive ones. They may struggle to come to terms with the emotional impacts of their high-mobility lifestyle and this may affect their academic attainment.

Who is responsible for service children?

Historically, the spouses and children of military personnel have often accompanied an army as it moved (Clifton, 2007). The facilities and arrangements made to support the British Army and meet the needs of these camp followers became increasingly sophisticated and records show that formal schooling for regimental children has been provided for over 300 years, in fact, the 'earliest established school was set up in Tangiers in 1675' (Clifton, 2007: 14).

Today, the Ministry of Defence (MOD) has responsibility for the education of service children who live overseas and they currently fund Service Children's Education (SCE) schools. Service children who live in the UK remain the responsibility of the local authority for the area in which they live, just like their non-service peers. 'However, the armed forces do provide some bespoke services, for example, Children's Education Advisory Service (CEAS), Community Development and Youth Services and social welfare services to Service families' (MOD Children and Young People's Trust Board, 2010: 18).

One final note of caution: this chapter may at times use broader explanations, but it is important to remember that every veteran's child or service child is different, one size will not necessarily fit all, and for that reason, I would ask that you take the content, and if appropriate, adapt it for the context in which you work and with the children you work with.

Review of the literature

Within the UK, the literature relating to service persons, veterans and families is very limited and literature relating to service children is even more restricted. Much of the research is usually focused on the 'returning service person or veteran, with very little attention being paid to the needs of their families and children' (Fossey, 2012: 7).

The body of research that is available in the UK comes broadly from four sources.

Studies looking at deployment or mobility, for example, The Royal Navy and Royal Marines Children's Fund (2009) or the on-going work of the King's Centre for Military Health Research. Unpublished undergraduate or postgraduate dissertations such as Edwards (2004), Clifton (2007), Coe (2007), O'Neill (2008), Beadel (2012) and Pexton (2012). Documents produced by the CEAS, SCE or the MOD Directorate of Children and Young People (DCYP) and national policy guidance, for example, the House of Common Defence Committee (2005/2006a, b), Department for Children, Schools and Families (2009a, b, c), Armed Forces Covenant in Action Part 3 Educating the Children of Service Personnel (2012/2013) and a small-scale study by the Department for Education School Standards Advisors in 2010, which considered 21 schools (11 primary and 10 secondary), looking for evidence of good practice that supports service children (Department for Education, 2010b).

For that reason, it has been necessary to consider US literature such as Blaisure *et al.* (2015), Ender (2002), Ginsburg (2007), Hodge (2010), Military Child Education Coalition (2012), Mines (2015) and Tick (2005). However, it should be remembered that there are marked differences between the UK and US militaries and their families. The cultural attitude towards the military, veterans and families is significantly different in the US.

Service children

Service life is unique and even amongst other groups of global nomads it has often been said that 'there's no life like it' (Harrison and Laliberte, 1994). Pollock and Van Reken (2001) identified military children as one of the traditional groups of children that belong to the collective known as 'Third Culture Kids or TCK'. Third Culture Kinds are children who have been raised outside of their parent's home culture for a significant portion of their life that includes the child's developmental years.

Usually, the time spent outside of the parent's culture would be time spent overseas and while many service children have experienced life overseas not all will have done. However, even within the UK, I would suggest that time spent living within the military community can often feel culturally very different for many families.

One benefit of a life lived in many geographic areas means that children can build relationships with each region and culture and this can enrich a child's 'life' experience. It is also important to note that this experience means that children are unlikely to feel completely settled or to have 'full ownership in any area' in which they have lived (Pollock and Van Reken, 2001: 13).

Life within the military community can bring both benefits and hardships that at times can leave children feeling extremely vulnerable. As we have already identified, the main issues for service children are moving home (mobility and transition), parental deployment, special educational needs and additional educational needs provision, bereavement and trauma and continuity of education.

I would suggest that this list could be further refined and broadly grouped into the academic and pastoral needs around high mobility and the emotional needs resulting from the separation with a parent due to events such as parental deployment. Military families need to be adaptable because life within the military community includes constant change (Jervis, 2011).

The subject of vulnerability within military families has often been subject of fierce debate. Many military parents can feel offended at the suggestion that their career has in some way harmed their loved ones. Culturally, there is a different perspective between the view of service children and families in the UK and the USA. In the UK, we tend to see the children as separate from the service person, whereas it is acknowledged that within the US, 'children serve as well' (Military Child Education Coalition, 2012).

My work in this area leads me to suggest that service children move through a spectrum of need or vulnerability depending on the circumstances within their lives at that time (O'Neill, 2008, 2010). They are not vulnerable *per se*, but, at times, they move through vulnerability or may even become 'stuck' on that spectrum (Jetten, 2013).

To focus on a deficit model and suggest that service children are all disadvantaged would be incorrect, but equally to assume that service children are not affected by the context in which they live would seem to be short sighted as the reality is far more nuanced than that.

Additionally, I would suggest that the reaction to the life event is very personal for each child or young person. Some children seem to cope with transition and/ or challenging issues while others experience anxiety or trauma. As professionals or academics, we need to ensure that we do not make judgements about what a child or young person finds stressful. 'What is anxiety provoking or traumatic for one child may not be for another child' (Trickey, 2013), but we still need to take that child's concerns seriously.

Veterans and their families

How does a service child become a veteran's child? A service child becomes a veteran's child when their parent or parents leave military service. All personnel will eventually leave military service. However, how or why they leave can have implications for them and for their families. All ex-service personnel are classed as veterans, regardless of their length of service.

Individuals join the services for a set period. This period of time will vary by service, job specialisation and rank and may range upwards from a minimum of four years. As a person's career progresses, they may be offered the opportunity to sign on for a longer period, usually up to a maximum age of 55. Where extensions are not offered, their original engagement will expire and the person will return to civilian life. Even where a person has signed on for a longer period of service initially, their terms of service usually offer several option points where they may give notice to leave the service if they so decide.

There are circumstances when a service person suffers injury or illness that means they are no longer physically fit for further military service and they may be medically discharged. More recently, the UK Armed Forces have undergone a period of significant reduction with several thousands of servicemen and women being offered redundancy and some personnel have been subject to compulsory redundancy.

Service leavers are given a package of support to assist with the transition back to civilian life, although the amount of support will often vary depending on the length of time served. This support can often include advice on employment, housing and financial guidance.

When a service person dies in service, the surviving family will be offered support with the bereavement and the transition back to civilian life (Child Bereavement UK, 2013). I would suggest that the effectiveness of this support varies depending on the personal perspective of each family. The additional loss of service community and many of the things that were so familiar in daily life can compound this grief.

What are the consequences of leaving the Armed Forces?

Leaving the services is not like leaving any other civilian job. A very structured hierarchical community has surrounded the service person throughout their military career. They have been provided with employment stability and housing, medical and dental care and educational services. They have been an integral part of a close-knit community quite unlike any other.

For their families, it is also a similar story. They too have been immersed in a community in which they share so much with their neighbours. They have experienced the same family upheaval of frequent postings, have been pushed from pillar to post as they follow the career of their serving member and had to share the burdens of worry when that person is deployed on military operations. The children too have often had many years of making and breaking friendships, being enrolled in school after school, worrying about a deployed parent and often having to help the remaining parent manage the family and look after younger siblings as well as other household tasks. Despite this upheaval, they have also been part of their own community of children undergoing similar experiences and often have a very strong sense of identity with their peers.

But, once the person leaves military service, they and their families often find that civilian life is very different both in reality and in their expectations. Some families have made the choice to leave after careful consideration of their future employment opportunities and planned where they are going to settle and where the children will go to school, as well as looking forward to moving on to a new phase in their life and this can be a very positive experience for the family.

However, where a service person's role has come to an end early and compulsorily, through redundancy or medical discharge, it can come as a real shock and families may struggle to deal with this experience. Not only are they losing their job unexpectedly, but also friends and colleagues, home, base, indeed, almost everything with which they are familiar. Finding rewarding employment may not be as achievable as they had been led to believe. Suitable housing may be hard to find, particularly where they have served for a long time, and they may not feel that they have a 'home area' that they can return to and settle in. Likewise, appropriate medical and dental care may be hard to access. The family may find it hard to integrate back into a society so different from everything they have known for many years, and whereas, some may make the transition relatively smoothly, others may struggle to settle for a very long time if ever.

Veterans' children

It is often said, by veterans' children, that the legacy of being a military child persists long beyond the period of service itself and in some cases, may have a lifelong influence upon them. Adult service children often talk about their desire to travel frequently, relocate regularly and change jobs often. Asked where they come from, they may struggle to answer (Musil, 2013).

What does this actually mean? How can a few years in childhood living within a military community make such a difference as you grow up?

In order to answer these questions, I want to consider Bronfenbrenner's ecological model (Bronfenbrenner, 1979: 92) because I believe that this provides a useful theoretical framework to consider how elements of a child's life are interrelated. This model allows practitioners to use multiple sources of knowledge to support the child effectively. The model looks like layers of an onion with the child at the centre.

Layer one is called the microsystem and contains the child's immediate environment such as family, friends and peers, school, health services, neighbourhood, parent's work and church or place of worship. Layer two is called the mesosystem and this connects the micro- and exosystem. Layer three is called the exosystem, the indirect environment, which contains educational, economic and political systems, law, government and media. Finally, layer four is called the macrosystem, which includes shared cultural beliefs, values, customs and laws.

For a child within a service family, it is possible that the majority of the ecological model is linked to the service community. The child will live in service family accommodation with their immediate family and live in a neighbourhood that is within a base. The base provides work and financial security for the service person and possibly the non-service spouse. Additionally, healthcare, early years' provision and places of worship will also be available on the base, although medical care is not as widely available for families as it once was. The local school will often sit just outside the base and the majority of the child's neighbours and peers will also attend that school.

As an employee of the Crown, the policies of the government of the day will also impact on the family and the service community will share beliefs, values and customs that will form the background to life as a service child.

Of course, there will be some families who choose not to live in service family accommodation, that send their child to other schools or who use the local church or doctors. There will also be families who choose to buy a house in one area while the service person commutes or lives away during the week and returns at weekends.

However, I would suggest that these families would still experience ripples from life within the service community but perhaps not as much. 'Nevertheless, the life style is demanding and the military always takes priority. In fact, the military has been called a greedy institution because of the exceptional demands that it makes both of its personnel and their families' (Jervis, 2011: 10).

Children who have lived within the service community will have experienced a life that has revolved around the military, they will have experienced moves, attachments and separations and these will have meshed and contributed towards a child's development, self-worth, self-identity and social relationships in the positive or negative (Foley and Leverett, 2008). On the day the parent leaves the military, these experiences do not cease to exist. Just because children suddenly find themselves becoming a civilian child does not mean that the service child issues have suddenly gone away (Fossey, 2012: 7). Many of these children will have experienced a significant portion of their lives living within the military culture and context and this cultural identity may not be understood or valued by the civilian community they now find themselves in.

Children and young people in their own words

The following are case studies of children and young people over the past three years. All names have been changed.

Mathew

Mathew was 17 years old and in the middle of taking his A-Level exams when his Head of Year got in touch. 'Mathew has changed so much and we're really concerned about him. He is such a bright boy and a solid member of his class, never a problem and never in trouble'. He continued, 'It's like he's stopped trying, he's putting on weight, he looks unkempt, dirty clothes and he smells. In fact, I don't think he's washing'. 'He's tired all the time, doesn't appear to pay any attention in class and his homework isn't being handed in and I think he's fallen out with his friends as well'.

After a few meetings with Mathew, he began to talk about his home and family and share what was going on. He explained that his dad had recently left the military and couldn't seem to settle in to a job even though they had bought a house in the area. The arguments between his mum and dad seemed to get worse until a few months ago, when his mum decided to leave the family. Mathew had older brothers and sisters but they had gone to university so it was just him and his dad at home. 'I miss mum so much but dad gets so angry if I mention her so I've stopped talking about her'. He wanted to see her but his dad said he couldn't.

Mathew told me that he couldn't sleep. So he often stayed up until the early hours of the morning playing computer games and then he was exhausted every morning and certainly did not want to get up and go to school or bother with washing and changing or doing his homework. He and his dad didn't have regular meal times so he just ate when he felt hungry and it wasn't necessarily healthy food. He didn't really want to see his friends because he found it hard to spend time with other people's families when he didn't have one anymore.

Twice weekly meetings were arranged with Mathew for the rest of the academic year to talk about how he felt. With the use of a worry board, problem-solving techniques were used taking each concern in turn and working through them. This support enabled him to feel confident enough to speak to his dad and let him know how he felt. He was also given academic help through a revision action plan.

The impacts this can have on children may not always be immediately recognised, even within the family itself. Some children may feel excluded from family discussions and that their views and worries are not being taken into account. Such feelings can have a negative influence on their emotional wellbeing and may impact on their educational attainment.

Will and James

Mrs Bolsey got in touch because her husband was due to leave the military in March. He had been expecting this and the family had been preparing for the move to 'Civvy Street' for some time. Mr Bolsey had found a new job several hundred miles away and the family was very excited to have bought their first house in a lovely new area.

Mr Bolsey would be moving into the new house in March to begin work but Mrs Bolsey had decided to stay in their military quarter with their sons until July to allow Will and James to finish the school year before the permanent move.

The Bolseys had applied for a short extension of their Service Families Accommodation and were surprised to receive a reply explaining that the extension would not be possible. Mrs Bolsey was very distressed when she made contact. 'We've tried to plan for the move and do our best for the whole family. My boys have had so many school moves because of my husband's postings so we wanted them to finish the school year in this school and I can't believe we can't do that'.

Mr and Mrs Bolsey made Will and James a priority because they knew the impact on their education because of all their previous moves. They were supported to persevere with their application to retain the quarter and to make use of the limited research available to strengthen their application.

Research into school transitions has highlighted the inconsistency faced by families as they move, such as those encountered when moving between the education systems of England, Scotland, Wales and Northern Ireland, and, of course, overseas locations (outside SCE schools). Pupils may arrive with very little prior notice and with little or no documentation from their previous school. Children may have gaps in their education, which can occur through missing certain parts of the curriculum, or, conversely, they may have covered a particular topic many times over. Many service children have had 13 to 14 moves by the time they reach secondary school and often for service families the only consistency is inconsistency (Ofsted 2011).

In the *House of Commons Defence Committee's Report 2005–06*, the emotional impact of mobility; educational attainment; deployment and special educational needs were considered. It was noted that 'moving schools was stressful for all children and frequent moves can have a significant detrimental impact on young people' (2005/2006a: 14). However, there was much disagreement about what these impacts are and reviews of the educational performance of service children in England were commissioned in 2009 and 2010 to compare them with their non-service peers. The Department for Children, Schools and Families (DCSF 2009a, b, c) three Rapid Analysis Papers, 'What are the characteristics of Service Children and how does their performance at Key Stages 1, 2 and 4 compare to their peers?' reported that the levels of attainment of service children were broadly better than their non-service peers. However, data in 2010 from the Department for Education (2010a) suggested that service children moving schools in Years 10 or 11 experienced a massive fall in performance at GCSE level compared with young people who were geographically stable during these years. Ofsted in 2011 commented that 'despite the relatively positive picture of service children's attainment overall, national data indicated that mobile service children did not perform as well as non-mobile service children across all key stages' (2011: 13).

Rana Family

A primary school teacher made contact, as she was concerned about a boy in her class. She realised that his parents had stopped bringing him to school or collecting him and that she hadn't seen either of them for several months. The teacher was also aware that Mrs Rana spoke no English but that Mr Rana or her sons often acted as her translator.

After spending several sessions with the younger son, he began to share news of his family. His dad had left the military eight months before and hadn't been able to find a new job. His mum had a new baby and he had an older brother who was in secondary school. When they left their military housing, the family became homeless and were placed by the local authority in a one-bedroom bedsit an hour's drive from the boys' schools.

He said of the house in which the bedsit was 'it's so noisy all day and at night it is very scary and my mum cries a lot because she's worried about the baby'. He also explained that they had no way of cooking any food or storing produce in their room. He and his brother got up early each day to catch the bus to school, which took one hour, and then they returned each day after school, which took another hour.

His teacher had no idea that this was the situation and was able to share this information immediately with the nearby secondary school his brother attended; they were also unaware of the situation.

A meeting with Mr Rana revealed that he was a very proud man and had not wanted to ask for help because he feared that people would think he was unable to look after his family. After liaising with local military charities, a new home was found for the family near the boys' schools. The charities also helped Mr Rana to find a new job.

The findings of my research showed that families felt more at ease to share problems and seek help in local schools as they found this less threatening than approaching the military (O'Neill 2014).

Phoebe

Phoebe, who was 14 years old, asked her teacher to get in touch on her behalf because she had no one to turn to.

Phoebe had arrived in the area about six months before. She explained that she was an only child and lived with her mum, it was just the two of them, she'd never met her dad but her mum did have a long-term partner, Pete, who she felt close to and often thought of him as a stepfather. Pete had never lived with her and her mum.

Mum had returned four months earlier from a tour in Afghanistan, and while mum was on deployment her grandmother had looked after her. While her mum was away, she'd been busy making lots of arts and craft gifts ready to give to mum but on her return her mum was completely different.

'I'm so confused she's broken off with Pete and I'm not allowed to see him'.

She couldn't understand why her mother changed. Previously, they had been very close and now her mum shouted all the time or made fun of her if she was upset or ignored her or hit her. Sometimes mum would say sorry and offer to take her out and then cancel at the last moment. 'She's never broken her promises before'. Phoebe began to think that she must have done something wrong, 'it must be my fault'.

In an effort to try to appease mum, she volunteered to clean the house and get the shopping after school and cook dinner every night. She also made gifts and cards but these were usually thrown away. The more Phoebe tried to help, the more mum shouted at her.

Phoebe's teacher was shocked by these disclosures as the school were not aware that her mum had been away on deployment, that Phoebe had become a young carer or that her mum and stepdad had separated.

Phoebe's mum would soon be leaving the military and Phoebe wanted to know 'what happens then?'

The school made contact with the padre of the base and asked if they could share some concerns confidentially. The padre offered to pass the information on to the medical officers on the base. The professionals supporting mum were reluctant to talk about the implications for Phoebe and the welfare organisations were reluctant to get involved.

Phoebe experienced a transition due to the move and her mum's deployment in quick succession and each of these issues brings with it challenges.

The transition cycle

Logan (1987) first identified the 'transition cycle' which has since been refined by psychologists working within SCE as consisting of five stages: settled, disconnecting, transition, reconnecting and settled (Service Children's Education, 2008: 3-4). Having an understanding of this cycle is important for teachers and other practitioners who work with highly mobile children to enable them to prepare for the changes that they are likely to observe.

Stage 1 – Settled. A period of stability living in one location enables families to feel 'settled and secure' and these emotions arise from feeling comfortable in that area. 'Knowing the area', being able to get around it and 'having friends' will all help families to feel settled.

Stage 2 – Disconnecting. 'As soon as a family hears that they are posted, they will begin a process of disconnecting from their current location'. All their energy will be focused towards their upcoming move rather than their present situation. Often, families will feel excited about the imminent move but also sad at leaving 'familiar places and people behind'. During this time, children may start to switch off and lose interest in their current school friends (and school work) and many school staff have told me that they have observed just this type of behaviour and worry about its impact on children's future attainment.

Stage 3 – Transition. During the move itself, families will experience significant upheaval and many of the usual routines will be disrupted. This experience 'can feel very unsettling, particularly for young children'. This stage may be prolonged for families that are moving to or from an overseas location, as they may have to 'vacate their quarter and move to temporary accommodation before getting their overseas passage'.

Stage 4 – Reconnecting. When a family finally arrives at their new location, they will be very busy initially as they start to explore the area, find their way around and (hopefully) start to make new friends. Some families have said that it may even feel like being on holiday at first. However, this rose-tinted image often fades quickly as the family copes with the actual practicalities of their new circumstances. 'It may take up to six months for individuals to feel settled in their new environment and develop the feelings of belonging, closeness and identity which they had prior to the move'.

Stage 5 – Settled. The family has re-established a sufficient sense of security and feels settled in their new location.

It would be beneficial for anyone who is due to move to visit the area before the relocation takes actually place. This would enable a family to visit their prospective new home and schools. This can go a long way towards reducing the uncertainly and stress involved in the move. But for many families, time and distance can mean that this is not a realistic option and in reality, families often move without having seen their new home beforehand (O'Neill, 2010).

Deployment is a challenge for every member of the family and for Phoebe and her mum this meant the added practical complication of who would look after Phoebe during the deployment. Deployment consists of the phase prior to the departure, the time away and the return. Anecdotal evidence from school staff suggests that many children are distracted in lessons during the deployment cycle and this in turn will have implications for school work.

Each child will react differently to the changes and often as the deployment progresses, many families learn to 'get on with' life and establish new routines. But for some, this period will continue to be very distressing and even children who normally appear to cope well, may actually be very vulnerable. Coe, in 2007, discussed how service children may face an increased risk of mental health problems as a result of separation from parents due to deployment. Therefore, it is vital that staff that work with children have a good understanding of the potential effects of parental deployment and the range of behaviours that children may display during this time.

This will help staff to decide when referrals to specialist professionals may be needed.

Families often tell me that the return and the time afterwards are the hardest part of the deployment as everyone finds their roles within the family dynamics again. This period of renegotiation and reintegration for the family may take anywhere from 'three to six months' (Pincus *et al.*, n.d.: 6). As in Phoebe's situation, this time can bring unexpected stresses especially if parents have returned with physical or mental injuries.

This period can be as challenging a time for children, as it is for the adult, and it is important that schools and other professionals continue to offer support to pupils and families during this time. Links with service welfare organisations could be useful as they can offer specialist knowledge and practical support to families and advise schools on the most appropriate way to support the needs of the families.

Children who cope successfully with these experiences may have developed key skills that will support them later in life and help to build resilience. 'Resilience is used to describe why some people struggle hard to cope with life experiences while others survive with self-esteem, identity and their level of wellbeing intact' (Johnston-Wilder and Collins, 2008: 54). It is resilience that enables people to recover after a trauma or allows them to function, even when living in difficult circumstances.

Conclusions, best practice and recommendations

'It was a strange and interesting childhood, cruel, magical, privileged and painful all at the same time' (Brats without Borders, 2016).

Growing up within a service community is a unique experience and life as a military child has both benefits and challenges. These benefits and challenges are further nuanced depending on individual perceptions, responses, previous experiences and the support systems around each child.

I have worked with several hundred service and veterans' children each year since 2009 and while each child will bring with them personal hopes, fears and concerns, the thread that binds all of these children is worry or anxiety. The anxiety may be mild, moderate or severe, relating directly to the child or indirectly to the child but nevertheless, it remains.

Service children are an often-invisible population that is under researched and while pockets of good practice do exist for service children across the country, these are generally under resourced.

The needs of veterans' children and the implications for them remain in place long after the service person leaves the military. Further research to investigate their context and lives and identify key information is needed. This research should form the basis for policy and practice changes that recognise where gaps in provision currently exist whether educational, health, housing or other areas.

Next steps for practitioners

Gaining an understanding of the issues that arise in service life and the implications for veterans' children is really the first step to providing them with effective support. It will also help to inform strategic planning for organisations such as schools.

Consider the holistic needs of the child and family and remember that all of the areas of a child's life are interlinked and will contribute towards their health and wellbeing.

A lack of knowledge can contribute to the uncertainty and professionals can help to remove this by establishing early contact with the incoming family and providing them with information about the new area, schools, health and so on, whilst also providing professionals with a useful opportunity to gather as much information about the children and family as possible. This will be particularly important if the child has special or additional educational needs.

Key points for schools

- Establish effective home/school links with the family as soon as possible.
- Establish effective multi-agency links with any other professionals involved in the children or families' life.
- Schools should actively encourage families to inform them of significant changes or events that may impact on their children.
- Schools should ensure that parents know that the school 'has time' for them and their children and that staff are in place to discuss their concerns such as any observed behavioural changes in their children.
- Schools should provide an opportunity for children to discuss their concerns or worries either within the school or by linking to an external professional agency if required.
- Schools should provide a safe and stable setting to promote continuity for children experiencing any trauma associated with the transition or previous issues such as separation during parental deployment.
- Some aspects of work may have been missed, or conversely, topics may have been covered many times over. Encourage teachers to consider creative approaches to subjects to help minimise these issues.
- Transition during exams such as GCSE's, A Levels, Highers or other similar qualifications is best avoided.
- Schools should consider the barriers to attainment and achievement for veterans' children who have issues as a result of their previously mobile lifestyle and actively plan to mitigate these issues.

- Carrying out base-line assessments enables teachers to plan in detail for each pupil, including, if required, any intervention support. Teachers should work with pastoral support managers/co-ordinators in school to create a supportive environment.
- Parents are an invaluable source of information about their child's educational history.
- Schools should make every effort to *really* understand the culture and context in which these children have lived when part of the service community and how this may impact on children going forwards.

So, in summary, military children are not vulnerable *per se* but due to the context in which they live, they move in and out of vulnerability. As practitioners, it falls to us to ensure that we support them during these transition periods to enable them to make changes as smoothly as possible.

References

Blaisure, K., Saathoff-Wells, T., Pereira, A., MacDermid Wadsworth, S., Dombro, A. (2015). *Serving Military Families: Theories, Research, and Application.* New York: Routledge.

Beadel, R. (2012). *Service Children and SEN.* Oxford: SCSN Research Conference, Department of Education, University of Oxford, September 2012.

Brats without Borders (2016). *Brats: Our Journey Home.* Denver: Brats Without Borders, Inc.

Bronfenbrenner, U. (1979). *The Ecology of Human Development: Experiments by Nature and Design.* Harvard: Harvard University Press.

Child Bereavement UK (2013). *Supporting Forces Families.* Saunderton: Child Bereavement UK.

Clifton, G. (2007). *The Experience of Education of the Army Child.* Unpublished thesis. Oxford: Oxford Brookes University.

Coe, N. (2007). *Reducing the Turbulence Associated with Transition.* Akrotiri: RAF Akrotiri School.

Department for Children, Schools and Families (2009a). What are the characteristics of service children and how does their performance at Key Stage 1 compare to their peers? *Rapid Analysis*, 3 April 2009.

Department for Children, Schools and Families (2009b). What are the characteristics of service children and how does their performance at Key Stage 2 compare to their peers? *Rapid Analysis*, 8 May 2009.

Department for Children, Schools and Families (2009c). What are the characteristics of service children and how does their performance at Key Stage 4 compare to their peers? *Rapid Analysis*, 30 January 2009.

Department for Education (2010a). *Research Report: The Educational Performance of Children of Service Personnel.* London: Department for Education.

Department for Education (2010b). *How Schools Secure the Progress of Children from Armed Forces Families: Good Practice Guidance.* DFE Effective Practice Team. London: Department for Education.

Edwards, L. (2004). *Service Children's Education: An Exploration of the Strategies Employed to Mitigate the Adverse Effects of Pupil Mobility on Social and Academic Progress.* Exeter: University of Exeter.

Ender, M. (ed.) (2002). *Military Brats and Other Global Nomads Growing up in Organization Families.* Connecticut: Praeger Publishers.

Foley, P. and Leverett, S. (2008). *Connecting with Children: Developing Working Relationships.* Bristol: The Policy Press in association with The Open University.

Fossey, M. (2012). *Unsung Heroes: Developing a Better Understanding of the Emotional Support Needs of Service Families.* London: Centre for Mental Health.

Ginsburg, K. (2007). The importance of play in promoting healthy child development and maintaining strong parent–child bonds. *Pediatrics,* 119, 182–91.

Harrison, D. and Laliberte. L (1994). *No Life Like It.* Toronto: Lorimer.

Hodge, C. (2010). *Once a Warrior-Always a Warrior: Navigating the Transition from Combat to Home-Including Combat Stress, PTSD, and MTBI.* Connecticut: Globe Pequot Press Life.

House of Common Defence Committee (2005/2006a). *Educating Service Children: Eleventh Report of Session 2005-06.* HC1054. London, House of Commons: The Stationery Office Limited.

House of Common Defence Committee (2005/2006b). *Educating Service Children: Government's Response to the Committee's Eleventh Report of Session 2005-06,* 21 November 2006. London, House of Commons: The Stationery Office Limited.

Jervis, S. (2011). *Relocation, Gender and Emotion: A Psycho-Social Perspective on the Experiences of Military Wives.* London: Karnac Books.

Jetten, P. (2013). *Emotional First Aid.* Service Children Training Day, Buckinghamshire, September 2013.

Johnston-Wilder, S. and Collins, J. (2008). Children negotiating identities. In Collins, J. and Foley, P. (eds). *Promoting Children's Wellbeing*: Bristol: The Policy Press in association with The Open University, 54.

Logan, K.V. (1987). The emotional cycle of deployment. *Proceedings,* February, 43–7.

Military Child Education Coalition (2012). *Professionals.* Available online at www.military-child.org/professionals (accessed 30 August 2012).

Mines, S. (2015). *They Were Families: How War Comes Home.* Stillwater: New Forums Press.

MOD Children and Young People's Trust Board (2010). Harnessing the positive benefits of living in a Services community to ensure that every Service child and young person's experiences and opportunities help them to achieve the best possible outcomes whilst also supporting, protecting and intervening where needed, to help those most vulnerable, to achieve their ambitions. *Children and Young People's Strategy and Improvement Plan 2010–2013.* London: Ministry of Defence.

Musil, D. (2013). *Brats on the Move.* Mobility Conference, Buckinghamshire, October 2013.

Ofsted. (2011). *Children in Service Families,* No. 100227, May 2011. London: Ofsted.

O'Neill, J. (2008). *What Would an Effective 'Transition and Induction' Policy Look Like in Relation to Service Children at Halton School?* Aylesbury: Halton School.

O'Neill, J. (2010). *'It's Hard for Me I Move a Lot'. Evaluating Policy and Practice: The Process of Designing and Implementing a One-Year Pilot Project to Support Service Children at Halton School during periods of Mobility and Parental Deployment.* Aylesbury: Halton School.

O'Neill, J. (2010). *Service Children. How do they Cope with Transitions Between schools?* Oxford: University of Oxford.

O'Neill, J. (2014). *The Service Children Coordinator Project,* Service Children's Training Project, Buckinghamshire.

Pexton, S. (2012). A pilot study: The welfare, emotional; wellbeing and support needs of primary school service children and their families separated during active service. A psychological assessment of the impact of deployment in school aged service children (Aged 8-11) and their families, DPsych. London: City University.

Pincus, S., House, R., Christenson, J., Lawrence, A. (n.d.). *The Emotional Cycle of Deployment: A Military Family Perspective*. Available online at https://msrc.fsu.edu/system/files/The%20Emotional%20Cycle%20of%20Deployment%20-%20A%20Military%20Family%20Perspective.pdf (accessed 19 January 2017).

Pollock, D. and Van Reken, R. (2001). *Third Culture Kids: The Experience of Growing Up Among Worlds*. London: Nicholas Brealey.

Service Children's Education. (2008). *Service Children in State Schools Handbook*. Upavon: CEAS.

The Royal Navy and Royal Marines Children's Fund. (2009). *The Overlooked Casualties of Conflict*. Portsmouth: The Royal Navy and Royal Marines Children's Fund.

Tick, E. (2005). *War and the Soul: Healing Our Nation's Veterans and Their Families from Post-Traumatic Stress Disorder*. Wheaton: Quest Books.

Trickey, D. (2013). *Building Resilience*, Service Children Training Day, Buckinghamshire, November 2013.

5

THE EX-ARMED FORCES OFFENDER AND THE UK CRIMINAL JUSTICE SYSTEM

Deirdre MacManus and Nick Wood

Introduction

Nations have historically been apprehensive about their returning veterans (Waller, 1944; Leventman, 1978), centred around concern about the prospects of their adaptive reintegration into civilian society. After the First World War, and then the Second World War, there were concerns about domestic upheaval, problems with reintegration and what we would now call social exclusion (Allport, 2009). Military personnel returning from the Second World War were treated less as heroes, as is the common misperception today fuelled by years of Hollywood film portrayals, and rather more as social problems, with aggression and crime high on the list of concerns (Allport, 2009; Emsley, 2013). The UK has recently withdrawn troops following prolonged conflicts in Iraq and Afghanistan, conflicts which have led to greater media, political and public scrutiny of the impact of these operations on military personnel involved than in previous periods in British history. Given the levels of media and political concern about offending (in particular, violent offending) among ex-serving personnel and the proportion who allegedly end up in the criminal justice system (CJS) (McGinnes, 2008; Doward, 2008; James, 2010), it seems these age-old concerns have not gone away. Media accounts have highlighted some of the challenges facing troops in their transition back to civilian life: social and housing problems; mental health problems; alcohol and substance misuse; and relationship and family breakdown (Hopkins, 2014; Townsend, 2008), and as before, a particular focus of interest has been on violent behaviour. But what is the reality (Caesar, 2010; Hattenstone and Allison, 2014)?

Around 20,000 (10 per cent) of the regular strength of the UK Armed Forces leave every year. Estimates suggest that there are around 6.2 million people in the ex-service community in the UK (The Royal British Legion, 2014). Most of the current generation of service leavers make successful transitions back into civilian life (Lord Ashcroft, 2014). However, a minority have a bleaker outlook as a result of health, behavioural and social problems, some of which, as already covered in Chapter 1, are related to their experiences in military service (Hatch *et al.*, 2013; Iversen *et al.*, 2009; MacManus *et al.*, 2012b, 2013; Rowe *et al.*, 2013).

Some find themselves involved in the CJS, which can have a very negative impact on their lives and the lives of their families, not to mention the impact of their behaviour on society (MacManus *et al.*, 2014a). There is an expectation, in light of the Armed Forces Covenant (Ministry of Defence, 2014), that more should be done to support those who enter the CJS and indeed to try to prevent this outcome following the end of military service.

In this chapter, we will review (i) recent estimates of the proportion of the ex-service population who are involved with the CJS; (ii) the growth in support for Veterans in the UK CJS and the drivers for this; (iii) whether ex-Armed Forces personnel who offend are different from general population offenders; and, finally, (iv) what interventions exist which may help reduce the risk of ex-service personnel entering the CJS and rehabilitate them back into civilian society. This chapter is written from a UK perspective, but where appropriate we have drawn on evidence from other countries, such as the United States.

Ex-service personnel in prison: The truth behind the headlines

There are currently over 85,000 people in prison in England and Wales (Ministry of Justice, 2014a), but the exact number of former Service personnel in prison, never mind those that pass through police custody and court, or who are subject to probation orders, is at present still a matter of debate. There have been a number of attempts to produce a reliable figure, each with its own methodological weaknesses, and all are based on varying degrees of conjecture or statistical extrapolation. The Home Office has conducted surveys of 2,000 prisoners at the point of release in 2001, 2003 and 2004, and found the proportion of veterans to be 6 per cent, 4 per cent and 5 per cent respectively. In 2007, the Ministry of Defence (MOD), based on a Prison in Reach (PIR) survey of prisoners on one wing at HMP Dartmoor, estimated that the figure could be as high as 17 per cent (Howard League, 2011a). There are obvious dangers in extrapolating the results from small non-representative samples to estimate the number of ex-servicemen in all prisons in England and Wales (Treadwell, 2010). Later research undertaken by the probation service union, the National Association of Probation Officers (NAPO), suggested that the number of ex-serving military personnel in UK prisons approximated 9.1 per cent (NAPO, 2009). NAPO relied in part on the aforementioned MOD data, and another study by Veterans in Prison (VIP), which surveyed ten prisons. The study identified 118 self-reported former service personnel out of a surveyed prison population of 1,191. On that basis, NAPO extrapolated these results to the entire prison estate (NAPO, 2009). They also estimated similarly that it is likely that 6 per cent of those currently subject to community supervision by the probation service have served in the UK Armed Forces (NAPO, 2009). A major weakness of prison surveys is the reliance on self-reported service history which is not officially verified (NAPO, 2009; MacManus and Wessely, 2011).

Subsequently, the Defence Analytical Services and Advice (DASA) of the Ministry of Defence collaborated with the Ministry of Justice (MoJ) on a linkage study, the findings of which were published as two separate reports (DASA, 2010a,b). The study used service records of approximately 1.3 million service leavers and linked these records with a database of all remand and sentenced prisoners in England and Wales on one day in November 2009, creating a one-day snapshot. The first report estimated that some 3.0 per cent of all those currently in custody in England and Wales had served in the Armed Forces (DASA, 2010a). While there are potential inaccuracies in this study (in that it omitted a number of individuals, for example, those whose military service predated 1979 for the Navy, 1972 for the Army and 1968 for the RAF, those under 18 years of age, reservists and those in secure psychiatric hospitals), it is likely to be a more comprehensive estimate than any produced previously. In September 2010, DASA published its second round of figures containing a further estimate revised upwards to take account of omissions in the original study (DASA, 2010b). It asserted that approximately 2,820, or some 3.5 per cent of all those currently in custody in England and Wales, had served in the Forces. The key finding from this second stage of DASA's research is the finding that regular veterans are less likely to be in prison than the non-veteran population. The number of male non-veterans in prison was found to be 496.3 per 100,000 compared with 298.4 for regular veterans. These figures were adjusted for age ratio to provide a finding that regular veterans are 30 per cent less likely to be in prison than non-veterans. While the revised estimate is likely to be more accurate, it is still only a partial picture. These figures still excluded reservists and those under the age of 18 years.

What was interesting about the second DASA study (DASA, 2010b) was that the revised estimate was broken down by service. It established that of the 2,820 ex-service personnel in prison, 77 per cent were ex-Army, 15 per cent ex-Royal Navy and 8 per cent ex-Royal Air Force. Furthermore, it estimated that 51 per cent of ex-service personnel in prison were over the age of 45 years and 29 per cent were over the age of 55, which compares with 9 per cent of the general prison population being aged 50 years or over (DASA, 2010b). These statistics suggest that many ex-service personnel in prison have offended or continued to offend a considerable time after their date of discharge. The DASA figures also provide a breakdown of offence types, indicating that approximately 1 in 3 ex-servicemen are held in custody for violence against the person, 1 in 4 for sexual offences and 1 in 12 for offences of dishonesty (26). The figures reveal that violent and sexual offences were recorded at higher levels than for the general prisoner population, whereas, conversely, the proportion of former service personnel in custody for acquisitive offences is significantly lower than in the general population; 33 per cent of veterans were in prison for violence against the person compared with 29 per cent of the non-veteran prison population. The difference was more marked when it came to sexual offences 25 per cent of veterans were in prison for sexual offences compared with 11 per cent of the non-veteran prison population (DASA,

2010b). Overall, veterans were shown to be less likely than the general population to be in prison, but more likely to have convictions for violent and sexual offences.

DASA undertook a further subsequent study to estimate the numbers of former service personnel offenders who were being supervised by probation services in England and Wales. The study concluded that 3.4 per cent (5,860) of offenders who were being supervised by probation were former service personnel. By combining the two figures 'custody' and 'probation', this would suggest that around 8,680 offenders who are former service personnel are in contact with the CJS on a daily basis. We urge a note of caution, however, as both DASA studies provided only 'snapshot' figures taken on one day of their respective years of study, therefore, they did not reflect the annual 'through flow', or total figures of offenders entering custody or receiving probation supervision and may increase if collated over a 12-month period.

More latterly, Her Majesty's Inspectorate of Prisons (2014) found that, of those who took part in the prisoners' surveys between 2012 and 2013 and 2013 and 2014, 6 per cent and 7 per cent respectively, identified themselves as ex-service personnel. Taking all the reports published to date into consideration, the estimates of the proportion of the prison population who have previously served in the Armed Forces range from 3.5 per cent to 17 per cent. This means that at any one time, between some 3,000 and 14,000 prisoners may be ex-service personnel (Treadwell, 2010).

To date, there have been few studies undertaken to estimate the number of former service personnel coming into contact with the CJS through police custody suites across England and Wales. An example of one such study is a project undertaken by Kent Police in 2010, which reported that over a 2-month period, 3.2 per cent, 232 out of a total of 7,200 arrested, self-reported a service history (The Royal British Legion, 2012).

In an attempt to address the need for a more accurate and accepted figure for the proportion of the prison population who have served in the Armed Forces, the Secretary of State for Justice's Inquiry into Former Armed Forces Personnel in the CJS (Phillips, 2014) called for all offenders entering custody as of 1 January 2015 to be asked if they had served in the Armed Forces. Her Majesty's Prisons (HMP) establishments will need time to adopt, embed, collect and share the new data within their own local and national processes. A cautionary note is that the 'identification' process only reflects veterans who 'self-disclose' their veteran status, so offenders who choose to keep their service history private, will not be identified. Anecdotal reports suggest that either (i) fear of retribution among other prisoners may discourage ex-service personnel from coming forward leading to underestimation or (ii) high levels of fabrication of service history could lead to a high false, positive rate leading to over-estimation of numbers unless service history is verified.

The debate over the numbers of and needs of former service personnel within the CJS has, over time, been raised to government level, and although understanding and support for service development continues to lag behind our US counterparts, there has been considerable development over the past decade.

Support for veterans in the UK CJS: The drivers behind service development

Prior to the Iraq and Afghanistan conflicts, the levels of awareness of the needs of veterans in the UK were low. Systems of support for ex-service personnel have been in place in other countries, such as the US, for many years. US veteran care systems developed after the First World War with a particular expansion since the Vietnam War. Individuals who have served in the US Armed Forces may be eligible for a wide range of programmes and services provided by the US Department of Veterans Affairs (VA) (Kizer *et al.,* 1997). For those who end up in contact with the CJS, the VA operates Veteran Courts (Howard League for Penal Reform, 2011a; Russell, 2010) and state-wide Justice Outreach Programmes which offer re-training, education, mental health treatment, assistance with housing among other supports (Howard League for Penal Reform, 2011b). The UK has lagged behind in recognising the specific needs of ex-Armed Forces personnel in the CJS, but over the past decade or so, there have been developments at a local and national level.

In 2003, following the publication of the MOD report 'Strategy for Veterans' (Ministry of Defence, 2003), the Prison In-Reach Project was established, a partnership between the MOD and the voluntary sector, national and local authorities and businesses to provide support to veterans who are serving prison sentences and to their families, with the aim of aiding rehabilitation and reducing the risks of re-offending. An Ex-Serving Offenders Government Working Group was established to ensure that the ex-service prison and probation offender population, their families and the resettlement services, were fully informed of the support available from the voluntary and community sector. In 2008, the MOD report, 'Nation's Commitment: Cross-Government Support to our Armed Forces, their Families and Veterans', called for increased interagency government working with third sector services to improve identification and support of the vulnerable who have left service (Ministry of Defence, 2008). This proved to be a key trigger for the establishment of the 'Veterans in Custody Support' (VICS) model, using ex-service prison officers to identify and offer support to veterans in prison (model described in more detail described later in chapter) (Figure 5.1). By 2010, over 100 HMP establishments had set up VICS services. The model was officially launched by the National Offender Management Service (NOMS) along with the publication of 'A *Guide to Working with Veterans in Custody*' (James and Wood, 2010) (Figure 5.2). VICS was subsequently adopted as a best practice model in prisons and probation services across England.

The seminal Government paper to drive the development of health services for the Veteran population was Dr Andrew Murrison MP's report, 'Fighting Fit' (Murrison, 2010), which set the agenda for planning mental health services for both serving and ex-service personnel (Fossey, 2010). His recommendations for an uplift in veteran mental health workers was followed by investment in regional NHS community veteran mental health services. A number of these services have expanded to provide in-reach support for veterans in the CJS. However, in the absence of national coherence on the provision of prison services for veterans, the distribution of such services remains patchy.

- Identifying former Armed Forces offenders at the earliest opportunity in the custodial setting
- Referral or sign posting into community organisations for resettlement assistance
- Contributing to the NOMS 7 pathway offender management and resettlement model
- Encouraging HMP establishments to identify a Veterans in Custody Support Officer
- Encouraging the sharing of veteran-specific resettlement information between custodial offender supervisors and community offender managers.
- Create a working partnership between custodial service providers and ex-Armed Forces community services
- Promote MOJ and MOD Prison In Reach (latterly ESOWG) and Armed Forces Covenant
- Comply with Equality agenda
- Create a national model of practice to be replicated in HMP establishments in England and Wales
- Ensure veteran-specific datum is included on the Prison National Offender Information System
- Ensure resettlement arrangements provided by ex-Armed Forces Charities are included on the Offender Assessment System
- Liaison with HMP and community NHS Health and Mental care staff
- Liaison with community offender managers and share resettlement information

FIGURE 5.1 The VICS project priority aims.

- Accommodation
- Health and Mental Health
- Drugs and Alcohol
- Children and Families
- Attitudes, thinking and behaviour
- Education, training and employment
- Finance, benefits and debt management

FIGURE 5.2 NOMS 7 pathway offender management model.

A number of key non-governmental reports, published in 2010 and 2011, high-lighted the growing recognition of problems in this area which were believed to contribute to the involvement of some Armed Forces personnel with the CJS: social problems, addictions, general mental health problems, relationship and fam-ily breakdown and poor educational attainment (Howard League for Penal Reform 2011a,b; Fossey, 2010). Concerns were raised in particular about early service leav-ers (ESLs; those who are discharged from service before their initial four-year term is complete for many reasons, including unsuitability for forces life, breaches of military codes of discipline, substance misuse or offending behaviour). Fossey (2010) highlighted the needs of 'single young men, with difficulties in adjusting to change, poor social skills and limited basic education, dyslexia and dyscalculia, who leave the services early'. An influential report by the Howard League for Penal Reform (2011b) drew on a series of qualitative interviews with 29 offenders. Though these 29 individual narratives were not considered to be a representative sample, and indeed were drawn from three prisons, one of which was a high secure dispersal prison, important themes emerged such as lack of support on transition into civilian life, difficulty re-establishing social and family relationships and struggles with employment. The analysis highlighted that mental health problems in general, and not just post-traumatic stress disorder (PTSD), were commonly associated with a difficult transition and a subjectively important factor on the pathway to offending along with alcohol misuse. The narrative developing was that this population of offenders was not significantly different from general population offenders in their range of needs, but that their experiences in the military may have shaped their presentation and problems associated with a difficult transition out of the military are key contributors to their offending. Better identification of veterans in the CJS and police custody suites was highlighted as a priority need and courts and prison reception processes were identified as providing 'an opportunity for timely intervention and assistance'. A further paper by Howard League for Penal Reform highlighted the similarities between veterans who offend in the UK and in the US, but yet also the discrepancy between the comprehensive support provided by the US Department of Veteran Affairs and Veteran Justice Rehabilitation Programmes and the patchy support provided in the UK (Howard League for Penal Reform, 2011c).

Over time, increased awareness of the difficulties faced by some during the transition out of the military has been reflected in a number of helpful reports such as '*Transition to Civilian Life: The Emotional Pathway*' (Ministry of Defence, 2015) and Lord Ashcroft's review '*The Veteran Transition*' (Lord Ashcroft, 2014). The latter highlighted issues of extreme social exclusion among the worst off in this population who fail to make the transition and cannot access help. By 2014, such was the level of public concern and political debate around the proportion of former Armed Forces personnel in prison and on probation for violent and sexual offences (MacManus *et al.*, 2012a; MacManus and Wessely, 2011) and increasing pressure on the government to be seen to be addressing this issue, that an independent review on behalf of the Secretary of State for Justice was commissioned into '*Former Members of the Armed Forces in the Criminal Justice System*'. The review, by Stephen Phillips QC MP, which involved wide consultation with individuals with a range of expertise in the area (research, mental health, social care, criminal justice and legal), highlighted the need for national guidance on the identification and management of former Armed Forces personnel in the CJS. The review was clear that identification across the CJS is patchy and in some cases non-existent. The recurring theme among the recommendations was for more training in the needs of this population for those working within the CJS and judiciary (Her Majesty's Inspectorate of Prisons, 2014). The integral link between poor mental health, alcohol and substance misuse and offending behaviour was acknowledged (MacManus and Wessely, 2011) and better co-working between criminal justice and mental health agencies, both NHS and third sector, was recommended. Growing concerns about domestic violence within military families, supported by new NHS England research (MacManus *et al.*, 2014b), were taken very seriously and formed the first of Phillips' recommendations:

> I recommend that within six months of the publication of the KCMHR research, the Secretary of State should make a statement to Parliament

addressing the issue of domestic violence by former service personnel and the steps being taken across Government to address any issues identified as affecting this cohort of offenders and to prevent their offending.

The review also highlighted the need for greater support and interventions not just within prison and probation (Murray, 2014), but also earlier in the criminal justice pathway.

In order to ensure the development and delivery of appropriate services and interventions, we must seek to understand the pathways to offending among those who have served in the Armed Forces.

Pathways to offending: Are ex-Armed Forces offenders different from offenders in the general population?

A UK-based study, which linked data from a large cohort study into the health and wellbeing of the UK Armed Forces with official MoJ criminal records, described, for the first time, the pattern of officially recorded offending among a large representative sample of military personnel (MacManus *et al.*, 2012a). Overall, 17.0 per cent of males in the sample were found to have committed any offence in their lifetime. This can be compared crudely with Home Office birth cohort data from 2006 which estimated that 28.3 per cent of men in the general population aged between 18 and 52 had a criminal conviction (Ministry of Justice, 2010). The proportion of the aforementioned military sample who had been sentenced to a custodial sentence in their lifetime (1.7 per cent) was also less than in a similarly aged general population birth cohort (7.0 per cent) (Prime *et al.*, 2001). The lower prevalence of lifetime criminal records and prison sentences in the military population in this study may partly be explained by the fact that the sample spent a median of 12 years in military service, which could be considered to restrict their time at risk of offending in the community. The peak age of both offending among males in the general population (Prime *et al.*, 2001) and enlistment in the military is 19 years. So young men are enlisting at a time when they are at highest risk of offending. We also know that offending 'in service' is recorded on a military police database and, until recent years, offences were less likely to be transferred to the Police National Computer database unless they crossed a certain threshold of severity (e.g. violent offences). This may, in part, explain the drop in non-violent offences during the in-service period. Other interpretations could be that the military instils more ordered behaviour or is more tolerant of low grade crime.

Interestingly, violent offenders are the most prevalent offender type among those who have served in the military (Howard League, 2011a; MacManus *et al.*, 2013), unlike in the general population, where there is a lower prevalence of male violent offenders than other types of offenders such as acquisitive offenders (i.e. those with a record of offences such as theft) (Prime *et al.*, 2001). Contrary to the figures for overall offending, the prevalence of lifetime male violent offenders in the military was found to be *higher* than in a similarly aged sample of males from the general population and the difference was most striking among men younger than

30 years (20.6 per cent in the military sample versus 6.7 per cent of males aged up to 30 years in England and Wales in 2001 (Prime *et al.*, 2001). So does the military just recruit disproportionately from a social group in society who would be more violent anyway or is this a consequence of their military service?

The same sociodemographic factors which are associated with violence in the general population have been found to be associated with violence among military personnel (MacManus *et al.*, 2012a; Simonoff *et al.*, 2004). The increased risk of violent offending among lower rank Army personnel is most likely a reflection of the social backgrounds and lower levels of education among lower ranks in the Army. These results reinforce the common perception that many of those entering the lower ranks of the military already have an excess of risk factors for violence. Pre-military antisocial behaviour and violent offending is shown to be one of the strongest predictors of violence (MacManus *et al.*, 2012b; MacManus *et al.*, 2013).

However, MacManus *et al.* (2013) also found that a greater proportion of their deployed sample offended in the post-deployment period compared with the rest of their in-service or pre-military periods for all types of offending, including violent offending (MacManus *et al.*, 2013). This suggests that deployment or aspects of deployment act to increase offending and violent offending. There is a growing international evidence base for the impact of aspects of military service, such as combat, on the mental health of service personnel and their risk of offending. There is also now a substantial body of literature which has used data ranging from conflicts in Vietnam (Calvert *et al.*, 1990; Yager, 1976), the 1990 to 1991 Gulf War (Black *et al.*, 2005) and Iraq and Afghanistan (Elbogen *et al.*, 2014; Fear *et al.*, 2010; Killgore *et al.*, 2008; MacManus *et al.*, 2012a, 2013, 2015a,b), which reports an association between combat exposure and subsequent aggression, violence and general antisocial behaviour among serving and ex-serving military personnel. Post-deployment mental health problems, such as PTSD, common mental disorders, anger management problems and alcohol misuse have also been shown repeatedly to be strong predictors of subsequent violent offending among military populations (Elbogen *et al.*, 2010; MacManus *et al.*, 2013; Zoricić *et al.*, 2003).

MacManus and colleagues further found that the rates of all types of offending among military personnel increase after leaving service, and that violent offending remains the most prevalent type of offending (MacManus *et al.*, 2013). It is perhaps of no surprise that offending increases after leaving service. Two possible explanations spring to mind. The first, drawing on the previous argument, is that military service acts to reduce offending by limiting the opportunity for crime, which thus increases again once they leave. But offending decreases with age in the general population. Does the military just delay offending that may have occurred at a younger age or is this a new pathway to offending, different from that seen in the general population, with new additional risk factors? This is supported by the DASA finding that out of 2,820 veterans identified, 577 (20 per cent) were aged 26 to 34 and 619 (22 per cent) were aged 45 to 54 (DASA, 2010b). The second possible explanation is that this peak in post-service offending is, in part, contributed to by ESLs. It is widely accepted that this particular group may have entered service with a higher than average burden of disadvantage and had little time to prepare for life outside of the Armed Forces. Research has confirmed that poor outcomes are clustered in ESLs and tend to be multiple (debt, antisocial behaviour, substance misuse, mental health problems, unemployment, marital difficulties and unstable housing) (Buckman *et al.*, 2012). It is important to explore the risk and protective factors for offending after leaving the services, which can better inform offending reduction intervention programmes.

Mental health problems, such as PTSD, common mental disorder, alcohol misuse and anger management issues, continue to be strongly associated with or even predictive of subsequent offending behaviour (MacManus *et al.*, 2013; Elbogen *et al.*, 2012a). This highlights the persistent impact of mental health on the behavioural outcomes among those who have left service, over and above the risk associated with sociodemographic and military factors. The transition from military to civilian life can be challenging and some ex-service personnel struggle to manage aspects of life, which were previously managed for them.

Accommodation and employment are common concerns for many offenders when resettling back into the community following a prison sentence. These have also been highlighted as hurdles for veterans on leaving the military and trying to settle into civilian life. The King's Centre for Military Health Research '*Fifteen Year Report*' highlighted how poor outcomes among veterans are multiple (debt, antisocial behaviour, substance misuse, mental health problems, unemployment, marital difficulties and unstable housing) and disproportionately present among ESLs (King's Centre for Military Health Research, 2013). The Howard League for Penal Reform observed:

> It is true that young single men are particularly vulnerable on discharge [from the military] because they often have nowhere to live when their military service end. Unstable arrangements can lead to a lack of stable accommodation, and this in turn can make it difficult for the ex-serviceman to find employment, sometimes leading to a cycle of social exclusion.
>
> (*Howard League for Penal Reform, 2011b*)

The association between socioeconomic risk factors, such as financial debt, unemployment, unstable housing and relationship problems and offending among veterans has been confirmed by research, and greater stability in these areas has also been shown to have a protective effect and to be associated with reduced risk of offending in the face of other risk factors, such as combat exposure or mental health risk (Elbogen *et al.*, 2012b; MacManus *et al.*, under review).

Some limited insight into how the needs of the ex-serving community of offenders compares with general population offenders has been gained from government offender surveys. The Offender Management Community Cohort Study surveyed a representative sample of 2,919 adult offenders on various levels of NOMS management across 10 Probation Trusts, who started Community Orders between October 2009 and December 2010. As part of the survey offenders were asked if they had ever served in the Armed Forces and 151 respondents self-identified as ex-service personnel (5 per cent) (Ministry of Justice, 2013). The Resettlement Surveys were conducted in 2001, 2003 and 2004 and surveyed prisoners shortly before their release to examine the prison population's resettlement needs (May et al., 2008). Data were collected on the requirements and characteristics of the prison population – 4,898 prisoners were interviewed from 74 different prisons, which included 232 ex-service personnel (5 per cent). Such surveys are limited by their self-report nature and the small numbers of ex-serving personnel contained in the samples, so the results must be interpreted with caution. Overall, the offending behaviour and needs of ex-service offenders and the general population offenders were not found to be dissimilar. The most notable difference was the much higher need for alcohol detoxification among ex-service personnel than among the other offenders. This was in contrast to lower reported levels of drug misuse. It is important to note that mental health needs were not enquired about.

So it seems that the characteristics of former Armed Forces personnel offenders look similar to other offenders in the general population; that is, younger males from more deprived areas of the country with a history of offending. However, their experiences in the military and on deployment and associated mental health and substance misuse problems can also play an important role on their pathway into the CJS. Layered on top of that, the socioeconomic and cultural impact of transitioning from the military into civilian life and issues of stigma and barriers to help-seeking (Iversen et al., 2011) are all important considerations when trying to understand why ex-service personnel end up in the CJS. The Armed Forces Covenant (House of Commons Defence Committee, 2011) in the UK, now enshrined in law, holds that society has a legal responsibility to ensure that appropriate support and treatment is provided for serving and ex-service personnel with mental health and social needs to ensure they do not suffer a disadvantage as a result of military service. So what is being done currently to support veterans in the UK CJS and prevent this outcome among new service leavers?

Current interventions for ex-Armed Forces offenders

Access to a good evidence-base is an essential when recommending interventions for a certain population. Unfortunately, there is little research into what works to reduce offending among veterans. The Phillips' report (2014) fell short in not making any recommendations for research on what interventions may be effective in ameliorating offending behaviour in ex-service personnel (Phillips, 2014). Perhaps we can build on what we already know to work from research in the field of general offender research (Ministry of Justice, 2014b). After all, the background risk profile of former Armed Forces personnel offenders is similar to other offenders; that is, younger males from more deprived areas of the country with a history of offending (MacManus et al., 2013). However, if it is assumed that the ex-military population is different, and if that were not the case there would have been no need for the recent government review, then it follows that we need an evidence base for its efficacy among the former Armed Forces offender population, as well as exploration of opportunities for preventative measures during an individual's service and on resettlement (House of Commons Defence Committee, 2014). Particular challenges in dealing with former Armed Forces personnel in the CJS may arise from their experiences in the military, the associated mental health problems and the socioeconomic, cultural and health impact of transitioning into civilian life. There are particular problems with stigma, barriers to help seeking (Iversen *et al.*, 2011) and issues of responsivity to interventions that need to be considered. The challenge is not only the adaptation of existing interventions for this population, but then also trialling them and building an evidence base on 'what works' on which to base future recommendations. Commissioning exclusive services may improve initial accessibility, but engagement with mainstream services will continue to be preferable to fit the goal of integration with the general population, provided there is evidence to support it. As the Philips review rightly points out, early interventions in offending reduction such as those in youth justice (Smith, 2014) and mental health (Scott *et al.*, 2013) should be the priority for the future.

Identification

As in most areas of health and social care, early identification and intervention is key in order to improve chances of successful rehabilitation. One major outcome following the Phillips report into veterans in the CJS (Phillips, 2014) is that, from January 2015, every prisoner coming into custody would be asked if they have been a member of the Armed Forces and prisons would be given new guidance on how to support them during their sentence. This obligation needs to be extended to courts and police custody. Barriers to self-disclosure are, however, many, ranging from fear (of being targeted by fundamentalist groups in prison), shame and stigma. Such barriers need to be addressed in order to improve identification and opportunities for intervention.

Court diversion and liaison

The US has been running Veteran Courts since 2008 (Howard League for Penal Reform, 2011a; Russell *et al.*, 2010). These are courts which operate solely for veterans and which prioritise treatment and support over custodial sentences wherever appropriate. In the current financial climate in the UK, it is unlikely that such a system could be supported and nor is it generally seen as something that is necessary to achieve the goal of recognising veterans' needs and considering appropriate disposals. Phillips (2014) was not of a mind to recommend such a judicial restructuring, concluding that criminal courts in England and Wales are able to take into account the special characteristics of defendants and that veteran courts would be unlikely to increase public confidence in the proper and equal administration of justice for all citizens of the United Kingdom (Phillips, 2014). This conclusion is predicated on the reliable identification of veterans coming through the court system. Hampshire has had a Court Diversion and Peer Mentoring project for a number of years, which aims to refer former service personnel from the CJS into appropriate support settings, such as mental health services, substance misuse services or service charities (Phillips, 2014). NHS England have now established ten Court Liaison and Diversion (or L&D) pilot services across England, which operate by 'identifying, assessing and referring offenders who have mental health problems, learning disabilities, substance misuse issues or other vulnerabilities, to an appropriate treatment or support service' (Phillips, 2014). The identification of veterans is part of the process at all ten sites. Following assessment, referrals can be made to generic or veteran specific health and social care services. The L&D pathway also provides information to agencies such as the police, prosecutors, judges and probation services contributing to decisions around case management, sentencing and disposal. Data emerging from the first year of this pilot venture will for the first time allow insight into the number of veterans coming through the magistrates' court, their pattern of offending and their health and social care needs.

Support in custody

The 'Veteran in Custody Support' model began with the process of identifying offenders who were former service personnel, based on self-report, a process which became known as 'Ask the Question' (James and Wood, 2010). Beyond identification, the model was designed to incorporate the custodial Offender Assessment System (OASYS) and the 7 pathway resettlement model. Among the aims of the service was to assist in veteran offender resettlement and to incorporate veteran-specific interventions into offender management systems and resettlement arrangements.

As increasing research has emerged which has identified key risk factors for offending and hence target risk groups among veterans, the NOMS pathway was developed and adapted in accordance with veteran-specific needs.

Despite widespread acceptance as a model of best practice, the VICS service has historically attracted no dedicated funding to operate within prison establishments, and in most cases, has relied on dedicated and enthusiastic voluntary staff, in some cases in their own time. Perhaps a marker of the increased recognition of the need for these services to be funded, NHS England recently funded The London Veteran Service, a collaboration between Camden and Islington NHS Trust and South London and Maudsley NHS Trust, to establish a Veterans Inreach Project in HMP Wandsworth. This is an expansion of the VICS model and not only utilises a Veteran in Custody Support Nurse and VICS officers but is part of a larger multidisciplinary service including welfare, housing and mental health, which provides support in prison, through the gate and into the community. Whilst the VICS model has received universal praise for its effectiveness in identification and support of offenders who are veterans, there is concern about the lack of consistent application across the custodial estate (Phillips, 2014). A similar model to VICS was developed and championed by Alan Lilly, a probation officer based in Cheshire. The probation role was to become known as VSO (Veterans Support Officer). VSO schemes are now operational in a number of Probation Trust areas across the country (e.g. Cheshire, Durham Tees Valley, Lancashire). The working relationship between the probation VSO and custodial VICS models facilitates pathways of support if an offender who is a former member of the Armed Forces moves from a community to custodial to community setting. Some services employ a Veterans Champion (VSO) to identify and support offenders who are veterans in police custody suites and court environments. The Durham, Tees Valley Probation project employs the use of 'Veterans Champions' who advise staff and endeavour to see offenders undergoing probation within ten days of referral. Again, in spite of pockets of good practice, there is, as yet, no national programme of VSOs.

Police custody support

Identification of veterans at the point of entering the court process is desirable, but even earlier identification and intervention could be achieved at the point of arrest. There are a number of projects in the UK that have been endeavouring to do this. In a number of regions, police officers routinely identify offenders who are veterans in the custody suites and refer on to Project NOVA, a pilot joint venture which is delivered by the Regular Forces Employment Association (RFEA) and the Veterans and Families Institute (VFI) at Anglia Ruskin University, who are undertaking a mixed-methods evaluation of the pilot. Project Nova is funded by Walking with the Wounded and the Forces in Mind Trust, both charitable bodies for the ex-military community. The aim of this project is to identify veterans at the point of arrest in police custody and provide advice, guidance and support utilising a recognised network of ex-Armed Forces charities and support organisations. An important feature of the NOVA project is to collect data to help to understand underlying factors contributing to offending behaviour, with the aim of developing interventions to reduce reoffending in this cohort. Data from the first 12 months of this project are eagerly awaited.

Care pathways out of the criminal justice system

The Phillips review called for coherent national guidance on working with former Armed Forces offenders and more coherent pathways into mental health, social, welfare and employment support for those who find themselves in contact with the CJS (Phillips, 2014). Given the recognised link between mental health, social problems and offending, clear pathways into mental health treatment and social support must be prioritised. High levels of need within this population (Iversen et al., 2011), at a time of greater fragmentation of services than ever before, mean this will not be easy. Social and welfare needs of this population are often enmeshed with mental health needs, and therefore greater cross-working between government, statutory and third sector agencies is essential if the ambitions of the Military Covenant are to be upheld.

Co-ordination of care and 'duplication' of 'Third sector' contact has been raised as an issue. Phillips (2014) highlights this, saying that 'former service personnel to whom I spoke in custody described incidents where they were visited by staff from two or more of the major charities about the same issues'. This was also a concern raised in Lord Ashcroft's (2014) Veteran's Transition Review where he recommends greater co-operation between the service charities. To address this particular issue, the Confederation of Service Charities (COBSEO) have created ten 'cluster' groups to enhance collaborative working within different fields of veterans' issues. One of these groups is the 'Veterans in the Criminal Justice System', which brings together Third sector, MOD, MoJ and ex-service charities to address and develop working with offenders who are veterans across the CJS. What impact this will have on the current duplication of resources remains to be seen. As a major provider of services for veterans, especially mental health, the NHS should also be represented in this group.

Conclusion

It is important to remember that the vast majority of those who serve in the military go on to successfully re-integrate into civilian life without problems. A small proportion do not, and can end up in the CJS. We have identified that this can partly be predicted by pre-military factors such as poor educational attainment, exposure to childhood adversity and contact with the CJS prior to enlistment. The perpetuation of these risks is evidenced by the clustering of offenders among those who served in the lower ranks of the Army. For some who have not had successful military careers and leave service early, their offending may be mostly associated with the problems they had prior to joining the military. Unfortunately, we have no data on the positive impact that military service may have on some who enter with histories of early life adversity. Research has shown that some military experiences such as exposure to combat trauma, and the associated mental health problems, are associated with an increased risk of offending, over and above the pre-existing risk factors. For some, it may be difficulties incurred during the transition period after leaving the military, problems with housing, employment, family relationships, resultant mental health and substance misuse problems. For some it may be all of the above.

The biggest hurdle to providing support and help has been difficulty identifying those who are veterans in the CJS. Alongside increased public attention and political momentum, government recommendations for changes to practice may improve the status quo. There is no shortage of goodwill and motivation to implement services to provide support, but these need to be co-ordinated at a national level and key to any improvement in offender management is an evidence base of what works to reduce re-offending in this population. There must be funding of research to provide this bedrock of evidence.

References

Allport, A. (2009). *Demobbed: Coming Home After the Second World War*. New Haven: Yale University Press.

Black, D. W., Carney, C.P., Peloso, P.M., Woolson, R.F., Letuchy, E., Doebbeling, B.N. (2005). Incarceration and veterans of the First Gulf War. *Military Medicine*, 170, 612–18.

Buckman, J.E.J., Forbes, H.J., Clayton, T., Jones, M., Jones, N., Greenberg, N., Sundin, J., Hull, L., Wessely, S., Fear, N.T. (2012). Early Service leavers: A study of the factors associated with premature separation from the UK Armed Forces and the mental health of those that leave early. *The European Journal of Public Health*, 23, 410–15.

Caesar, E. (2010). From hero to zero. *The Sunday Times*, 4 April 2010. Available online at www.thesundaytimes.co.uk/sto/incoming/article256838.ece (accessed 20 January 2017).

Calvert, W.E., Hutchinson, R.L. (1990). Vietnam veteran levels of combat: Related to later violence? *Journal of Traumatic Stress*, 3, 103–13.

DASA (2010a). *Estimating the Proportion of Prisoners in England and Wales who are ex-Armed Forces*, Defence Analytical Services Advice (ed.). London: Ministry of Defence.

DASA (2010b). *Estimating the Proportion of Prisoners in England and Wales who are ex-Armed Forces–further analysis*, Defence Analytical Services Advice (ed.). London: Ministry of Defence.

Doward, J. (2008). Record numbers of ex-soldiers in UK jails as combat trauma blamed. *The Guardian*, 31 August 2008. Available online at www.theguardian.com/uk/2008/aug/31/military.prisonsandprobation (accessed 20 January 2017).

Elbogen, E.B., Wagner, H.R., Fuller, S.R., Calhoun, P.S., Kinneer, P.M., Mid-Atlantic Mental Illness Research Education, Clinical Center Workgroup, Beckham, JC. (2010). Correlates of anger and hostility in Iraq and Afghanistan War veterans. *The American Journal of Psychiatry*, 167, 105–8.

Elbogen, E.B., Johnson, S.C., Newton, V.M., Straits-Troster, K., Vasterling, J.J., Wagner, H.R., Beckham, J.C. (2012a). Criminal justice involvement, trauma, and negative affect in Iraq and Afghanistan War era veterans. *Journal of Consulting and Clinical Psychology*, 80, 1097–102.

Elbogen, E.B., Johnson, S.C., Wagner, H.R., Newton, V.M., Timko, C., Vasterling, J.J., Beckham, J.C. (2012b). Protective factors and risk modification of violence in Iraq and Afghanistan War veterans. *The Journal of Clinical Psychiatry*, 73, e767–73.

Elbogen, E.B., Johnson, S.C., Wagner, H.R., Sullivan, C., Taft C.T., Beckham, J.C. (2014). Violent behaviour and post-traumatic stress disorder in US Iraq and Afghanistan veterans. *The British Journal of Psychiatry*, 204, 368–75.

Emsley, C. (2013). *Soldier, Sailor, Beggarman, Thief: Crime and the British Armed Services since 1914*. Oxford: Oxford University Press.

Fear, N.T., Jones, M., Murphy, D., Hull, L., Iversen, A.C., Coker, B., Machell, L., Sundin, J., Woodhead, C., Jones, N., Greenberg, N., Landau, S., Dandeker, C., Rona, R.J., Hotopf, M., Wessely, S. (2010). What are the consequences of deployment to Iraq and Afghanistan on the mental health of the UK armed forces? A cohort study. *The Lancet*, 375, 1783–97.

Fossey, M. (2010). *Across the Wire: Veterans, Mental Health and Vulnerability*. London: Centre for Mental Health.

Hatch, S.L., Harvey, S.B., Dandeker, C., Burdett, H., Greenberg, N., Fear, N.T., Wessely, S. (2013). Life in and after the Armed Forces: Social networks and mental health in the UK military. *Sociology of Health and Illness*, 35, 1045–64.

Hattenstone, S., Allison, E. (2014). 'You don't ever get over it': Meet the British soldiers living with post-traumatic stress disorder. *The Guardian*, 18 October 2014. Available online at www.theguardian.com/society/2014/oct/18/collateral-damage-ex-soldiers-living-with-ptsd (accessed 20 January 2017).

Her Majesty's Inspectorate of Prisons (2014). *People in Prison: Ex-service personnel. A findings paper by HM Inspectorate of Prisons*. London: HMIP.

Hopkins, N. (2014). Number of UK war veterans seeking help for mental health issues on the rise. *The Guardian*, 12 May 2014. Available online at www.theguardian.com/uk-news/2014/may/12/uk-war-veterans-mental-health-issues-rise (accessed 20 January 2017).

House of Commons Defence Committee (2011). *The Armed Forces Covenant in Action*. London: The House of Commons Defence Committee.

House of Commons Defence Committee (2014). *The Armed Forces Covenant in Action Part 5: Military Casualties, a review of progress*. London. The House of Commons Defence Committee. Available online at www.publications.parliament.uk/pa/cm201415/cmselect/cmdfence/527/52709.htm (accessed 20 January 2017).

Howard League for Penal Reform (2011a). *Inquiry into former Armed Service personnel in prison*. London: Howard League for Penal Reform.

Howard League for Penal Reform (2011b). *Leaving Forces Life*. London: Howard League for Penal Reform.

Howard League for Penal Reform (2011c). *Leave No Veteran Behind*. London: Howard League for Penal Reform.

Iversen, A., van Staden, L., Hacker Hughes, J., Browne, T., Hull, L., Hall, J., Greenberg, N., Rona, R., Hotopf, M., Wessely, S., Fear, N.T. (2009). The prevalence of common mental disorders and PTSD in the UK military: using data from a clinical interview-based study. *BMC Psychiatry*, 9, 68.

Iversen, A., van Staden, L., Hacker Hughes, J., Greenberg, N., Hotopf, M., Rona, R., Thornicroft, G., Wessely, S., Fear, N. (2011). The stigma of mental health problems and other barriers to care in the UK Armed Forces. *BMC Health Services Research*, 11, 31.

James, E. (2010). Why are so many former soldiers in prison? *The Guardian*, 9 February 2010. Available online at www.theguardian.com/society/2010/feb/09/erwin-james-soldiers-prison (accessed 20 January 2017).

James, S., Wood, N. (2010). *A Guide to Working with Veterans in Custody*. London: NACRO. Available online at http://northeastveterans.net/downloads/vic130510.pdf (accessed 20 January 2017).

Killgore, W.D.S., Cotting, D.I., Thomas, J.L, Cox, A.L., McGurk, D., Vo, A.H., Castro, C.A., Hoge, C.W. (2008). Post-combat invincibility: Violent combat experiences are associated with increased risk-taking propensity following deployment. *Journal of Psychiatric Research*, 42, 1112–21.

King's Centre for Military Health Research (2013). *King's Centre for Military Health Research: A Fifteen Year Report*. London: King's College London.

Kizer, K.W., Fonseca, M.L., Long, L.M. (1997). The veterans healthcare system: Preparing for the twenty-first century. *Hospital and Health Services Administration*, 42, 283–98.

Leventman, S. (1978). Epilogue: Social and historical perspectives on the Vietnam veteran. In: *Stress Disorders Among Vietnam Veterans*, Figley, C. (ed.). New York: Brunner/Mazel, pp. 291–5.

Lord Ashcroft (2014). *The Veterans' Transition Review*. London: Lord Ashcroft KCMG PC.

McGinnes, J. (2008). One in ten inmates are former servicemen, research shows. *The Sunday Times*, 15 July 2012. Available online at www.thesundaytimes.co.uk/sto/news/uk_news/Defence/article1082223.ece (accessed 20 January 2017).

MacManus, D., Wessely, S. (2011). Why do some ex-armed forces personnel end up in prison? *BMJ*, 342, d3898.

MacManus, D., Dean, K., Al Bakir, M., Iversen, A.C., Hull, L., Fahy, T., Wessely, S., Fear, N.T. (2012a). Violent behaviour in UK military personnel returning home after deployment. *Psychological Medicine*, 42, 1663–73.

MacManus, D., Dean, K., Iversen, A., Hull, L, Jones, N., Fahy, T., Wessely, S., Fear, N.T. (2012b). Impact of pre-enlistment antisocial behaviour on behavioural outcomes among UK military personnel. *Social Psychiatry and Psychiatric Epidemiology*, 47, 1353–8.

MacManus, D., Dean, K., Jones, M., Rona, R.J., Greenberg, N., Hull, L., Fahy, T., Wessely, S., Fear, N.T. (2013). Violent offending by UK military personnel deployed to Iraq and Afghanistan: a data linkage cohort study. *The Lancet*, 381, 907–17.

MacManus, D., Fossey, M., Watson, S.E., Wessely, S. (2014a). Former Armed Forces personnel in the criminal justice system. *The Lancet Psychiatry*, 2, 121–2.

MacManus, D., Thandi, G., Trevillion, K., Howard, L., Fear, N.T. (2014b). *Intimate Partner Violence: A Systematic Review of Prevalence and Risk Factors. Internal Report for NHS England.* Redditch: NHS England.

MacManus, D., Burdett, H., Jones, M., Hull, L., Wessely, S., Fear, N. T. (under review). Risk and protective factors for offending among UK military personnel after leaving service, in press.

MacManus, D., Rona, R., Dickson, H., Somaini, G., Fear, N.T., Wessely, S. (2015). Aggressive and violent behavior among military personnel deployed to Iraq and Afghanistan: Prevalence and link with deployment and combat exposure. *Epidemiologic Reviews*, 37, 196–212.

May, C., Sharma, N. and Stewart, D. (2008). *Factors Linked to Reoffending: A One-Year Follow-Up of Prisoners Who Took Part in the Resettlement Surveys 2001, 2003 and 2004.* London: Home Office.

Ministry of Defence (2003). *Strategy for Veterans.* London: Ministry of Defence.

Ministry of Defence (2008). *Nation's Commitment: Cross-Government Support to our Armed Forces, their Families and Veterans.* London: Ministry of Defence.

Ministry of Defence (2014). *Fulfilling the Commitments of the Armed Forces Covenant.* London: Ministry of Defence.

Ministry of Defence (2015). *Transition to Civilian Life: The Emotional Pathway.* London: Ministry of Justice.

Ministry of Justice (2010). *Conviction Histories of Offenders between the Ages of 10 and 52: England And Wales, Ministry of Justice Statistics Bulletin.* London: Ministry of Justice.

Ministry of Justice (2013). *Offender Management Community Cohort Study (OMCCS) Baseline Technical Report.* London: Ministry of Justice.

Ministry of Justice (2014a). *Prison Population Bulletin, December.* London: Ministry of Justice.

Ministry of Justice (2014b). *Transforming Rehabilitation; A Summary of Evidence on Reducing Reoffending,* 2nd ed. London: Ministry of Justice. Available online at www.gov.uk/government/uploads/system/uploads/attachment_data/file/305319/transforming-rehabilitation-evidence-summary-2nd-edition.pdf (accessed 20 January 2017).

Murray, E. (2014). Post-army trouble: veterans in the criminal justice system. *Criminal Justice Matters*, 94, 20–1.

Murrison, A. (2010). *Fighting Fit: A Mental Health Plan for Servicemen and Veterans.* London: Department of Health. Available online at www.gov.uk/government/uploads/system/uploads/attachment_data/file/27375/20101006_mental_health_Report.pdf (accessed 20 January 2017).

NAPO (2009). *Armed Forces and the Criminal Justice System.* London: NAPO.

Phillips, S. (2014). *Former Members of the Armed Forces and the Criminal Justice System: A Review on Behalf of the Secretary of State for Justice*. London: Ministry of Justice.

Prime, J., White, S., Liriano, S., Patel, K. (2001). *Criminal Careers of Those Born Between 1953 and 1978*. London: Home Office.

Rowe, M., Murphy, D., Wessely, S., Fear, N.T. (2013). Exploring the impact of deployment to Iraq on relationships. *Military Behavioral Health*, 1, 13–21.

Russell, R.T. (2010). *Buffalo Veterans Treatment Court: Buffalo Veterans Court and Veterans Mentor Handbook*. Cambridge: Harvard University Press.

Scott, D.A., McGilloway, S., Dempster, M., Browne, F., Donnelly, M. (2013). Effectiveness of criminal justice liaison and diversion services for offenders with mental disorders: A review. *Psychiatric Services*, 64, 843–9.

Simonoff, E., Elander, J., Holmshaw, J., Pickles, A., Murray, R., Rutter, M. (2004). Predictors of antisocial personality: Continuities from childhood to adult life. *The British Journal of Psychiatry*, 2004, 184, 118–27.

Smith, R. (2014). Re-inventing diversion. *Youth Justice*, 14, 109–21.

The Royal British Legion (2012). *Literature Review: UK Veterans and the Criminal Justice System*. London: The Royal British Legion.

The Royal British Legion (2014). *A UK Household Survey of the Ex-serving Community*. London: The Royal British Legion.

Townsend, M. (2008). They're back from the front line - so why are these ex-soldiers still fighting their own wars? *The Guardian*, 3 February 2008. Available online at www.theguardian.com/uk/2008/feb/03/afghanistan.iraq (accessed 20 January 2017).

Treadwell, J. (2010). Counterblast: More than casualties of war? Ex-military personnel in the criminal justice system. *The Howard Journal of Criminal Justice*, 49, 73–7.

Waller, W. (1944). *The Veteran Comes Back*. New York: Dryden Press.

Yager, J. (1976). Postcombat violent behavior in psychiatrically maladjusting soldiers. *Arch Gen Psychiatry*, 33, 1332–5.

Zoricić, Z., Karlovic, D., Buljan, D., Marusić, S. (2003). Comorbid alcohol addiction increases. aggression level in soldiers with combat-related post-traumatic stress disorder. *Nordic Journal of Psychiatry*, 57, 199–202.

6

THE HEALTH AND SOCIAL CARE OF OLDER VETERANS IN THE UK

Raising Awareness of Needs in Later Life

Karen Burnell, John Crossland and Neil Greenberg

Introduction

When we talk about the transition of veterans, we most often refer to the move from serving to formerly serving status, but veterans are likely to experience multiple transitions during their lives, including into and out of service, into and out of another career and, of course, into later life. Currently, the transition out of service to civilian life appears to be a key concern for policy makers and service providers (Forces in Mind Trust, 2013), and awareness is growing in terms of the mental health and wellbeing of veterans (Greenberg, 2014). However, there is relatively scant attention given to the impact of service experience in the context of ageing and the lifespan, which has yet to gain the momentum it deserves (Settersten and Patterson, 2006; Spiro and Settersten, 2012).

This chapter is embedded in gerontological theory and particularly that of the life course perspective (George, 1996). This theory suggests that to understand the circumstances of older people, we must consider the major social and psychological forces they have experienced throughout their lives. The accumulation of life events should be considered at both the individual and societal level. Given that the experience of military service, particularly when personnel are operationally deployed, is both an individual and societal event, it is important to have an awareness of this from a theoretical and practice perspective.

Linked with this is the concept of life course development, which is concerned more with the individual tasks and challenges that people face as they age. Among these ideas is that of the *life review* (Butler, 1963, 2002), which is the 'progressive return to consciousness of memories and unresolved past conflicts for re-evaluation and resolution' (2002: 7). Originally, it was thought that this happened at the later stages of life and involved the reflection of the life events and the (re)emergence of unresolved conflict. This complements the work of Erik Erikson, writing in the

1950s, who spoke of integrity versus despair in later life (Erikson, 1994), and the purpose of life stories to maintain identity and wellbeing throughout life, particularly in later life.

Underpinning life review is the concept of reminiscence as being a vital aspect of successful ageing. Reminiscence is the act of recalling the past, and it serves several purposes, including integration of events across the lifespan. It can otherwise serve to reduce boredom, but may also have negative outcomes particularly if it is obsessive or ruminating in nature (Webster et al., 2010). When reminiscence is used to integrate experiences and events, adding meaning and continuity, it has been found to enhance feelings of wellbeing in later life.

Interestingly, as identified by Bender (1997), Erikson, in his strive towards developing a universal theory of ageing, did not consider cohort differences, much less the impact of conflict or military service in later life. Perhaps this absence of acknowledgement can be explained if we consider who these older people were when Erikson was originally writing; these men were not of a war generation. Career soldiers quite possibly, but not the war generations created by World Wars I (WWI) and II (WWII), and their experiences may have gone unnoticed in an otherwise non-military cohort. This may well mirror the experiences of the cohorts of younger veterans today as they age; their experiences may also be lost within otherwise non-serving generations. The shrinking size of the military and the changing demographics and ethnic makeup of United Kingdom (UK) society might mean that knowledge of the military and military service is likely to become more scarce over time.

It is interesting to note that the impact of service experience in later life came to the fore in the literature in the late 1980s and 90s as those who lived through WWII as servicemen and women, civilians and survivors of atrocities reached later life; their memories emerging, perhaps for the first time. For instance, Peter Coleman's seminal work on older adults' reminiscences indicated that reminiscence, far from being a fun activity for some older people, was troubling to those who recalled war experience and actively avoided by others (Coleman, 1986). Around a similar time, oral history work was beginning to report the emergence of memories of the Holocaust for older people who lived through this time (Bornat, 1989).

The idea that reminiscence and life review only occur in later life is no longer held by gerontological theory. It is acknowledged that people are constantly striving to make sense of their lives, particularly through story form (see McAdams, 1993). If we then see life review in later life as not the creation of a life story, but the reflection on and modification of an existing story, the concept of life course comes to the fore. Using this framework, research was carried out nearly a decade ago to try to understand veterans' reconciliation of traumatic memories across the lifespan and the types of social support associated with this (Burnell, 2007; Burnell et al., 2011b). The underlying premise was to understand whether veterans could reconcile memories of service experience in earlier life, before cognitive and social resources, that might be useful in the process, change or decline over time. Findings indicated that when social support facilitated meaningful communication, reconciliation could be achieved regardless of age or cohort. Also of importance was the impact of perceived societal perceptions; that is, the societal narrative or story of particular wars and conflicts (see also Burnell *et al.*, 2011a).

Of course, interventions can and should be put in place to support younger veterans. One such programme is the Veterans Transition Program (Westwood *et al.*, 2010), which provides support for career transition, (re)building and strengthening family relationships, post-traumatic stress disorder (PTSD) and understanding availability of resources. While there is a great and pressing need for earlier life resolution, reconciliation and transition, it cannot be that all veterans will get such timely intervention. The literature to date suggests that there will always be an element of avoidance or need emerging only in later life. It is also the case that such transition programmes capture those currently serving or recently formerly serving. As such, there are generations of veterans who left the military years ago, who did not have this opportunity and who may require support in later life. It is essential that we continue to recognise this need in our older veteran populations, who may reach later life without resolution and whose natural reminiscences may become more focused on achieving this.

Impact of service experience on later life

Given the potential concerns of later life, one might question whether service experience impacts sufficiently enough to warrant being concerned about the health and wellbeing of older veterans. Are their experiences unique enough to justify the development of specific services? Are their needs any greater than those of older people generally? They may not be greater, but they are arguably different. In the past ten years, there have been three special issues in leading gerontological journals highlighting the seriousness of the impact of service experience in later life (Settersten and Patterson, 2006; Spiro and Settersten, 2012; Albright *et al.*, 2015). In some cases, those who have been exposed to combat fare worse than those who have not (i.e. MacLean and Elder, 2007*)*, the differences being most marked in later life. Veterans are also more likely to experience depression, PTSD, the breakdown of personal and intimate relationships and experience even greater levels of social isolation (Erickson *et al.*, 2001; Krause *et al.*, 2006). Importantly, in each introduction, the authors called for the need to acknowledge the impact of service experience in later life from both a theoretical and practice perspective and from a perspective of both negative (Settersten, 2006) and positive impact, such as good employment prospects and marital satisfaction and the emergence of wisdom and resilience (Jennings *et al.*, 2006; Lee *et al.*, 1995; Settersten, 2006).

Much interest has been given to changes in physical, cognitive and social resources experienced in later life. As one ages, it becomes harder to avoid remembering the past due to age-related changes in cognition and, in the absence of social support, the problem is exacerbated. Social changes may mean that positive memories cannot be shared in later life. As a result, wellbeing may be significantly affected in later life (e.g. Bender, 1997; Davison *et al.*, 2006; Elder and Clipp, 1989;

Hunt and Robbins, 2001a). As argued by Baltes and Lang (1997), how well individuals cope with change over the life course is, in part, due to available resources. Cognitive ageing due to natural changes or organic disease, such as dementia, may be responsible for re-experiencing memories in later life that have been avoided for decades (Floyd *et al.*, 2002). Through the life course, veterans may lose family and comrades who may have helped them cope (Hunt and Robbins, 2001b), or there may be a natural reduction in the size of social networks (Isaacowitz *et al.*, 2003). Difficulties may emerge in later life around retirement when the routines that have helped to maintain their ability to function change (Allen, 2008), or may heighten the impact of traumatic memory (Busuttil, 2004). Equally, for those whose military experience impacted in positive ways, an opportunity to share these experiences is valued but not always available.

Trauma throughout the life course

Traumatic events can affect military personnel during service for many reasons. Whilst traditional military narratives assume that operational deployments, including combat exposure, are the main cause of traumatic exposure, contemporary studies have shown that non-combat factors are as important predictors of a service person suffering from PTSD (Jones *et al.*, 2013). However, during later life, it may be that the symptoms of unreconciled trauma, which veterans have been able to cope with, become more problematic as cognitive function declines and support structures become less available (Hamilton and Workman, 1998; Schreuder *et al.*, 2000). It may thus be that, during later life, significant PTSD symptoms may present as being clinically significant for the first time (Lindman Port *et al.*, 2001). The (re)emergence of trauma in later life may be due to a number of factors, such as a decline in physical health in later life (Ong and Carter, 2001), the stress and loss of routine associated with retirement (Busuttil, 2004), changes in cognition and changes in social support resources in later life, which may have previously aided the avoidance of memories (Hunt and Robbins, 2001b).

As previously noted, traumatic war memories and reminiscence have a reciprocal relationship, with one affecting the other (Coleman, 1999). As reminiscence and life review are linked to meaning making, the avoidance of looking back can impact on the ability to find meaning in events (Krause, 2005). Of course, experiencing trauma is not exclusive to older people who have served but, as a cohort, those who have served may be more likely to have experienced such events. While military forces have paid more attention to encouraging troops to speak about traumatic experiences over recent years (Hunt *et al.*, 2014), traditionally troops have been encouraged not to speak openly about their experiences, which may inhibit the ability to make meaning in later life.

Fundamentally, Krause also determined that trauma incurred between the ages of 18 and 30 is particularly associated with difficulties in finding meaning in throughout life. In the case of veterans, the ages of 18 to 30 may be more likely to be the years in which they served. In addition, the reminiscence bump associated with later life focuses on incidences that occur at the age of 18 to 30 (Conway and

Holmes, 2004). As meaning is gained from these experiences in later life, and individuals are more likely to reminisce about them, one can see the potential impact of this in later life. Whilst the life review process may resurrect difficult memories or traumatic symptoms, the process of life review and the search for meaning can be used to integrate these events into the life that has been lived (Frankl, 2004).

Cognitive change, memory loss and dementia

Natural age-related changes in cognition may lead to the emergence of involuntary memories in later life, leading to the post-traumatic symptoms in some cases. Floyd *et al.* (2002) argue that an age-related decrease in attention increases the likelihood of experiencing intrusive flashbacks. These flashbacks may heighten distress associated with traumatic or difficult memories. The loss of attention associated with cognitive ageing can be explained by the two-part process of facilitation (selection of information) and inhibition (repression of information), which is said to become less effective with age. Research focusing on changes in attention indicates that older adults can experience more frequent distraction from goals (Hasher and Zacks, 1988). Older adults with post-traumatic symptoms may find that, after years of inhibiting and switching their attention from ruminations, avoiding memories is no longer a viable coping strategy. As such, post-traumatic symptoms may worsen with age and older people's mental health services may not recognise these symptoms due to a lack of experience in dealing with them. Equally, practitioners may not ask about these symptoms and older veterans may not volunteer this information.

Changes in long-term memory can be divided into changes within explicit (episodic) memory and implicit (semantic) memory. Implicit memory relates to subconscious imagery, and due to its subconscious nature, shows very little decline. Explicit memory relates to information regarding specific events and the narrative surrounding them, which can be affected by age-related change (Smith and Earles, 1996). The implication here is that if access to explicit memories decreases with age, intervention may be required to limit the potential negative impact (Busuttil, 2004). It is also recognised that this will not be relevant to all older veterans but, at the very least, the potential impact must be recognised.

There is increasing evidence from research carried out in the US suggesting a link between PTSD resulting from military exposures and increase risk of developing neurodegenerative diseases such as Alzheimer's disease (AD). Weiner *et al.* (2013) provide a brief, informative review paper of the potential underlying pathological changes underlying such an association. This review suggests that there appears to be changes in synaptic connectivity associated with learning, such as fear conditioning. Veterans with PTSD may also have reduced hippocampal volume that correlates with impaired memory and impaired brain function in the medial prefrontal cortex, amygdala and hippocampus (Bremner, 2007), potentially influenced by PTSD severity (Apfel *et al.*, 2011; Cardenas *et al.*, 2011). However, chronic stress due to PTSD has also been shown to cause hypertrophy of the amygdala, an area of the brain that has evolved to deal with stressful, dangerous and threatening situations.

Thus, it may be that hippocampal atrophy represents an adaptive change in response to high stress rather than a form of brain damage. Another possibility is that individuals with smaller hippocampi are at higher risk of developing PTSD. A study in Gulf War veterans (Apfel *et al.*, 2011), showed that current, but not lifetime, PTSD symptoms were associated with smaller hippocampal volume. This may mean that hippocampal size reverts to normal when PTSD symptoms abate or that individuals with small hippocampi fail to recover from PTSD. However, another study of identical twin pairs discordant for combat exposure in Vietnam found that hippocampal diminution was shared by the combat-unexposed twins of combat veterans with PTSD (Gilbertson *et al.*, 2010).

Another important military-related problem which may be linked to cognitive decline and dementia is that of alcohol misuse (Ridley *et al.*, 2013). There is plenty of evidence that the UK Armed Forces consume far more alcohol than similarly aged members of the civilian population (Thandi *et al.*, 2015) and that harmful use of alcohol is reported by around 13 per cent of serving personnel (Fear *et al.*, 2010), which is more than double the rate found in civilian studies. It therefore follows that military personnel are likely to be at increased risk of this condition. One important facet of alcohol-related dementia is that, during the early stages at least, if abstinence from alcohol is maintained, then a good degree of cognitive recovery is usually possible (Ridley *et al.*, 2013).

Social resources, loneliness and isolation

Increased concerns around social isolation and loneliness in later life (Department of Health, 1999, 2001) further compound the issue (Cook and O'Donnell, 2005). With changes in the nature of war and conflict, and reduction of personnel in the British Armed Forces, it may be argued that the veteran population will become increasingly dispersed and invisible. The recent Household Survey conducted by The Royal British Legion (2014) found that the British veteran population is currently elderly and declining in size. This may become increasingly so if we pace forward to those who have served in less well-known conflicts post-WWII and what the needs of these small cohorts of veterans may be as they age. As Hunt (2007) argues, those living with the impact of their service experience must be acknowledged and be provided with appropriate and suitable services and interventions.

Just as social support has been found to be fundamental for younger veterans, it is equally important for older veterans, but social support networks are also affected by the ageing process. For instance, loss of support through illness or death of comrades or family results in reduced social support networks as we age (Hunt and Robbins, 2001b). Another reason is the natural reduction of social support networks, which is specific to later life. Laura Carstensen (1992) and colleagues (Isaacowitz *et al.*, 2003), argue that this natural decrease in social activity is an adaptive process of successful ageing because the older adult can devote more emotional resources to fewer relationships (Lansford *et al.*, 1998). As long ago as the 1960s, Cumming and Henry (1967) documented this downward trend in social activity, but interpreted it as isolation and disengagement from society. Carstensen casts a positive light on this decrease, suggesting that social activity does not indicate social support. As one ages, the resources available to invest in networks decrease, and so older adults maintain the most important and fruitful contacts, these being close friends and family.

Although often adaptive, the reduction in social networks for older veterans highlights again where the needs of older people who have served may be different from those who have not. This is because support networks, including family and friends, may help older veterans avoid their negative memories of service. Where memories are positive, having a small, but meaningful, network can provide an important opportunity to share memories, reinforcing feelings of identity. In both cases, wellbeing is likely to be maintained.

Conversely, if the friends invested in are emotionally significant individuals for older veterans, it is feasible to suggest that these individuals may be comrades. Whilst this may be positive in some cases, a problem shared is not necessarily a problem halved. In a study conducted with Holocaust survivors, Isaacowitz *et al.* (2003) found that these individuals experienced more negative emotional experiences within their social networks because they were composed of fellow Holocaust survivors. Furthermore, communication about these memories was infrequent because these relationships were marked by some degree of trauma-related negative affect. Whether a reduced support network be adaptive or otherwise, it is clear that they may exacerbate the impact of service experience in later life. It is also notable that research carried out with younger military personnel has also shown that veterans who continue to associate primarily with still serving personnel also report worse mental health outcomes than service leavers who manage to establish a non-military social network (Hatch *et al.*, 2013). This perhaps again reflects that continuing to dwell on trauma-related aspects of military service is detrimental to mental health no matter what age the veteran may be.

To focus only on the relationship between support and negative emotions would be wrong. Looking back on memories can be an enjoyable and rewarding experience, with implications for wellbeing in later life. And so, this natural desire to reflect on the life that has been lived is not only relevant for those whose service experience was traumatic, but also for those whose service experience was entirely positive. Veterans value the opportunity to share memories (i.e. Sixsmith *et al.*, 2014) and we must consider the implications when veterans have no one to share these experiences with.

Cohort differences and the impact of different wars

Over the years, the needs of older veterans have changed, and will continue to change. Each cohort of older veterans represents individuals who have experienced different wars and conflicts, different reasons for joining the Armed Forces, different societal reactions in terms of *justness* of war and homecoming reactions, different circumstances after service and different attitudes to the stigma of mental illness (Fontana and Rosenheck, 1994). All these factors will influence their wellbeing in later life.

Glen Elder (1986) has argued that war represents a turning point in the life of a young person. WWII presented opportunities to men and women that they may not have had otherwise, such as travel, training, responsibility at an earlier stage of life and for US veterans, education after service through the GI Bill (Elder *et al.*, 1991). However, Elder also found that the older the service person at the time of conscription, the more negative the impact of war, because the service interrupted an already established life. Indeed, Elder *et al.* (1994) found that as the age of mobilisation increased, financial and employment opportunities after service decreased.

Another cohort difference is societal involvement in the conflict and subsequent reaction to veterans. Research investigating direct comparisons between the homecoming of WWII and Korean War veterans suggests that, due to stressful homecoming experiences, Korean War veterans experienced more negative outcomes associated with their service. They returned to a society which was not directly involved in the conflict and who were perceived to be unsupportive of the war effort and losses incurred by these veterans (McCranie and Hyer, 2000). In truth, our knowledge of the *transition process* has not necessarily recognised the nuanced experiences of previous generations or acknowledged the power of societal opinions on service personnel. Research in areas of gerontology, psychology, sociology, human geography and history is beginning to look more closely at this and at the importance, for instance, of memorialisation and remembrance as forms of societal support.

Current policy

If the impact of service experience in later life presents a unique set of needs, the question becomes one of awareness and action. Do current policies recognise the needs of older people who are veterans? Of relevance here are the Armed Forces Covenant and the Care Act 2014, which, in turn, influence local authority strategies for older people's health and wellbeing.

The Armed Forces Covenant

Whilst the Armed Forces Covenant is not a legal document, its key principles have been enshrined in law in the Armed Forces Act 2011. The Armed Forces Covenant aims to be the expression of the moral obligation that the government and the nation owe to the Armed Forces Community because they, and their families, sacrifice some freedoms and often face dangerous situations. The Covenant operates two key principles; first, that the Armed Forces community faces no disadvantage in the provision of public and commercial services. Second, that special consideration should be given when required, such as to the injured or the bereaved (Ministry of Defence, 2015). In theory, veterans can be expected to receive fast-tracked treatment via primary care trusts and via the veteran pathway for Improving Access to Psychological Therapies (IAPT) services. Whilst the Covenant does not place any time limits on how long an obligation is owed to the Armed Forces community, it does not mention the needs of ageing veterans or their families specifically. Furthermore, many older people may well not identify themselves as being veterans and thus may not be able to use the provisions of the Covenant to encourage providers to provide them with relevant services.

Care Act 2014

In England, the primary legal responsibility for ensuring the organisation and provision of care and support services for all adults lies with local councils, referred to in the legislation as 'local authorities'. In the single most significant reform of care and support in more than 60 years (Lamb, 2014), the new Care Act brings together, and strengthens, the core elements of previously existing policy and legislation into a single statute (Law Commission, 2010). Importantly here, it embeds the personalisation policy agenda (Department of Health, 2007), with a strong focus on developing person-centred systems and strengths-based, community focused approaches. The concept of 'individual wellbeing' sits at its heart, creating a general legal duty for local authorities to promote individual wellbeing in the exercise of its care and support functions. Vitally, the legislation takes an outcome focused asset-based response to support people in their own communities, using existing resources and strengths.

In addition to the outcomes previously set out, there are several additional key principles embedded in the Act. Of particular relevance here are: that individuals are best placed to judge their own wellbeing; the necessity in a person-centred system to consider the particular views, feelings or beliefs of an individual; and the requirement to see people not simply as individuals in need of care but to understand them in the context of their families and support networks.

Combining the policies

The Care Act must also comply with its related public law duties too. Arguably, this could include the Armed Forces Community Covenant (Ministry of Defence, 2015), to which all councils have now signed up. The Care Act specifically requires that a local authority must provide services, facilities or resources which will contribute towards preventing, reducing or delaying the development by adults or carers in its area of needs for care and support. In doing so, it must 'have regard to' the importance of identifying adults and carers with needs for care and support that are not being met. In terms of assessment, the purpose here is to identify the person's needs and how these impact on their wellbeing and the outcomes that the person wishes to achieve in their day to day life. Once again, what is essential here is that consideration must be given to the person's own strengths and capabilities, and what support might be available from their wider support network or within the community to help.

For assessment, eligibility and service provision, the underlying assumptions here are that the individual will identify as a veteran and that their existing support

networks are adaptive. However, there is a clear opportunity here for the identification of, and provision for, unacknowledged needs amongst specific groups,
including older veterans, with implications for commissioning strategies. As such,
it would be beneficial if social workers and other local authority staff involved in
assessment are aware of the particular ways military service in earlier life can impact
on individuals' wellbeing in later life stages in order to ensure their assessments are
appropriately sensitive to particular experiences.

Possible interventions

The statutory guidance of the Care Act 2014 outlines a range of ways that a local
authority can address its responsibilities to prevent, reduce or delay the need for
care and support at various levels. For example, with regards to primary prevention
(aimed at adults with no current health or support needs) community-based activity or befriending services are highlighted as particularly effective in reducing social
isolation and the guidance explicitly requires local authorities to consider how they
can work with different partners, including voluntary sector organisations, to identify unmet needs for different groups (Section 2.31), which could include different
cohorts of veterans.

Befriending is a popular, cost-effective, intervention for older people and it
has a good evidence base (Windle *et al.*, 2011). In recent years, there has been
a move towards providing peer support for older people, rather than befriending. The difference here is that peers are lay people with similar experiences
to the person they are befriender to, rather than lay people more generally.
In a recent study conducted by the first author, older veterans were consulted
with to develop a peer support programme for older veterans. The underlying
principle was that peer support given by older veterans to older veterans would
provide the comradeship often missed when networks reduce in size. Importantly, however, ensuring the peer was trained and well supported themselves
would go some way to ensuring that communication was appropriate, aiding
processing rather than avoidance, which addresses the concerns introduced in
this chapter (see also Burnell *et al.*, 2011b). It is also notable that peer support,
delivered by appropriately trained service personnel, has also been found to be
highly beneficial and acceptable in still serving military personnel (Greenberg
et al., 2010).

There is also an opportunity to further explore reminiscence therapies for older
veterans. Previous work in this area has found that the concepts of 'restorying'
(Kenyon and Randall, 1999), and guided autobiography conducted with groups of
WWII veterans can aid the reconciliation of traumatic memories through the provision of social support (Shaw and Westwood, 2002). Reminiscence therapies are
also used extensively to provide quality of life for people with dementia and their
carers (e.g. Schweitzer and Bruce, 2008). Emerging research concerning an evaluation of a reminiscence and activity group specifically for veterans with dementia and
their carers. Findings suggests that general chatting within the group using language

common to the veterans from their military service was the single most beneficial aspect of the activity group. This highlights the importance and value of shared experiences and reinforces the concept of peer support for its added value in aiding the continuity of identity. Both pieces of research were exploratory in nature and more research is needed to evaluate these veteran focused initiatives. Initial findings suggest that they are both suitable and feasible approaches.

What is important about both examples is that they can exist within services that cater for older people generally. With the numbers of veterans decreasing and becoming more dispersed in general, non-military, cohorts of older people, the idea that services can exist purely for the benefit of older servicemen and women exclusively is financially unstainable. This is before we remember that these exclusive services would only be used by those self-identifying as *a veteran*. More appropriate, then, is that services for older people are primed to recognise the potential impact of military experience in later life so that needs can be met, and issues prevented, by these services.

Conclusion

This chapter argues that military service, including deploying in a combat or peace support role, can impact on veterans' wellbeing in later life. At present, our understanding is almost entirely based on male veterans' life courses, and there is a clear need to understand the impact of service on the increasing proportion of military women better as they grow older. While current policy in theory recognises the concept of how military service impacts in later life, assumptions are implicit, and the needs of older veterans must be raised for those who work with this group of individuals. As long ago as 1997, Bender concluded that as services were provided by a younger generation unaffected by the direct experience of WWII, 'mental health services need to be readily available and they need to be staffed by personnel who understand the impact of war, in both its immediate and long-term effects' (1997: 346). This is precisely the awareness that is as essential for service provision for older veterans now, who have served in *forgotten wars* such as the Korean War, as it will be in years to come when formerly serving personnel, hidden in an otherwise non-serving generation, move through life's stages. That we have not acted on Bender's advice voiced some 20 years ago, indicates that there is still much to do in this important area.

References

Albright, D.L., Weiss, E.L., Nedjat-Haiem, F.R. (2015). Introduction to the aging military veterans special section. *Journal of Gerontological Social Work*, 58, 382–5.
Allen, J. (2008). *Older People and Wellbeing*. London: Institute for Public Policy Research.
Apfel, B.A., Ross, J., Hlavin, J., Meyerhoff, D.J., Metzler, T.J., Marmar, C.R., Weiner, M.W., Schuff, N., Neylan, T.C. (2011). Hippocampal volume differences in Gulf War veterans with current versus lifetime posttraumatic stress disorder symptoms. *Biological Psychiatry*, 69, 541–8.

Baltes, M.M., Lang, F.R. (1997). Everyday functioning and successful aging: The impact of resources. *Psychology and Aging*, 12, 433–43.

Bender, M.P. (1997). Bitter harvest: The implications of continuing war-related stress on reminiscence theory and practice. *Ageing and Society*, 17, 337–48.

Bornat, J. (1989). Oral history as a social movement: Reminiscence and older people. *Oral History*, 17, 16–24.

Bremner, J.D. (2007). Neuroimaging in posttraumatic stress disorder and other stress-related disorders. *Neuroimaging Clinics of North America*, 17, 523–38.

Burnell, K. J. (2007). *The Reconciliation of Traumatic War Memories Throughout the Adult Lifespan: The Relationship Between Narrative Coherence and Social Support*. Doctoral thesis. Southampton: University of Southampton.

Burnell, K.J., Boyce, N., Hunt, N. (2011a). A good war? Exploring British veterans' moral evaluation of deployment. *Journal of Anxiety Disorders*, 25, 36–42.

Burnell, K.J., Coleman, P.G., Hunt, N. (2011b). Achieving narrative coherence following traumatic war experience: the role of social support. In G. Kenyon, E. Bohlmeijer, W. Randall (eds.), *Storying Later Life: Perspectives, Investigations, and Interventions in Narrative Gerontology*. New York: Oxford University Press, pp. 195–212.

Busuttil, W. (2004). Presentation and management of post traumatic stress disorder and the elderly: A need for investigation. *International Journal of Geriatric Psychiatry*, 19, 429–39.

Butler, R. (1963). The life review: An interpretation of reminiscences in the aged. *Psychiatry*, 26, 65–76.

Butler, R. (2002). The life review. *Journal of Geriatric Psychiatry*, 35, 7–10.

Cardenas, V.A., Samuelson, K., Lenoci, M., Studholme, C., Neylon, T.C., Marmar,C.R., Schuff, N, Weiner, M.W. (2011). Changes in the brain anatomy during the course of posttraumatic stress disorder. *Psychiatry Research*, 193, 93–100.

Care Act 2014 (2014). *Legislation.gov.uk*. Available online at www.legislation.gov.uk/ukpga/2014/23/contents/enacted (accessed 28 July 2016).

Carstensen, L.L. (1992). Social and emotional patterns in adulthood: Support for socioemotional selectivity. *Psychology and Aging*, 7, 331–8.

Coleman, P.G. (1986). *Ageing and Reminiscence Processes*. Chichester: Wiley.

Coleman, P.G. (1999). Creating a life story: The task of reconciliation. *The Gerontologist*, 39, 133–9.

Conway, M.A., Holmes, A. (2004). Psychological stages and the accessibility of autobiographical memories across the life cycle. *Journal of Personality*, 72, 461–80.

Cook, J.M., O'Donnell, C. (2005). Assessment and psychological treatment of posttraumatic stress disorder in older adults. *Journal of Geriatric Psychiatry and Neurology*, 18, 61–71.

Cumming, E., Henry, W. (1967). *Growing Old: The Process of Disengagement*. New York: Basic Books.

Davison, E.H., Pless, A.P., Gugliucci, M.R., King, L.A., King, D.W., Salgado, D.M., Spiro, A., Bachrach, P. (2006). Late-life emergence of early-life trauma: The phenomenon of late-onset stress symptomatology among aging combat veterans. *Research on Aging*, 28, 84–114.

Department of Health (1999). *Saving Lives: Our Healthier Nation*. London: Stationery Office.

Department of Health (2001). *National Service Framework for Older People*. London: Department of Health.

Department of Health (2007). *Putting People First*. London: Stationery Office.

Elder, G.H. (1986). Military times and turning points in men's lives. *Developmental Psychology*, 22, 233–45.

Elder, G.H., Clipp, E.C. (1989). Combat experience and emotional health: Impairment and resilience in later life: *Journal of Personality*, 57, 311–41.

Elder, G.H., Gimbel, C., Ivie, R. (1991). Turning points in life: The case of military service and war. *Military Psychology*, 3, 215–31.

Elder, G.H., Shanahan, M.J., Clipp, E.C. (1994). When war comes to men's lives: Life-course patterns in family, work, and health. *Psychology and Aging*, 9, 5–16.

Erickson, D.J., Wolfe, J., King, D.W., King, L.A., Sharkansky, E.J. (2001). Posttraumatic stress disorder and depression symptomatology in a sample of Gulf War veterans: A prospective analysis. *Journal of Consulting and Clinical Psychology*, 69, 41–9.

Erikson, E.H. (1994). *Identity and the Life Cycle*, 2nd edn. New York: W.W. Norton & Company, Inc.

Fear, N.T., Jones, M., Murphy, D., Hull, L., Iversen, A.C., Coker, B., Machell, L., Sundin, J., Woodhead, C., Jones, N., Greenberg, N., Landau, S., Dandeker, C., Rona, R.J., Hotopf, M., Wessely, S (2010). What are the consequences of deployment to Iraq and Afghanistan on the mental health of the UK armed forces? A cohort study. *Lancet*, 375, 1758–60.

Floyd, M., Rice, J., Black, S.R. (2002). Recurrence of posttraumatic stress disorder in late life: A cognitive aging perspective. *Journal of Clinical Geropsychology*, 8, 303–11.

Fontana, A., Rosenheck, R. (1994). Traumatic war stressors and psychiatric symptoms among World War II, Korean, and Vietnam War veterans. *Psychology and Aging*, 9, 27–33.

Forces in Mind Trust (2013). *The Transition Mapping Study: Understanding the Transition Process for Service Personnel Returning to Civilian Life*. London: Forces in Mind Trust.

Frankl, V.E. (2004). *Man's Search for Meaning*, 5th edn. London: Elbury Press.

George, L.K. (1996). Missing links: the case for a social psychology of the life course. *Gerontologist*, 36, 248–55.

Gilbertson, M.W., McFarlane, A.C., Weathers, F.W., Keane, T. M., Yehuda, R., Shalev, A. Y., Pitman, R.K. (2010). Is trauma a causal agent of psychopathologic symptoms in posttraumatic stress disorder? Findings from identical twins discordant for combat exposure. *Journal of Clinical Psychiatry*, 71, 1324–30.

Greenberg, N. (2014). What's so special about military veterans? *International Psychiatry*, 11, 79–80.

Greenberg, N., Langston, V., Everitt, B., Iversen, A., Fear, N.T., Jones, N., Wessely, S. (2010). A cluster randomized controlled trial to determine the efficacy of Trauma Risk Management (TRiM) in a military population. *Journal of Traumatic Stress*, 23, 430–6.

Hamilton, J.D., Workman, R.H.J. (1998). Persistence of combat-related posttraumatic stress symptoms for 75 years. *Journal of Traumatic Stress*, 11, 763–8.

Hasher, L., Zacks, R.T. (1988). Working memory, comprehension, and aging: A review and a new view. In G.H. Bower (ed.), *The Psychology of Learning and Motivation*. San Diego: Academic Press, pp. 193–225.

Hatch, S.L., Harvey, S., Dandeker, C., Burdett, H., Greenberg, N., Fear, N.T., Wessely, S. (2013). Life in and after the Armed Forces: Social networks and mental health in the UK military. *Sociology of Health Illness*, 35, 1045–64.

Hunt, E.J.F., Wessely, S., Jones, N., Rona, R.J., Greenberg, N. (2014). The mental health of the UK Armed Forces: where facts meet fiction. *European Journal of Psychotraumatology*, 5, 23617.

Hunt, N. (2007). The long term effects of war experience. *Aging and Mental Health*, 11, 156–8.

Hunt, N., Robbins, I. (2001a). The long-term consequences of war: The experience of World War II. *Aging and Mental Health*, 5, 183–90.

Hunt, N., Robbins, I. (2001b). World War II veterans, social support, and veterans' associations. *Aging and Mental Health*, 5, 175–82.

Isaacowitz, D.M., Smith, R.B., Carstensen, L.L. (2003). Socioemotional selectivity and mental health among trauma survivors in old age. *Ageing International*, 28, 181–99.

Jennings, P.A., Aldwin, C.M., Levenson, M.R., Spiro A. III, Mroczek, D.K. (2006). Combat exposure, perceived benefits of military service, and wisdom in later life. *Research on Aging*, 28, 115–34.

Jones, M., Sundin, L., Goodwin, L., Hull, L., Fear, N., Wessely, S., Rona, R. (2013). What explains posttraumatic stress disorder (PTSD) in UK service personnel? Deployment or something else? *Psychological Medicine*, 43, 1703–12.

Kenyon, G.M., Randall, W.L. (1999). Introduction: Narrative gerontology. *Journal of Aging Studies*, 13, 1–5.

Krause, N. (2005). Traumatic memories and meaning of life: Exploring three age cohorts. *Ageing and Society*, 25, 501–24.

Krause, E.D., Kaltman, S., Goodman, L., Dutton, M.A. (2006). Role of distinct PTSD symptoms in intimate partner reabuse: A prospective study. *Journal of Traumatic Stress*, 19, 507–16.

Lamb, N. (2014). *Care Bill becomes Care Act 2014*. London: Department of Health.

Lansford, J.E., Sherman, A.M., Antonucci, T.C. (1998). Satisfaction with social networks: An examination of socioemotional selectivity theory across cohorts. *Psychology and Aging*, 13, 544–52.

Law Commission (2010). *Adult Social Care: A Consultation Paper*. London: Law Commission.

Lee, K., Vaillant, G., Torrey, W., Elder, G. (1995). A 50-year prospective study of the psychological sequelae of World War II combat. *American Journal of Psychiatry*, 152, 516–22.

Lindman Port, C., Engdahl, B., Frazier, P. (2001). A longitudinal and retrospective study of PTSD among older prisoners of war. *American Journal of Psychiatry*, 158, 1474–9.

McAdams, D. P. (1993). *The Stories We Live By: Personal Myths and the Making of the Self*. New York: Oxford University Press.

McCranie, E.W., Hyer, L.A. (2000). Posttraumatic stress disorder symptoms in Korean conflict and World War II combat veterans seeking outpatient treatment. *Journal of Traumatic Stress*, 13, 427–39.

MacLean, A., Elder, G.H., Jr. (2007). Military service in the life course. *Annual Review of Sociology*, 33, 175–96.

Ministry of Defence. (2015). *Armed Forces Covenant: 2015 to 2020*. Available online at www.gov.uk/government/publications/armed-forces-covenant-2015-to-2020 (accessed 30 September 2015).

Ong, Y.L., Carter, P. (2001). I'll knock elsewhere: The impact of past trauma in later life. *Psychiatric Bulletin*, 25, 435–6.

Ridley, N.J., Draper, B., Withall, A. (2013). Alcohol-related dementia: An update of the evidence. *Alzheimer's Research and Therapy*, 5, 3.

Schreuder, B.J.N., Kleijn, W.C., Rooijmans, H.G.M. (2000). Nocturnal re-experiencing more than forty years after war trauma. *Journal of Traumatic Stress*, 13, 453–63.

Schweitzer, P., Bruce, E. (2008). *Remembering Yesterday, Caring Today. Reminiscence in Dementia Care: A Guide to Good Practice*. Philadelphia: Jessica Kingsley Publishers.

Settersten, R.A., Jr. (2006). When nations call: How military service matters for the life course and ageing. *Research on Aging*, 28, 12–36.

Settersten, R.A., Jr., Patterson, R.S. (2006). Military service, life course, and aging: An introduction. *Research on Aging*, 28, 5–11.

Shaw, M.E., Westwood, M.J. (2002). Transformation in life stories: The Canadian war veterans life review project. In J.D. Webster, B.K. Haight (eds.), *Critical advances in*

Reminiscence Work: From Theory to Application. New York: Springer Publishing Co, pp. 257–74.

Sixsmith, J., Sixsmith, A., Callender, M., Corr, S. (2014). Wartime experiences and their implications for the everyday lives of older people. *Ageing and Society*, 34, 1457–81.

Smith, A.D., Earles, J.L.K. (1996). Memory changes in normal aging. In F. Blanchard-Fields, T.M. Hess (eds.), *Perspectives on Cognitive Change in Adulthood and Aging*. New York: McGraw-Hill, pp. 192–220.

Spiro, A., III., Settersten, R.A., Jr. (2012). Long-term implications of military service for later-life health and well-being. *Research in Human Development*, 9, 183–90.

Thandi, G., Sundin, J., Knight, T., Jones, M., Hull, L., Jones, N., Fear, N.T. (2015). Alcohol misuse in the United Kingdom Armed Forces: A longitudinal study. *Drug Alcohol Dependence*, 156, 78–83.

The Royal British Legion. (2014). The UK Ex-Service Community: A Household Survey. Available online at http://www.britishlegion.org.uk/get-involved/campaign/public-policy-and-research/the-uk-ex-service-community-a-household-survey/ (accessed 29 September 2015).

Webster, J.D., Bohlmeijer, E.T., Westerhof, G.J. (2010). Mapping the future of reminiscence: A conceptual guide for research and practice. *Research on Aging*, 32, 527–64.

Weiner, M.W., Friedl, K.E., Pacifico, A., Chapman, J.C., Jaffee, M.S., Littleg, D.M., Manley, G.T., McKee, A., Petersen, R.C., Pitman, R.K., Yaffe, K., Zetterberg, H., Obana, R., Bain, L.J., Carrillo, M.C. (2013). Military risk factors for Alzheimer's disease. *Alzheimer's and Dementia*, 9, 445–51.

Westwood, M. J., McLean, H., Cave, D., Borgen, W., Slakov, P. (2010). Coming home: A group-based approach for assisting military veterans in transition. *The Journal for Specialists in Group Work*, 35, 44-68.

Windle, K., Francis, J., Coomber, C. (2011). *Preventing Loneliness and Social Isolation: Interventions and Outcomes.* SCIE Research Briefing 39. London: Social Care Institute for Excellence.

7

VETERANS AND RESERVES MENTAL HEALTH PROGRAMME FOR BRITISH FORCES

Meeting Need ... or Managing Expectation?

Jeya Balakrishna

Introduction

In three years of leading the Veterans and Reserves Mental Health Programme (VRMHP) at Chilwell in Nottingham, UK, the author has met many engaging ex-service personnel (veterans) and reserves of the British Forces. A majority appreciate the opportunity to talk about their past military service in what they perceive to be an 'enabling' setting for the conversation. For many, it is a first opportunity that they have found the courage to do so. A significant minority among these individuals carry long-standing misgivings about their military service or struggle to cope with post-deployment issues.

Each has a story to tell, and they want us, the healthcare practitioners, to listen and to understand, even when they know – consciously or subconsciously – that we may not always be able to meet all their needs or solve their mental health problems.

In this chapter, the author provides an account of the service delivered by the VRMHP and the people who have used the service. In using case examples from the programme, the author has created composite case histories from many different stories in order to make anonymous the individuals and also to illustrate common attributes of veterans and reserves who present to the programme. The author shares his reflections from the work within VRMHP, drawing on experience of work in the psycho-trauma field and military service, and considers implications for healthcare practice in the care and treatment of ex-service personnel.

History of the programme

The Gulf Veterans Medical Assessment Programme (GVMAP) was established in July 1993 at The Baird Medical Centre, an Army Medical Centre located in

St Thomas' NHS Hospital in central London. The programme was originally for UK Gulf veterans who had mainly physical health concerns after the 1990/1991 Gulf Conflict. The programme became simply the Medical Assessment Programme (MAP) in 1996 when it provided for other groups of veterans. Consultant physicians were involved in assessments, and where mental health issues were raised, individuals were referred for psychiatric assessment elsewhere.

By 2007, the MAP was extended to provide mental health assessments for former service personnel with experience of deployment. A consultant psychiatrist fielded referrals, typically from NHS general practitioners (GPs).

Meanwhile, in November 2006, a nurse-led mental health team was established in Chilwell, Nottingham, to support the Reserves Mobilisation Centre, alongside the Medical Centre in Chetwynd Barracks. Reserves who attended this site for training exercises or in preparation for mobilisation to operational tours could access help from this team.

In March 2012, a process of relocation began, with the MAP being moved from The Baird in London to Chetwynd Barracks in Chilwell by December 2012, merging with the existing nurse-led team for reserves to become the VRMHP in 2013, the clinical lead being a consultant psychiatrist (the author).

A review of military Departments of Community Mental Health (DCMH) concluded in 2016, with the VRMHP relocating to the DCMH in Colchester Garrison and a plan for assessments of veterans and reserves to be undertaken at a DCMH nearest to where the individual lives.

Accessing the programme

Veterans and reserves can ask to be seen by the national VRMHP if they have concerns about their mental health in relation to operational experiences since 1982. The programme is a national advisory service which receives referrals from NHS GPs, and sometimes from other NHS mental health services and service charities.

The objectives of an assessment with the programme are to:

1 Help the veteran or reserve better understand (often for the first time) any mental health problems arising since deployment; and
2 Provide advice and guidance about appropriate treatment and care pathways, including where known, sign-posting to local service providers in the NHS and service charities.

While the NHS remains the mainstay for providing care and treatment to veterans and reserves, the programme can direct reserves to access DCMH care and treatment, if assessment determines that the reserve has suffered operationally related mental health problems. As such, the programme does not provide treatment for veterans or reserves who do not have operationally related mental health problems.

An individual could wait several weeks, sometimes months, for an appointment for assessment, mainly because of time taken to retrieve military records (both service and healthcare) from the Ministry of Defence (MoD) and healthcare records from the NHS GP. Delay also occurs from the individual not promptly returning forms sent by the programme, in which the individual is asked to give details about service, deployment, health and personal history.

Veterans referred to the programme

The first 75 veterans seen by the author under the auspices of the VRMHP in Nottingham came from some 275 referrals received during a period of 30 months, a mix of self-referrals and GP referrals. The programme encouraged those who sought self-referral to consult with their GP in the first instance to clarify need, but most of these did not do so. The did–not–attend (DNA) rate of offered appointments was under 10 per cent.

It is interesting that, of 275 referrals of ex-service personnel, nearly 58 per cent – mostly self-referrals – either failed to return forms to the programme (including consent forms for disclosure of records) or if they did, then chose not to progress the referral when invited to do so once all records had been retrieved. Palmer[1] (2012) observed that the MAP probably missed seeing veterans who did not want their service record to be scrutinised or to be seen by a military or government service, or chose not to access the service out of pride or because they felt shame about their condition.

In essence (as Dr Palmer observed), the author found that most veterans referring to the VRMHP are seeking help, similar in characteristics to those already seeking help from the NHS or service charities such as Combat Stress, Hidden Wounds (Help for Heroes) or Headstart (Walking with the Wounded). Their help-seeking is more often than not prompted by a partner or spouse, a characteristic common in referrals to the charity Combat Stress.

Sometimes, a referral would be triggered by a significant life event, often a stressful experience associated in some way with personal circumstances around the time when the individual returned from deployment. For example, a soldier leaving service to return to civilian life and family feuds that he had managed to avoid by being away in the Army, became unsettled by a nasty rift instigated by a sibling, which then brought back memories of his family situation when he had returned from deployment. This soldier did not become mentally unwell immediately after deployment or consult military healthcare for his remaining period of service, but did present to the VRMHP several years after leaving, with symptoms suggestive of delayed-onset post-traumatic stress disorder (PTSD) related to deployment experiences. The findings of a study by Andrews *et al.* (2009) are relevant in this regard. In comparing delayed-onset PTSD with immediate-onset PTSD, this study found individuals in the former group gradually accumulating symptoms throughout their military career. Veterans with delayed-onset were more likely (than veterans without PTSD) to report a severe life stressor in the year before PTSD onset. The study concluded that delayed onset PTSD involves more general stress sensitivity and a progressive failure to adapt to continued stress exposure.

Guardedness and being unwilling to talk about past experiences is common among ex-service personnel seen by the VRMHP. Both depressive disorders and alcohol misuse or dependence are common co-morbid conditions of operationally related PTSD. While many younger veterans (in their thirties and forties) have often consulted healthcare (GPs at military medical centres or DCMH) about mental health problems during service, military health records of older veterans (in their fifties and sixties) rarely reveals evidence of similar consultation. The case example of 'Scott' is illustrative.

Nonetheless, it is an important step being taken by the cautious and anxious veteran, to agree referral to, and attendance at, the VRMHP. The author suggests that leaving military service is a significant factor in allowing some opening up of previously bottled-up emotions. Jones *et al.* (2013) acknowledged the need to investigate further the increased risk of PTSD in those who left service – was there a real increase in PTSD or a greater willingness to report symptoms having left service?

Case example: 'Scott'

It was a proud day – his father stood up when Scott received his Green Beret. He was deployed to Afghanistan within nine months of passing out.

He did not know what to make of the place – they walked into one village where folks would offer them fruit and cake, then into another, they'd be pelted with eggs and stones.

There were many casualties and fatalities in their Company during the tour. Scott saw his best mate John being blown up by an improvised explosive device (IED). He said, 'I saw body parts everywhere and tried to retrieve them … I saw the local children kicking about and spitting on what looked like a burnt slab of meat; it was John's leg'.

Scott struggles with emotions; he tried to ignore these while still in service, for fear of being seen as weak. He never told the DCMH therapist the full story. It has been five years since he left the Army.

He said, 'I get angry all the time, sometimes I aim it at the wife, but mostly I direct it at myself'. He admitted being highly self-critical. He does not like tight, enclosed places with lots of people about – 'I snap, I get really angry, and then I run right through the crowd to get outside'.

Fortunately for Scott, he was able to face his demons in therapy with an NHS service and a charity, several years after leaving the Army. When seen by the Programme, he had started work as a despatch driver.

Some 15 per cent of veteran referrals to the VRMHP were not seen, as the individuals had already been assessed elsewhere and had received treatment in the recent past or were in treatment in relation to mental health problems arising from deployment experiences. A typical example, a veteran in his fifties, had been struggling with moderate mood problems and periods of sick leave from work, treated with antidepressants by his GP. As his condition was not improving, he was taking to alcohol, and his wife told the GP that he was becoming increasingly short-tempered with the children. He was referred to be seen by local NHS mental health services. He met nurses and psychiatrists who were able to explore his history of traumatic events in both military deployment and his early life at home. Diagnoses were explained to him, treatment was planned and delivered, including alcohol psycho-education, psychological therapy and antidepressant medication. As with other referrals to VRMHP like this one, the author appreciates the importance of reviewing both military and NHS healthcare histories in a comprehensive letter to formulate the health problems, to concur with the views already expressed by healthcare counterparts and to support the treatment plan being undertaken. This letter to the NHS GP is usually copied to the referred individual as well, as is the procedure for all assessments undertaken.

Reserves referred to the programme

Since being established in 2006 as a mental health team in Nottingham, the programme for reserves has seen an average of 40 individuals yearly. Having hitherto been mostly self-referrals, reserve referrals to the newly formed VRMHP since 2013 have increasingly been from their NHS GPs. The programme assesses reserves who have demobilised since January 2003 following deployment as a reservist to an overseas operation, and who have concerns about their mental health as a result of this deployment.

Of appointments given to reserves, 12 per cent cancelled their appointments and 4 per cent did not attend; 70 per cent of those seen were referred on to a DCMH nearest to the reserve's home address, for treatment of operationally related mental health problems.

Jones *et al.* (2011) describing follow-up of reserves treated for post-deployment mental health problems in the nearest DCMH, comment on how the reserves service within the VRMHP functions well as a 'triage process' allowing reserves to access assessment and suitable interventions following demobilisation, and to return to good levels of health and occupational functioning. The programme deserves a better uptake through higher visibility amongst military units, military healthcare, service charities and the NHS, given that there are several groups of reserves who are unknown to the VRMHP, such as:

- Reserves being looked after by NHS GP and/or a local mental health trust, and not known to military healthcare
- Reserves who seek help directly from service charities (notably Combat Stress)
- Reserves seen by Field MH Team during operational tour, and not referred back to parent Unit or DCMH or VRMHP
- Reserves with mental health problems who have never been deployed on operational tour

The programme has also assessed a small number of reserves who are former regulars – such an individual would have deployed during regular service on a challenging tour, but did not present with mental health problems post-deployment or on leaving service. As a reserve, this individual then presents to the programme having demobilised after deployment as a reserve, to describe psychological issues attributed primarily to the previous deployment, with the latest tour possibly acting

TABLE 7.1 The differences in reserve and regular experiences, post-deployment

Reserve	Regular
• Getting back to civilian life (and non-military routine)	• Return to Unit (and military routine)
• Partners not always supportive; relationship tensions or changes	• Partners more likely to support (or resigned to the life expected!)
• Mental health stigma, but if treatment needed would prefer NHS to being picked up by military healthcare	• Mental health stigma, but realises healthcare is integral to military and complies
• Healthcare history patchy (depends on accuracy/ completeness of NHS record, if made available)	• Full healthcare history (being within military) is known

as a trigger for manifestation of symptoms or as an aggravating factor for low-grade symptoms already present before the reserve deployment. This has practice implications for military healthcare in relation to either unrecognised or unrevealed mental disorder in regular service leavers. The former requires rigorous application of structured mental health assessment at the Release Medical Examination (undertaken just before a service personnel leaves), the latter is a challenge.

That the reserve is someone balancing two careers (sometimes more!) in civilian life and in military service, is central to understanding the particular challenges which the reserve faces post-deployment. The reserve typically relishes every opportunity to get away from the humdrum of his or her day job, to take part in weekend exercises, the annual camp, regimental dinners and, of course, to mobilise for deployment on operations abroad. But the transition experience between the 'battle front' and the 'home front' can differ somewhat for the reserve, in comparison to the regular. This is described in Table 7.1.

What we already know from research such as Browne *et al.* (2007) and Hotopf *et al.* (2006) is that deployed reserves have higher rates of mental health problems (including higher rates of PTSD) than deployed regulars and non-deployed reserves. In the same way that Palmer (2012) reminds us to contextualise a veteran's narrative of deployment experiences in terms of the military trade the veteran was in (such as infantry soldier or aircraft mechanic or medic or driver or clerk or chef on a ship), we need to appreciate the context of civilian life with family, job and home in which the reserve sits, when he or she engages in his or her military role. The transition between the different roles can become an important factor in how the reserve is then affected in mental health by deployment experiences.

Some reserves can be understandably cautious about how much is known of their personal, civilian job and health circumstances, for fear that this may jeopardise their continuing commitment to the reserve role. Consider the case example of 'Dan'.

Case example: 'Dan'

As a Reservist Corporal, he was pleased to be put in charge of a section, a 12-man team of both reserves and regulars in a platoon location. He was just about to go on rest and recupera-

tion (R&R), so he swapped places with the section leader and was placed in the Observation Post (OP) while the sections went out on patrol in the local village.

He watched them doing so from the OP.

Dan saw white flags go up around the village where the patrol was moving to – this was a local signal about imminent attack by insurgents. He radioed the platoon commander. Then he saw an explosion – the fifth man in the patrol had hit an IED and one soldier lost a leg. He watched as another explosion happened a few minutes later; this time a soldier lost his life. Dan said, 'There was nothing I could do. I tried to warn them. Was there anything else I could have done? I could see the signs of what was going to happen ...'

He said this incident played on his mind more than instances when he was himself out on patrol and had got shot at.

Since returning from Afghanistan, Dan described having broken sleep and becoming increasingly isolative and distant from his wife Sue. He said, 'I can't do Bonfire Night or New Year's Eve [on account of noise of fireworks], I lock myself away ... I've been very alert most days, I'm sensitive to floorboard noises, there's a fire station near my house, when the sirens go off, I jump out of bed'.

When assessed and recommended for treatment at the nearest DCMH, Dan initially declined, preferring to take prescribed antidepressants from his NHS GP and maintain some semblance of normality both at civilian workplace and during reserve weekends. This quickly unravelled when he lost his rag one night at a local pub and got into an altercation with strangers, became disoriented about where he was, and imagined he was fighting to protect his Army section from harm.

Dan eventually agreed to see the local NHS veterans' mental health service.

Jones *et al.* (2011) comment on the possible advantage of allowing self-referrals to overcome perceived stigma and encourage help-seeking. Drawing on the clinical experience thus far with reserves in the VRMHP, there are limitations to relying only on the individual's narrative about his health, experiences and being able to cope with a part of his or her life which is not fully known to the VRMHP assessor. Mental health assessment requires a comprehensive healthcare history – the military health record for the reserve is often patchy because it describes the occasional contacts with a military medical centre for exercises, occupational fitness review, or pre- and post-mobilisation. The NHS health record becomes a very important source of information to provide some context about the individual. The author's view is that referral of the reserve by the NHS GP (or by a GP in a military medical centre) remains essential. The programme is informing occupational fitness review as well as informing the individual about how to cope with post-deployment mental health problems.

How does work with reserves mental health inform lessons about veterans' mental health?

Apart from reserves becoming ex-reserves (therefore veterans themselves) and the regular reserves (ex-regulars becoming reserves), serving reserves provide a valuable opportunity to help an understanding about transition between military life and civilian life – they are doing this all the time that they serve! Albeit that the regular undergoes a usually one-time-only transition into civilian life on leaving a full-time military career, the transition of roles and how deployment experiences impact on civilian life, are common to both the veteran and the reserve.

The meaning of psychological trauma

Individuals experience psychological trauma in different ways, depending on the circumstances in which trauma arises. The author's experience of working with refugees of war-torn nations is that these individuals do not talk in Western psycho-pathology terms: they talk more about political cause, threat to personal integrity and loss of racial or national identity. Telling a refugee that he or she suffers from PTSD means little to this individual.

The author has in the past also been involved in community mental health services for victims of domestic violence. Victims of childhood abuse and domestic violence often experience repetitive trauma, the cumulative effects of which can limit meaningful engagement in trauma-focused therapies.

So how does military psycho-trauma compare? In terms of 'event-specific' psychological trauma, military psycho-trauma is more about guilt and shame (and can be harder to treat) than the fear and anxiety often seen in victims of a road traffic accident or sports injury.

The psycho-trauma picture which veterans and reserves present is usually not simple – it is complicated by early life events, alcohol misuse, transition difficulties and housing, job and relationship issues. Medical history matters, too – endocrine abnormalities in the thyroid, for example, can aggravate anxiety, irritability and arousal, neurological deficits can impair cognitive function and alter perception of people and things. Prolonged drug and alcohol misuse can cause brain damage and behaviour change.

Case example: 'Ron'

Ron is in his fifties, an Army veteran of Northern Ireland tours.

His GP said he is alcoholic, chronically depressed and persistently unemployed. Ron is divorced with grown up children. Both his parents died not long after he left eight years of military service in the 1980s.

He did foot patrols in Northern Ireland – 'The pub and club checks were my biggest nightmare … we would arrive in a crowded pub and the lights would go out, the girls would to try to disarm us in the dark. If any of us got isolated, he'd be taken through an exit door and never heard of again'.

The past couple of decades have been a hazy passage in his life, as if nothing of any purpose happened.

The example of 'Ron' typifies the longstanding and damaged presentation of many veterans of his generation assessed by the VRMHP. There are often recurrent anxiety and depressive mood states over many years after leaving service, complicated by alcohol misuse and dependence. On leaving military service, the veteran faces a challenged mindset to return to home life, often not helped by marital breakdown and loss of being in a family. There is a failure to re-engage adequately in interpersonal or occupational life more generally.

Post-deployment physical injury is an important factor in mental health problems that is not always taken account of by healthcare professionals, especially in non-military settings. The National Audit Office (2010) describing statistics from the Defence Analytical Services and Advice (DASA) reveals rising numbers of physical injuries treated at field hospitals in operations each year from 2006 to 2009. Until 2006, most personnel treated at the Defence Medical Rehabilitation Centre (DMRC) at Headley Court, Surrey, were recovering after road traffic injuries, parachuting accidents or musculoskeletal injuries. Patterns of operational injuries changed thereafter, mainly because of the increase in injuries caused by IEDs.

The VRMHP assessed a small number of ex-service personnel and reserves with a variety of musculoskeletal injuries sustained either during deployment or during military training. In cases where long periods of rehabilitation with DMRC and being medically downgraded eventually resulted in medical discharge, any mental health issues relating to deployment tended to be overshadowed by physical rehabilitation and chronic pain management. Presenting to VRMHP then represented a first opportunity for the individual to address mental health problems – both relating to traumatic experiences and as a consequence of injury causing constraints to daily functioning and knocking self-confidence. Not surprisingly, such individuals would express bitterness in relation to their sense of loss about normal physical functioning. The author found that such individuals were not in the proper frame of mind to explore possible traumatic events during deployment; this was set aside in favour of giving time and space to the individual to give full voice to their frustration and bitterness. Advice could then be given in writing to the NHS GP and if involved, the NHS specialists (for example, in the Pain Clinic) about areas to explore psychologically in the future, taking account of a comprehensive review of the military service and healthcare record (provided in letter by the author to the specialist) of which the NHS professionals were unlikely to be fully aware.

Palmer (2012) assessing ex-service personnel in the MAP described a spread of diagnoses similar to civilians with history of traumatic experiences. At least half of his 150 cases had anxiety-related problems, obsessional features were prominent in 30 per cent, and a fifth revealed alcohol misuse. Most of the 15 per cent diagnosed with PTSD had co-morbid depression and/or alcohol misuse.

Referrals to the MAP and VRMHP are a self-selecting population, not representative of the whole veteran population in the UK. In the VRMHP, the author found that mood disorder and prolonged adjustment problems were commonest amongst veterans, with PTSD diagnosed in between 30 and 40 per cent of the first 75 veterans seen. While nightmares, flashbacks, irritability and depressive symptoms are common, it is important for healthcare practitioners to recognise that there are

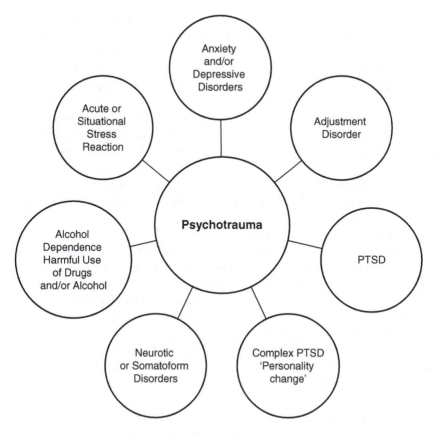

FIGURE 7.1 Diagram showing the diverse diagnostic manifestations of psychological trauma.

diverse clinical manifestations of psychological trauma, as shown in Figure 7.1. Two or more diagnoses could apply in an individual case, typical of the co-morbid presentation by veterans (and indeed reserves).

Veterans and civilian healthcare services

The author has the highest regard for the excellent support and expertise of the NHS Veterans' Mental Health Network, services which are distributed by region across England, Scotland and Wales, each hosted by an NHS mental health trust. Many of these regional services are delivered by mental health nurses and psychology graduates, typically utilising the service model of Improving Access to Psychological Therapies (IAPT). A number of these are specialist traumatic stress services with consultant psychologists as clinical leads. Some have clinicians who have served as regulars or reserves.

The VRMHP and the NHS Veterans' Network enjoy good professional relations, including sharing of expertise and exchange of clinical information, to ensure that veterans receive appropriate care and treatment from services local to where they live. The NHS regional services refer some veterans to the programme to seek advice about psychiatric diagnosis and to clarify service and military health record. In turn, the author relies on these regional services to accept responsibility for psychological treatment and other local mental health service support for veterans assessed by the programme.

Likewise, there are strong relations between the VRMHP and service charities such as Combat Stress, Help for Heroes and Walking with the Wounded, which also refer veterans to the programme, typically to clarify diagnosis and guide treatment plans.

MacDonald (2010) quotes Dr Palmer in relation to his work in the MAP in London. Dr Palmer describes the transition difficulties into civilian life, that charities, the NHS and other agencies 'cannot re-create the military milieu and the social and psychological support inherent in service'.

Dr Palmer notes that GPs referring veterans to the MAP do not appreciate the many different trades that service personnel can engage in, not many of which involve combat duties. In terms of mental health, he said, 'It may seem counterintuitive, but most personnel can serve on operations without psychiatric sequelae. They are of course changed by their experiences, but we should be aware of the urban myth that such change will invariably be negative'.

The author identifies with Dr Palmer's comments about GP perceptions of the ex-military patient. The author frequently receives referral letters to the VRMHP from the NHS GP with the following content:

> *Please see Mr X who tells me he served in the Army for many years and went on overseas operations. He is increasingly unhappy at work and at home. His wife tells him he is restless in bed and has nightmares. I am prescribing antidepressant medication. I think he has PTSD.*

Benedek *et al.* (2004) find that deployment itself is not a significant cause of psychiatric disorder. The US and UK have deployed service personnel around the world for decades, without substantially increased risk of PTSD. However, it is the nature of the deployment experience – traumatic events, loss of attachments such as good friends and the psychological and physical demands that increase the risk of mental disorder.

Palmer (2004) states that observers – mainly civilian – talk of military culture in terms of 'institutionalisation' being imposed on apparently passive service personnel, but they ignore the social and psychological processes and benefits derived from enlistment and military 'acculturation'.

This is interesting – in conversations with counterpart practitioners in the NHS, the author encounters views about perceived rigidity and order of service personnel, entirely dependent on the military infrastructure to meet occupational, social, welfare and health needs. MacManus and Wessely (2013) suggest that resilience and strength emphasised by military culture is at odds with 'traditional mental health discourse' about victims, sufferers and mental health problems. They suggest that this can explain the difficulty veterans have in the transition into civilian healthcare.

The author takes a different view: while there is some truth in how this can affect transition into civilian life, there is also adaptability and resilience in the face of change, which service personnel learn in structured training exercises and in preparation for deployment to countries with diverse cultures. This happens, necessarily, with time and experience; those with longer service fair better. It lends an understanding perhaps, to the body of research such as Buckman *et al.* (2013) and Woodhead *et al.* (2011) which finds that early service leavers are at greater risk of mental health problems.

Reflections and implications for practice

Many researchers in this field have queried the extent to which mental disorder in veterans can be attributed to deployment, or indeed to military service. This author believes that 'cause and consequence' is not an exact science. Should early life history influence our view about attributing 'cause' to later life events such as deployment?

As referenced earlier, Jones *et al.* (2013) wonder whether the increased rates of PTSD after leaving service are a real increase or the result of veterans becoming more willing patients. Whatever the answer, the findings have implications for military health practitioners in how they should explore more thoroughly traumatic events unrelated to deployment, occurring in service or pre-dating service.

Goodwin *et al.* (2012) reach a different view about the effect of leaving service on PTSD rates. They describe the prevalence of delayed-onset PTSD (defined as onset at least six months after a traumatic event) in a two-phase study. The cohorts were interviewed in periods between two and six years after deployment to operations in Iraq and Afghanistan. They found that sub-threshold PTSD, other mental disorders such as anxiety and depression, poor self-reported health and onset of alcohol misuse (between the phases) were associated with delayed-onset PTSD. They did not find a significant association with leaving military service.

Whichever part of the veteran's life – before service, during service or after service – features in our assessment of his or her mental health problems, healthcare practitioners should help the veteran to understand the illness experience in context (of both military and civilian life). The veteran also needs to understand the impact on family life and relationships.

Transition between 'battle front' and 'home front' is an important element of how service personnel are affected by deployment experiences. This is the essence of 'Battlemind', a training programme developed by the United States Armed Forces, which is group-based, interactive and psycho-educational, as described by Adler *et al.* (2009a, b). The US model (which has been adapted for use by British Forces as a more didactic model) uses psychological techniques to help personnel re-frame any problems they may have encountered during deployment, and to help them with adapting to life back home after deployment (Table 7.2). The author uses 'Battlemind' as a conversation tool during the assessment interview with a veteran or reserve to help the individual appreciate how his or her deployment experiences are manifest in a range of feelings and behaviours, which the individual often easily identifies with.

TABLE 7.2 How the 'Battlemind' rotates from 'battle front' to 'home front'

Deployment Battlemind		Home front problems
Buddy Buddy System	→	Withdrawal
Accountability	→	Controlling at home
Targeted aggression	→	General aggression
Tactical awareness	→	Being on edge
Limited alcohol	→	Lagered up
Emotional control	→	Detachment and numbness
Mission operational security	→	Secretiveness
Individual responsibility	→	Guilt
Non-defensive (combat) driving	→	Unnecessary risk-taking
Discipline and ordering	→	Conflict with friends and family

'Battlemind'– the anglicised version described in Mulligan *et al.* (2012) – as a conversation tool during the assessment interview with a veterans or reserve, to help the individual appreciate how his or her deployment experiences are manifest in a range of feelings and behaviours, in which the individual often easily identifies.

In relation to this rotation between deployment and home-base, Ursano *et al.* (2007) highlights the importance of properly managing duration of deployment for serving regulars and reserves, so that they can sustain skills in mental and physical strength when back home.

In terms of civilian healthcare services, the author recognises the importance of always writing to the veteran's NHS GP. General practitioners are busy professionals under huge demands, and may or may not be able to implement suggested actions or undertake effective care and treatment. Nonetheless, military mental health practitioners, NHS mental health services, independent therapists and charities providing treatment do need to keep good and regular contact with the veteran's NHS GP. The letters, reports and clinic notes we provide constitute an important health record for the individual. When any service has the veteran's consent to peruse this record, there is better knowledge of what help the veteran is receiving and where from.

The author supports Dr Palmer's view – as quoted by MacDonald (2010) – that GPs can improve their understanding of veterans by including 'exploration of trade in service, rank attained, length of service, as well as experiences' in history taking. The NHS GP has a valuable role to play in gathering helpful information about health needs of veterans.

It is unhelpful and therapeutically counter-productive to duplicate assessments by different services or for therapy to be delivered by different services in succession (the author finds that this sometimes happens simultaneously!). Some veterans can become frustrated by a lack of progress in one episode of treatment and seek an alternative service, or they fail to engage properly; they may well shop around!

Some veterans are open about seeking financial compensation for their operationally related mental health problems, but it is important to establish with such individuals that they are willing to address psychological issues and to recover.

Ex-service personnel may complain about NHS practitioners; they might say that they prefer to talk to practitioners with military experience. But many also can be wary of returning to consult with military healthcare; some have even formed strong, adverse views about service charities, depending on their experiences of any of these. Bitterness about service (people or organisation) is not uncommon, and frustration with transition difficulties clouds perspective.

And yet, most military patients – regular, reserve or ex-services – have a story to tell; they want to share it with us, or learn how to. It often takes time for the whole story to come out. They want us to listen. As Helman[2] (2003) states:

> The art of medicine is a literary art. One that requires of the practitioner the ability to listen in a particular way, to empathise, but also to imagine. To try to feel what it must be like to be that other person lying in the sick bed, or sitting across the desk from you. To try to understand the storyteller, as well as the story.

Many veterans do want to recover from their mental health problems, and to make a fresh start in life after military service. 'Ron', for example, wrote to the author following the VRMHP assessment at a DCMH near his home:

> *I took notice of your straight and direct no-nonsense approach (gave me something to think about while driving home). So, on my return home, I went to the Jobcentre and signed on for a course ... I also took on board what you said regarding my drinking. So from this day on I will only drink at weekends and not before 1700 hours. I do want to re-start my life. I feel I do have a lot to offer to any employer in the near future.*

Conclusion

MacManus and Wessely (2013) are uncertain whether the veteran population warrants an independent mental health service or just training NHS mental health practitioners to be more aware of veterans' needs. The author takes the view that we promote the valuable service provided by the NHS veterans' mental health services in every region; these can easily become centres of excellence in veterans' mental health practice in the public sector. Likewise, with the various charities that provide evidence-based mental health treatment by qualified and experienced practitioners, those charities which match the rigorous governance standards of the NHS and Defence Primary Healthcare should be supported and integrated into the wider network.

An idea for the future of mental health services for British veterans perhaps lies in the public health model proposed by Kudler (2007), which incorporates progressive outreach and engagement of all new veterans rather than a traditional medical model which focuses only on those with a biological disorder. Work with new veterans and their families requires facilitation of their own adaptive processes – psychological, social and indeed, spiritual.

The author supports the idea of NHS veterans' services and service charities providing an 'in-reach' service on a regional basis for service personnel in transition into civilian life and work. The military DCMH provides care, support and treatment to service leavers for up to six months after their last date of service, so this is a valuable period during which to link the military and civilian healthcare services and to ensure seamless transfer of care and information.

The VRMHP provides an opportunity for the veteran or reserve to make better sense of their operationally related experiences. It is important for healthcare providers working in this field to recognise that helping these individuals involves understanding their expectations about life, work and family, in addition to meeting any identified health need. In conjunction with the revised VRMHP providing assessments of veterans and reserves at a DCMH local to the individual, the future is certainly positive for an improved network of regional military and civilian healthcare services, alongside links with local service charities and other support agencies.

Notes

1   Dr Ian Palmer is a former MoD consultant psychiatrist who was head of the MAP in London.
2   The late Professor Helman, a GP and an academic in medical anthropology.

References

Adler, A.B., Bliese, P.D., McGurk, D., Hoge, C.W., Castro, C.A. (2009a). Battlemind debriefing and Battlemind training as early interventions with soldiers returning from Iraq: Randomization by platoon. *Journal of Consulting and Clinical Psychology*, 77, 928–40.

Adler, A.B., Castro, C.A., McGurk, D. (2009b). Time-driven Battlemind psychological debriefing: A group-level early intervention in combat. *Military Medicine*, 174, 21–8.

Andrews, B., Brewin, C.R., Stewart, L., Philpott, R. Hejdenberg, J. (2009). Comparison of immediate-onset and delayed-onset posttraumatic stress disorder in military veterans. *Journal of Abnormal Psychology*, 118, 767–77.

Benedek, D.M., Ursano, R.J., Holloway, H.C. (2004). Military and disaster psychiatry. In Saddock, H., Kaplan, B.J. (eds.), *Comprehensive Textbook of Psychiatry*, 8th edn. New York: Lippincott Williams and Williams, pp. 2426–35.

Browne, T., Hull, L., Horn, O., Jones, M., Murphy, D., Fear, N.T., Greenberg, N., French, C., Rona, R.J., Wessely, S., Hotopf, M. (2007). Explanations for the increase in mental health problems in UK reserve forces who have served in Iraq. *British Journal of Psychiatry*, 190, 484–9.

Buckman, J.E, Forbes, H.J., Clayton, T., Jones, M, Jones, N, Greenberg, N, Sundin, J., Hull, L., Wessely, S., Fear, N.T. (2013). Early service leavers: A study of the factors associated with premature separation from the UK Armed Forces and the mental health of those that leave early. *The European Journal of Public Health*, 23, 410–15.

Goodwin, L., Jones, M., Rona, R.J., Sundin, J., Wessely, S., Fear, N.T. (2012). Prevalence of delayed-onset posttraumatic stress disorder in military personnel: is there evidence for this disorder? Results of a prospective UK cohort study. *Journal of Nervous Mental Disorder*, 200, 429–37.

Helman, C. (2003). Cecil Helman (in Dissecting Room). *The Lancet*, 361, 2252.

Hotopf, M., Hull, L, Fear, N., Browne, T., Horn, O., Iversen, A., Jones, M., Murphy, D., Bland, D., Earnshaw, M., Greenberg, N., Hughes, J.H., Tate, A.R., Dandeker, C., Rona, R., Wessely, S. (2006). The health of UK military personnel who deployed to the 2003 Iraq War: A cohort study. *The Lancet*, 367, 1731–41.

Jones, M., Sundin, J., Goodwin, L., Hull, L., Fear, N.T., Wessely, S., Rona, R.J. (2013). What explains post-traumatic stress disorder (PTSD) in UK service personnel: Deployment or something else? *Psychological Medicine*, 43, 1703–12.

Jones, N., Wink, P., Brown, A. B., Berrecloth, D., Abson, E., Doyle, J., Fear, N.T., Wessely, S., Greenberg, N. (2011). A clinical follow-up study of reserve forces personnel treated for mental health problems following demobilisation. *Journal of Mental Health*, 20, 136–45.

Kudler, H. (2007). The need for psychodynamic principles in outreach to new combat veterans and their families. *Journal of American Academy of Psychoanalysis and Dynamic Psychiatry*, 35, 39–50.

MacDonald, H. (2010). The long road to recovery. *British Medical Journal*, 7744, 450–3.

MacManus, D., Wessely, S. (2013). Veteran mental health services in the UK: Are we headed in the right direction? *Journal of Mental Health*, 22, 301–5.

National Audit Office (2010). *Treating Injury and Illness Arising on Military Operations*. London: Ministry of Defence. Available online at www.nao.org.uk/treatinginjury2010 (accessed 20 January 2017).

Mulligan K., Fear N.T., Jones N., Alvarez H., Hull L., Naumann U., Wessely S., Greenberg N. (2012). Post-deployment Battlemind training for the UK armed forces: a cluster-randomized controlled trial. *Journal of Consulting and Clinical Psychology*, 80, 331–41.

Palmer, I. (2004). Soldiers, learning and fear. *British Army Review*, 135, 64–7.

Palmer, I. (2012). UK extended Medical Assessment Programme for ex-military service personnel: the first 150 individuals seen. *The Psychiatrist (formerly the Psychiatric Bulletin)*, 36, 263–70.

Ursano, R.J., Benedek, D.M., Engel C.C. (2007). Mental illness in deployed soldiers. Editorial. *British Medical Journal*, 7620, 571–2.

Woodhead, C., Rona, R.J., Iversen, A., MacManus, D., Hotopf, M., Dean, K., McManus, S., Meltzer, H., Brugha, T., Jenkins, R., Wessely, S., Fear, N.T. (2011). Mental health and health service use among post-national service veterans: Results from the 2007 Adult Psychiatric Morbidity Survey of England. *Psychological Medicine*, 41, 363–72.

PART II

Models of Service Provision

8

THE NORTH WEST PERSPECTIVE

Alan Barrett, Claire Maguire and Helen Lambert

Introduction

Hosted by Pennine Care NHS Foundation Trust (PCFT), based in Greater Manchester, the Military Veterans Service (MVS) has been providing dedicated, targeted and tailored evidence-based therapies to ex-service personnel who present with complex and chronic mental health issues since 2011. This chapter will briefly outline the journey from its inception to becoming one of the most highly regarded, award-winning, dedicated National Health Service (NHS) psychological treatment services for military veterans and their families in the UK. It will also describe some of the contextual backdrop of the North West, some features of the MVS model and information about its service users.

The set-up

In January 2010, a specially established Clinical Steering group reviewed the needs of ex-service personnel across the north west of England with support from the North West Strategic Health Authority (SHA). Comprised of a broad range of dedicated clinicians who already provided some services to the military veteran community, these individuals came together because they were passionate about developing better services for veterans within the NHS. Very quickly, the steering group also established a veteran service user group with the assistance of both national veteran charities and some of the smaller local third sector groups. It was clear from the outset that there was a lack of evidence regarding the clinical needs of UK veterans and a poor understanding of the numbers of veterans requiring specialist services. So, early on it was decided that any regional NHS service model would need to build up a body of evidence about the needs of military veterans.

Recommendations from the evaluation of the first six community mental health pilot projects for veterans (Dent-Brown *et al.*, 2010) were considered and broadly embraced, including:

• Ensuring that the service offered both assessment and treatment rather than referrals on
• That clients had access to staff members who were veterans and those with experience of working with the client group
• Being badged for military veterans
• Using a range of venues
• Travelling to remote clients
• Accessing military service and medical records

The Clinical Steering group also reviewed the King's Centre for Military Health Research report entitled '*Health and Social Outcomes and Health Service Experiences of UK Military Veterans: A Summary of the Evidence*' (Fear *et al.*, 2009), which stated that 'the most common mental health problems for ex-Service personnel are alcohol problems, depression and anxiety disorders'. It added that military personnel with mental health problems were at 'increased risk for adverse outcomes in post-service life', such as social exclusion and ongoing ill health. The steering group was then tasked with additionally looking at the particular needs of veterans in the north west to come up with a model of care that would break down some of the barriers to accessing help more promptly.

The Improving Access to Psychological Therapies (IAPT) model was seen to be a good starting point. It could be enhanced to become a vehicle to providing veterans and their families with timely access to evidence-based treatments for conditions such as anxiety, depression and post-traumatic stress. It was clear that several adaptations would be needed to suit the needs of the veterans' cohort. A consultation event was set up with over 100 veterans and their families to identify what they viewed to be the key issues regarding engagement with treatment services. Several important themes emerged:

• The veterans wanted to access services that would not immediately reject them if they were drinking too much or had had problems with the criminal justice system.
• It was not critical to the veterans that the therapists had served in the Forces but it was important that they understood the military culture.
• The veterans wanted the services to be delivered in a range of settings.
• The veterans wanted to be able to self-refer.
• The veterans did feel it was important that the therapy offered had an evidence base and therefore did not mind completing validated self-report measures provided this would be handled sensitively.
• The families were keen to be able to access help and support even if their family member was not able to engage in therapy.

- They preferred to be referred to as 'clients' rather than 'service users' which had connotations of military service or other descriptors such as 'customers'.

Following the consultation process, and with support from the North West Strategic Health Authority, the service was initially established as an extension of the National Improving Access to Psychological Therapies programme (IAPT): completely IAPT compliant, but with added extras to make it a 'plus' model, including a family and couples therapist, an offender and substance misuse case manager and freedoms to spend more time engaging with veterans and a greater number of therapy sessions offered. Initially established to deliver evidence-based psychological therapies to military veterans and their families who were experiencing moderate to severe common mental health disorders, the 'IAPT Plus' model emerged to form the basis of the first incarnation of the MVS.

The MVS formed a large part of the region's response to the government's 'Fighting Fit' report (Murrison, 2010). It fulfilled the need to uplift the number of mental health professionals conducting veterans outreach work, but instead of locating this in one or two people, the pilot provided a region-wide service and was able to forge strong links across all of the region's mental health services. It also ensured that the two mental health pledges within the Armed Forces Covenant (AFC) were delivered on behalf of the region by providing a culturally sensitive service:

> For those with concerns about their mental health, where symptoms may not present for some time after leaving Service, they should be able to access services with health professionals who have an understanding of Armed Forces culture.
>
> (*MOD, 2011*)

In addition to contributing to the 26 Primary Mental Healthcare services in the region offering 'priority treatment':

> Veterans receive their healthcare from the NHS, and should receive priority treatment where it relates to a condition which results from their service in the Armed Forces, subject to clinical need.
>
> (*MOD, 2011*)

Staffing

The workforce was recruited with veterans on the interview panels for the key staff positions. The makeup of the workforce was different from a traditional IAPT in that it included a dynamic psychotherapist (this was before the National IAPT programme included dynamic interpersonal therapy). This was on account that the Clinical Steering Group predicted that the pilot would have referrals from many individuals with pre-service and childhood difficulties, for whom this type of therapy would be beneficial. There was also the inclusion of a systemic family therapist so that the service could offer family and couples interventions (Fossey, 2012). The service also included a substance misuse and offender case workers. This was because above all, it was agreed that the service would not reject those who often found there were numerous barriers to them accessing care in traditional mainstream and charitable mental health services.

Another decision made early on was that the service would be better served through the appointment of a clinical psychologist as clinical lead. On account of their comprehensive training and experience in assessment and treatment of the whole life cycle of mental and behavioural presentations, including developmental, learning disabled and neuropsychological conditions, the clinical lead appointed had a strong track record of supporting disadvantaged groups and of working with complexity and clinical risk. With solid clinical integrity and a background within the Mental Health Act Commission (MHAC) and the Care Quality Commission (CQC), the lead had good exposure to what good clinical services looked like and, perhaps more importantly, what poor clinical services looked like, at the same time always keeping the service user at the forefront.

The appointed service coordinator had expertise in the commissioning of quality services, and a valuable political background. With a wealth of experience in bringing a whole system approach to the health and welfare needs of individuals, the service coordinator ensured internal standards and supports were in place, whilst also driving the intensive externally facing engagement agenda for the service.

Additionally, the service benefited from an experienced clinician and clinical adviser, who acted as a strategic lead for the project. Her willingness to go over and above in order to best serve the veteran community was recognised in her term of office as interim Chair of the North West's Armed Forces Network. The importance of securing the right individuals in key roles cannot be underestimated, as the MVS, comprising of a small number of clinicians with excellent administrative support, were expected to cover a large geographical area.

Non-diagnostic

Controversial in some circles, the service was set up to be broadly non-diagnostic. Although several staff were fully qualified in providing diagnosis and, on occasion (usually in relation to the courts) would have to diagnose, the use of diagnosis was the exception rather than the rule. Considering the relationship between the mental health needs of military veterans and the Armed Forces Compensation Scheme and war pension entitlements, it was considered probable that a specialist service would attract some individuals who were only seeking a diagnosis rather than treatment. This had been a feature reported in the original pilots (Dent-Brown et al., 2010). However, being non-diagnostic was important for several reasons. Principally, it allowed the service to accept and be of meaningful help to the most excluded veterans, while promoting the tailoring of intervention to individual needs. It also reduced any perverse incentives that may exist in a veteran looking to emphasise how unwell they are for the purpose of exceeding diagnostic thresholds to achieve a greater monetary return from the MOD or insurance companies.

With veterans, UK claims assessors consulting with medical advisers to determine outcome decisions, with neither having expertise in psychological injury, are likely to use what Gill (2008) refers to as 'the safety blanket' of requiring the client to have been provided with a particular diagnosis. To require veterans to have a diagnosis before awarding payment may be legal, but is also frequently unjust. Those military veterans who do not 'tick all the boxes' are frequently more distressed and functionally impaired than those that do. A prime example are the large numbers of morally injured veterans we have seen, whose psychological disturbance and clinical risk amount to more serious mental injuries but they will not be afforded the same financial remuneration. Even some of those clinicians involved in originally placing post-traumatic stress disorder (PTSD) into the Diagnostic and Statistical Manual (DSM) warn of its inherent deficits, reminding us, for example, that 'traumatic events are neither necessary nor sufficient to produce PTSD' (Rosen et al., 2008). We have often heard veterans discussing the issue, and on more than one occasion we have heard 'veteran A' informing 'veteran B', 'if you want a diagnosis of PTSD go to [x charity] but if you want treatment you need to go to the NHS'. As we do not provide a formal diagnosis to the client, they have less need to embellish or convey checklist symptoms, and are more likely to be able to have us formulate useful treatment plans based on their actual psychological difficulties. Access to military service and medical records, as we have, are of more use in determining the credibility of the client. A client who self-reports that he was an upstanding high-functioning soldier before a particular incident can have his account cross-checked with factual records. This may explain the smaller number of fabricators and embellishers seen in comparison to other services.

The British Psychological Society's '*Position Paper on Diagnosis*' has subsequently been issued, and we are in agreement that 'using everyday understandable language to describe a client's difficulties is a more honest and useful way to conduct a treatment service' (British Psychological Society, 2013). The use of a minimum data set of symptom outcome measures, with some being completed sessionally, provides consistent, demonstrable improvement, and is not dependent on idiosyncrasies of individual clinician opinion. Such psychometric self-assessment symptom measures are hugely more useful to clinicians than diagnostic classifications of clients. The World Health Organisation (WHO), of which the UK is a member, defines mental health as 'a state of complete physical, mental and social wellbeing and not merely the absence of disease or infirmity'. Making the service demographically inclusive (the military veteran living within the catchment of the service) allows it to reach more veterans in need compared with diagnostically exclusive services.

Regional background factors

The north west of England comprises of the five counties of Cheshire, Cumbria, Greater Manchester, Lancashire and Merseyside. It is the third largest English region with 7.1 million people, accounting for 11 per cent of the total UK population. The Office of National Statistics (ONS, 2013) states that the region has the second highest population density in the UK, and the second highest proportion of its population living in urban areas (89.4 per cent). The North West has the lowest life expectancy in England (77.4 years for men and 81.5 years for women), the second highest unemployment rate (8.2 per cent) and 17.8 per cent of children in the region live in workless households. For the last ten years, the North West has alternated with the North East for having the highest suicide rate per head of population.

The UK is ranked 24th out of the 29 developed countries for educational well-being (Adamson, 2013). Considering adults where English is their first language, the North West is in the bottom 3 areas of England for those achieving level 1 literacy. (Department of Business, Innovation and Skills, 2012). Brigadier G Morris, The Army's Director of Educational Capability, described that 'an adult at this level may be able to read an article in a newspaper, but slowly and with limited understanding' (House of Commons, Business, Innovation and Skills Committee, 2014). The report goes on to describe how 'in 2013, around 38% of trainees joining the Army were assessed with literacy skills below Level 1' (House of Commons, Business, Innovation and Skills Committee, 2014), in comparison with around 15 per cent of adults in England.

Despite the North West only accounting for 11 per cent of the population, it is from this socioeconomic and educational backdrop that more than 25 per cent of the Army infantry is recruited. This is a cohort that is associated with high levels of mental health difficulties (MacManus *et al.*, 2014). Many understandably return to the region when leaving the armed services as military veterans. Additionally, the North West provides a significant proportion of Army reservists, which is another cohort with frequently higher rates of mental health among deployed reserves.

Evolution of the Military Veterans' Service

Pennine Care's MVS started life as a two-year pilot, and opened to clients on 1 September 2011. The first phase of the pilot service ran until March 2013, and the feedback from the independent external evaluation, funded by the SHA, was presented to the 33 Clinical Commissioning Groups (CCGs) in the North West. This was led by Bury CCG, as the host CCG who had taken over from the SHA following the reorganisation of the health service in 2012. Based on the evaluation, 32 of the 33 CCGs, appreciative that the service had achieved as good outcomes but with a more complex and difficult to engage client group, agreed to an extension of the pilot for a further year, thus becoming the largest collaborative commissioning arrangement in the UK. Cumbria CCG departed from the arrangement at this stage, subsequently replacing the multidisciplinary and multimodality offer with a capable primary mental healthcare clinician in the role of veterans' champion. By this time, the service had lost the IAPT label, as although it was still IAPT compliant in terms of robust outcome data collection and tough waiting targets, the service had been responsive to client need and had adapted accordingly. The single point of entry function was enhanced with the appointment of dedicated duty staff to manage referrals, coordinate assessments, conduct all the telephone triage calls, and respond to crisis or information calls from clients and professionals alike. Further enhancements had been made to the clinical offer too, including the addition to the workforce of a dedicated art psychotherapist to assist in the treatment of those not yet ready to communicate with spoken word. Case working capacity for the more chaotic, complex and clinically risky clients was also increased.

Another 1-year extension followed, with only 1 of the 32 CCGs (Liverpool) no longer wanting to commission a dedicated service for military veterans. The MVS continued to offer free support to the NHS in Liverpool, including training to its mental health inpatient staff to help create 'veteran friendly wards'. Finally, the argument was won that the North West deserved a dedicated psychological therapies service for military veterans and the service was put out to a formal tendering process for a three-year contract. However, this was on the basis that the large North West region, which Pennine Care had been servicing for four years, was reduced to three, easier to commission, 'geographical lots'. Following a competitive tendering process, where tens of organisations expressed their interest, Pennine Care was successfully awarded the contract for Greater Manchester, the largest area in terms of activity, in 2015. It was also the lead bidder in the successful award of the Lancashire contract, where it works now in partnership with Lancashire Care NHS Foundation Trust. For various reasons, Pennine Care did not bid for the smallest remaining 'lot' that covered Cheshire and Merseyside. This was awarded to Greater Manchester West NHS Foundation Trust, with support from the veteran welfare charity, Combat Stress.

Referral data

The top three primary presenting problems were depression, mixed anxiety depression and trauma. Some broad referral information based on the first 2,000 clients is presented as follows:

- 74% of referrals were from non-mainstream NHS services (Criminal justice system, addiction services, veteran charities, MOD)
- 33% were self-referrals
- 93% male
- 81.5% had served fewer than 10 years
- 21% had served fewer than 4 years – early service leavers
- 46% accessed the service within 10 years of leaving the military
- 29% accessed the MVS within 5 years of leaving from the military
- 84% of clients had been operationally deployed

Branch of Armed Forces:

- 85% Army
- 5% Royal Navy
- 6% RAF

- 2% Reservists
- 2% Royal Marines

Age:

- 9% Aged under 26 years
- 27% Aged 26-35 years
- 29% Aged 36-45 years
- 23% Aged 46-55 years
- 12% Aged over 56years

Individualised, targeted and tailored

Pennine Care's MVS does not provide the same treatment to everyone; rather, it provides the same consideration of everyone. As one might expect, this leads to varying clinical care packages. We do not provide a blanket service to clients; they do not have to attend the same manualised treatment programme, group or residential programme, as these things are more suited to a research trial than real life clinical practice of providing individualised care. Henceforth, the service is fully compliant with national guidance on improving the experiences of care for people using NHS services (NICE 2012). It was in part due to the high levels of collaborative individualised interventions offered that the service won the national service user-led 'Positive Practice in Mental Health' award in 2014 for best mental health service. Like other good psychological models, the MVS assists individuals by heeding the guiding principles of acceptability, proportionality, authenticity, recovery and evidence.

Interventions

As expected from a psychological therapies service, a broad range of therapeutic modalities have formed part of the offer to clients. Our selection of clinical staff who can offer more than one therapeutic approach has been key to achieving this. Over the first four years of the project, interventions informed by the following approaches have featured: cognitive behavioural therapy (CBT), including trauma-focused CBT (tCBT) that incorporates both prolonged exposure and cognitive processing; eye movement desensitisation and reprocessing (EMDR); psychodynamic psychotherapy; families and couples therapy; acceptance and commitment therapy (ACT); cognitive analytic therapy (CAT); compassion focused therapy (CFT); mindfulness-based cognitive therapy (MBCT); art psychotherapy; narrative exposure therapy (NET); dialectic behaviour therapy (DBT); mentalisation-based therapy (MBT); and formulation-driven clinical psychology.

It has been the aim that interventions have been both relationally intelligent and trauma-informed. This has been especially helpful in working with pre-service childhood trauma, personality difficulties and with cases of moral injury. Therapy interventions are complimented by case management, and a duty function, discharged by an approved mental health practitioner (AMHP) and registered mental nurse (RMN). Psychopharmacology prescribing expertise is accessed as when required via a network of psychiatrists and pharmacists in the region, in addition to using the Veteran and Reserves Mental Health Programme. Some medically run veteran charities are also happy to offer clients medication. Further complimentary support is provided via both short message service (SMS) and web-based digital packages, at no cost to the client.

Sequenced and phased

Many traumatic stress services have recognised the utility of ensuring that treatment is offered in a way that maximises client engagement and readiness to undertake what is frequently challenging work. Pennine Care's MVS is no different in that it offers a stepped, sequenced intervention that can be undertaken in phases. This would typically be targeting those with multiple combat trauma who exhibit poor coping styles, poor impulse control or high-risk behaviours. In practice, the client would initially be offered a period of stabilisation work, incorporating elements from psychoeducation, mood regulation, anger management, grounding techniques, mindfulness, sleep hygiene, communication skills and problem solving. Sometimes, clients feel that they have improved adequately and seek discharge after this stage. The treatment is phasic because they are encouraged to return, and frequently do, in order to tackle more long standing or deeper difficulties. In 2016, this component was externally and independently evaluated and early indications (awaiting full analysis and publication) suggest positive outcomes for this client group.

Therapeutic rehearsal

Developed in early 2012, we initiated a somewhat similar but fundamentally different pre-trauma intervention for which we coined the name 'therapeutic rehearsal'. Essentially, this uses the experience that military personnel have of pre-deployment training to engage them in less threatening one-to-one therapy. Within therapeutic rehearsal, a client may be allocated to a more junior clinician, such as a psychological wellbeing practitioner (PWP), to work on less challenging aspects of their difficulty. The client gets to practice and have experience of meeting with a clinician on a regular basis at a particular time and venue. They get used to talking about things and recording information. This may involve, for example, working on social anxiety, and keeping a log of socially anxious thoughts. By the time they start the tougher task of trauma-focused therapy, they will have some 'early wins under their belts' and experience of broad therapy processes. The shift to substituting socially phobic thought records for keeping a log of nightmares or other intrusions now feel less of a step for the client. We believe that this intermediary phase encourages greater numbers of military veterans to stay engaged in trauma-focused interventions where traditionally they may have avoided and dropped out of treatment services.

Early intervention, in-reach and outreach

Pennine Care's MVS was the first dedicated NHS veteran service to offer early intervention in-reach to the MOD's regional Personnel Recovery Unit (PRU), and at no cost, thus enabling a smoother transition of military personnel who are on a medical discharge pathway for being 'Wounded Injured or Sick' (WIS). The service has additionally always taken a steady stream of referrals directly from the Departments of Community Mental Health (DCMH) that cover the North West. One of the most fitting quotes that the MVS received was from the Commanding Officer of the PRU who stated, 'The thing I like most about your service is that you under promise and continually over-deliver. In contrast to most veteran organisations where the opposite is true'.

The MVS has also offered in-reach into prisons, whereby an offender caseworker with prison clearance can visit a veteran prisoner with mental health needs in their last 12 weeks of their sentence. If the individual is due to be discharged to an address in the geographical area covered by the MVS, with a probation package, then an appointment can be planned to contribute to a smooth transition between mental health services. Probation remains a significant referral source, a group within which we have seen the highest levels of client fabrication and embellishment. Accessing clients within police custody suites has now by and large been taken on by some of the veteran charities, alongside generalist statutory liaison and diversion schemes. Forensic history was found to be the only statistically significant variable in which veterans dropped out or did not take up therapy having been accepted by the service (Giebel et al., 2014).

The ongoing work with the regional drug and alcohol services have been a challenge, because of the frequently changing hands of these services. Typically requiring clients to want to help themselves, we have found that military veterans who may be self-medicating their psychological difficulties require more of a facilitative and enabling approach. Thus, the substance misuse caseworker role, part educative and part encourager, prevents many clients from dropping out of services. Outreach to these services has resulted in significant numbers of referrals into therapy.

The 'undesirables'

Everybody wants to be seen to be helping the nation's heroes, but what happens to those at the other end of the spectrum? The official research statistics may minimise their existence, institutions may attribute their conduct as having nothing to do with their military service and some veteran charities and support organisations may turn their backs on them as undeserving. Nonetheless they exist and, unsurprisingly, it is left to the statutory agencies such the NHS to provide the required care and support with ever reducing funding. Pennine Care's MVS has found itself assisting large numbers of military veterans on account that they have been excluded by other agencies, for things such as 'unacceptable behaviour', 'abusive language', 'violent conduct' and 'being under the influence of alcohol and/or drugs'.

Confounding additional needs of the first 2000 clients seen were as follows:

- 40% reported being charged with a criminal offence in a court of law
- 30% regularly exceeding governmental alcohol limits
- 17% regularly using illicit drugs
- 40% having a long-term health condition (LTC), including mobility difficulties

Additionally, the MVS has seen high numbers of individuals with chaotic psycho-social problems, such as housing instability, debt and issues related to family courts. It sees higher numbers of sex offenders than we may have anticipated. However, this could be in part be due to factors such as the NHS commissioned residential service being unable to assist this group. Much of the forensic histories relate to violent offences against the person, which fits with the literature (MacManus *et al.*, 2013), with high levels of domestic violence. Less common are those clients involved with radicalisation and known to counter-terrorism. We also support several veterans as both witnesses and perpetrators of war crimes, and assist them psychologically as well as to navigate the legal processes surrounding this. As can be imagined, safeguarding has become a core function of the work of the MVS.

Pre-service factors

From an audit of 132 veterans receiving psychological therapy within the service (Barrett, 2015), 63 per cent had been exposed to significant pre-service adversity in at least one of the following areas:

- 54% sustained psychological abuse
- 40% repeated physical abuse
- 32% significant neglect
- 18% sexually abused

Frequently, these early life issues are treated first in therapy before tackling purely military-related issues. However, there is an expected crossover and factors are rarely exclusive. Whether it is the bullied school boy who sought refuge in the military only to find himself the scapegoat of regimental bullying, the sexually abused child who finds themselves as a victim of sexual assault at the hands of their peers in barracks or where childhood trauma themes of helplessness, responsibility or fear for safety are magnified during military traumatic experiences.

Training, consultation and supervision

The SHA also stipulated that the pilot service had a responsibility to improve the understanding and awareness of the needs of the veterans' community across a range of North West services. From awareness raising to bespoke training packages, the MVS has enhanced the knowledge and skills across the regions workforce. This included delivering teaching events across the region to the existing IAPT teams, mental health trusts, probation services and third sector groups, hosting visits and speaking at conferences, commissioning a number of short films, both with clients sharing their stories and pieces of engaging award winning drama. All of this training, in addition to supervision and consultation, has been delivered free of charge. Disappointingly, some of the information produced by the MVS has been reproduced uncredited by others as if their own. At the end of the day, though, it is likely that the benefit to the ultimate end-users of services has been a tolerable price, and the MVS will continue to be generous with its learning. MVS staff also contribute to the training of Mental Health First Aid trainers, and university training of psychological wellbeing practitioners (PWPs), high intensity CBT therapists (HITs) and clinical psychologists in the region.

Transparent outcomes

Initially, the MVS would report back to the North West IAPT programme board, the NW Armed Forces Forum, the SHA and to PCFT as the host Trust. As though four masters were not enough, the one SHA was then replaced with 32 CCGs, each initially wanting different feedback on activity. The service has always been heavily scrutinised in this way, with continuous reporting, evaluation and scrutiny. The MVS continues to demonstrate excellent value for money with consistently good outcomes for some of the most chronic and multiple need veterans in the country, especially considering that it receives no money for accommodation, travel or advertising in the budget. External independent evaluation, commissioned by the SHA, showed that the service was having as good outcomes with comparable services, but with a much more complex and chronic client group (Giebel et al., 2014). The report by the Personal Social Service Research Unit (PSSRU) at the University of Manchester has showed treatment for depression was more than twice as effective as antidepressant medication. It went on to state that 'The largest effect sizes and the greatest treatment improvements were seen with the Early Service Leavers across all the outcomes (depression, anxiety, and functioning)' (Giebel et al., 2014: 272). This was particularly pleasing as this is a specifically targeted cohort of the service. Despite very high self-reported scores at assessment on routinely used validated measures of depression and anxiety, the service achieves favourable rates of recovery to general IAPT services. (Clarkson et al., 2016)

Key successes and innovations

The MVS continues to deliver innovation in addition to good clinical practice. It has a track record of co-production with service users. It is evidence-based and outcome driven and provides whole person, ethical and safe care, supported by strong and passionate leadership. It has had comprehensive media coverage, challenging myths that the NHS cannot help, and challenging stereotypes that either see veterans as heroes or as damaged, instead, showing them as real people.

The MVS has worked in partnership with a wide range of external services to collaborate on innovative projects, from training veterans as community reporters to interview their own communities, to the SMS campaign that told us that veterans prefer to be contacted about appointments via SMS and to receive clinical appointments between the hours of 11am and 3pm (Pennine Care, 2016). Innovative partnerships have also involved: art; cinema; employment; film; technology; theatre; physical activity; tele-therapy; SMS mood monitoring; education; peer mentoring; pain management; online interventions; and history and heritage projects.

Crowded landscape

Starting out as a simple spreadsheet in the MVS office in 2011, it soon became clear when the number reached 1,000 that it would be too much for a clinical provider service or the co-located social wraparound service to manage the database of veteran charities. The datum was passed back to the SHA who added more agencies, and then it was briefly passed to Advancing Quality Alliance (AQuA) before returning to the NHS and becoming an online directory of almost 2,000 agencies purporting to support military veterans in the North West, with many being national charities. Libor funding was provided to one such charity to enhance the then 'Armed Forces Directory' and roll it out beyond the region.

The sheer number of organisations makes it difficult for potential users of services to make meaningfully informed decisions about receiving support. Clearly, the vast majority are genuine, well meaning, organisations that make real, tangible and valuable differences to the lives of military veterans. Although unable to officially endorse, we know which organisations do what they say and avoid mission drift. However, it would be remiss of us not to inform the reader about some of the difficulties we have encountered operating in the world of veteran care. Therefore, in the interests of raising awareness of the damage that can be caused – both to vulnerable individuals and to the wider reputation of the veteran community – we will provide an overview of the types of problems we have encountered.

We have experienced 'exaggerators', who sometimes dramatically inflate the extent of the problems faced by military veterans. 'Deniers', who minimise the extent of the problems, thereby making it harder for those experiencing genuine military-related difficulties to come forward for help. 'Misleaders', who offer false hope to veterans about what they can do for them, before disappointing them. 'Military hobbyists', who busy themselves dabbling in military veteran circles but appearing to add no discernible benefit to service users. Finally, 'exploiters', who target vulnerable or institutionalised veterans, or soft organisations, for ulterior motives such as personal financial gain.

All of those with an interest in providing evidence-based, compassionate care to veterans need to remain alert to the possibility of vulnerable veterans being exploited. Ensure both you as a provider, and the veteran client, is fully informed of the offers made by individuals and organisations, and assist them to unpick potential warning signs of future problems. These would include being suspicious if the client is asked not to have contact with any other organisations, is asked for payment or is offered rapid treatments that sound too good to be true. Ensure basic things such as the organisation having an address you can visit, has a complaints procedure and are appropriately accredited with a recognised body. You can always get support in checking these things out from your local NHS military veteran service provider.

Conclusion

There are lots of services in the NHS, some specialist and some generalist, who excellently support this client group as they do the civilian population. Military veterans share lots of common characteristics with the general population and frequently do not require their own services. There is established expertise out there already, and we should continue to use it and build on it. There is precious little resource to be working in silos and generating competition. If considering working in this arena, do your research, visit and talk to people and listen to where the gaps in service are, rather than contribute to the confusion. There are plenty of military veterans who will benefit from meaningful assistance. Think how your service can add value rather than repeating what others already do.

The MVS has excellent working partnerships with several veteran and third sector organisations. One particular success is embedding staff provided by veteran charities into clinical services to add value and enhance the offer to clients. Another is the sharing of training and work experience for peer mentors. We hope to continue to grow and develop both these areas going forward.

We continue to seek genuine allies and funding to co-conduct research to enable us to better understand how best to adapt clinical practice, to ensure it offers the greatest efficacy for military veteran clients. The large cohort studies of the mental health needs of serving personnel are interesting but may under-report mental health symptoms, due to responses being considered as not being confidential (Hunt *et al.*, 2014). Anecdotal evidence from both clients in our service and conversations with personnel who administered the Operational Mental Health Needs Evaluations (OMHNE – a self-report questionnaire to be completed by a sample of personnel on tour; Greenberg and Lamb, 2016) indicated that there was an implicit, if not explicit, direction not to report anything negative unless you wished to be returned home. Regardless of accuracy however, such studies remain of little clinical utility to provider services tasked with supporting and treating veterans presenting with mental health difficulties. The MVS continues to welcome researchers willing to work in partnerships to evaluate practice-based evidence and client-focused research. We also continue to welcome intervention partnerships that are safe, well governed and genuine about adding something extra. Pennine Care's MVS currently accept referrals from military veterans in Greater Manchester and Lancashire, whose issues are related to their military service and are unwilling or unable to access mainstream mental health services, or who prefer to access a service that is sensitive to their cultural needs. Please get in touch.

Finally, we would like to acknowledge the advice and support that we have received from NHS colleagues, both within the veteran sphere and within civilian specialist services. We thank a number of independent and community-based third sector providers of clinical services who have also been there for us and we acknowledge the sometimes bumpy but invaluable ongoing relationships with some of the veteran charities. Thanks also to some of our allies within the Ministry of Defence and in academia. We acknowledge the unwavering dedication of the staff within the MVS who routinely give many more hours than they are paid for. Lastly, but especially, we thank all the men and women of the Armed Forces community, including family members, who continue to be a continuous inspiration.

References

Adamson, P. (2013). *Child Well-being in Rich Countries: A Comparative Overview*. Florence: The UNICEF Office of Research.

Barrett, A. (2015). Emerging themes from a psychological treatment provider perspective. Paper presented at The British Psychological Society. *Military Veterans: Transition from Military to Civilian life*, Manchester, 18 March 2015.

British Psychological Society (2013). Division on Clinical Psychology Position Statement. *Classification of Behaviour and Experience in Relation to Functional Psychiatric Diagnosis: Time for a Paradigm Shift*. Leicester: British Psychological Society.

Clarkson, P., Giebel, C.M., Challis, D., Duthie, P., Barrett, A., Lambert, H. (2016). Outcomes from a pilot psychological therapies service for UK military veterans. *Nursing Open*, 3, 227–35.

Dent-Brown, K., Ashworth, A., Barkham, M., Connell, J., Gilbody, S., Hardy, G. (2010). *An Evaluation of Six Community Mental Health Pilots for Veterans of the Armed Forces: A Case Study Series*. A Report for the Ministry of Defence. Sheffield: University of Sheffield. Available online at www.sheffield.ac.uk/polopoly_fs/1.120472!/file/Sheffield-evaluation-published-version-15-Dec-2010.pdf (accessed 20 January 2017).

Department of Business, Innovation and Skills (2012). *BIS Research Paper Number 81. The 2011 Skills for Life Survey: A. Survey of Literacy, Numeracy and ICT. Levels in England*. London: Department of Business, Innovation and Skills. Available online at www.gov.uk/government/uploads/system/uploads/attachment_data/file/36000/12-p168-2011-skills-for-life-survey.pdf (accessed 20 January 2017).

Fear, N., Wood, D., Wessely, S. (2009). *Health and Social Outcomes and Health Service Experiences of UK Military Veterans: A Summary of the Evidence*. London: King's Centre for Military Health Research.

Fossey, M. (2012). *Unsung Heroes: Developing a Better Understanding of the Emotional Support Needs of Service Families*. London: Centre for Mental Health.

Giebel, C.M., Clarkson, P., Challis, D. (2014). Demographic and clinical characteristics of UK military veterans attending a psychological therapies service. *Psychiatric Bulletin*, 38, 270–5.

Gill, D. (2008). Proving and disproving psychiatric injury. *Medico-Legal Journal*, 76, 143–54.

Greenberg, N., Lamb, N. (2016). Operational Mental Health Needs Evaluation. Available online at www.kcl.ac.uk/kcmhr/research/admmh/OMHNE.aspx (accessed 20 January 2017).

House of Commons, Business, Innovation and Skills Committee (2014). *Adult Literacy and Numeracy, Fifth Report of Session 2014–15*. London: House of Commons, Business,

Innovation and Skills Committee. Available online at www.publications.parliament.uk/pa/cm201415/cmselect/cmbis/557/557.pdf (accessed 20 January 2017).

Hunt, E.J.F., Wessely, S., Jones, N., Rona, R.J., Greenberg, N. (2014). The mental health of the UK Armed Forces: where facts meet fiction. *European Journal of Psychotraumatology*, 5, 23617.

MacManus, D., Dean, K., Jones, M., Rona, R.J., Greenberg, N., Hull, L., Fear, N.T. (2013). Violent offending by UK military personnel deployed to Iraq and Afghanistan: a data linkage cohort study. *The Lancet*, 381, 907–17.

MacManus, D., Jones N., Wessely S., Fear, N.T., Jones, E., Greenberg, N. (2014). The mental health of the UK Armed Forces in the 21st century: resilience in the face of adversity. *Journal of the Royal Army Medical Corps*, 160, 125–30. Available online at www.kcl.ac.uk/kcmhr/publications/assetfiles/2014/resilience-paper.pdf (accessed 20 January 2017).

MOD (2011). *The Armed Forces Covenant*. London: Ministry of Defence.

Murrison, A. (2010). *Fighting Fit: A Mental Health Plan for Servicemen and Veterans*. London: Ministry of Defence. Available online at www.gov.uk/government/uploads/system/uploads/attachment_data/file/27375/20101006_mental_health_Report.pdf (accessed 20 January 2017).

NICE (2012). *Patient Experience in Adult NHS Services: Improving the Experience of Care for People Using NHS Services. Clinical Guideline 138*. London: NICE. Available online at www.guidance.nice.org.uk/CG138 (accessed 20 January 2017).

ONS (2013). *Region and County Profiles*. Available online at www.ons.gov.uk/ons/rel/regional-trends/region-and-country-profiles/region-and-country-profiles---key-statistics-and-profiles--october-2013/index.html (accessed 20 January 2017).

Pennine Care (2016). *Overcoming Barriers to Mental Health Services for Ex Service Personnel*. Available online at www.penninecare.nhs.uk/media/494516/160212-summary-sms-report-january-2016-1.pdf (accessed 20 January 2017).

Rosen, G.M., Spitzer, R.L., McHugh, P.R. (2008). Problems with the post-traumatic stress disorder diagnosis and its future in DSM–V. *The British Journal of Psychiatry*, 192, 3–4.

9

VETERANS' NHS WALES (VNHSW)

The Only NHS National Veterans' Service in the UK?

Neil Kitchiner

Introduction

In the UK, there has traditionally been no special provision made for the estimated 4.7 million plus veterans and their dependents. Veterans' health and social needs are officially catered for by statutory services such as the National Health Service (NHS) and local authorities, and the Medical Assessment Programme (MAP) offers an assessment-only service for those with operational service after 1982. The Service Personnel and Veterans' Agency (SPVA), various charities and other organisations, some with central funding, also play a major role in supporting veterans and supplementing the input provided by statutory services. Concerns about the current provision for veterans have been widely reported, with some arguing for dedicated services as in the US, Canada and Australia (IUA/ABI, 2004).

England's Improving Access to Psychological Therapies (IAPT) initiative has recognised veterans as a population with specific needs and published a positive practice guide (IAPT, 2009). This notes that veterans may have different needs to non-veterans, that they can be reluctant to access NHS care and that they are vulnerable to social exclusion including homelessness and unemployment. The document identifies a number of barriers which need to be addressed to fully engage veterans with NHS services including stigma, shame, disenchantment with previous contacts and lack of understanding of their needs by some health professionals.

In 2008, the Command paper, *'The Nation's Commitment: Cross-Government Support to our Armed Forces, their Families and Veterans'* (Ministry of Defence, 2008) was presented to parliament. It asserts that regular military personnel, reservists, veterans and their families must not be disadvantaged and that this will sometimes call for degrees of special treatment. For example, all veterans with 'service-related conditions' are now entitled to accelerated treatment through the NHS priority treatment scheme, although it is clear that this may not always occur (Health in Wales, 2008).

The Command paper committed to raising awareness of veterans' needs among healthcare professionals and noted the introduction of the six pilot community mental health services across the UK to improve veterans' timely access to mental health services and inform the development of future services. This initiative, funded by the Ministry of Defence (MOD) ran for two years and was formally evaluated by Sheffield University (Dent-Brown *et al.*, 2010). The devolved governments in Scotland and Wales had co-funded veterans' services. Including in March 2008, the Welsh Veterans Pilot was launched in Cardiff to cover the catchment areas of the Cardiff and Vale and Cwm Taf NHS Trusts, a population of around 1 million people. The evaluation data suggest that this project has proved successful at identifying veterans and enabling them to access appropriate NHS and welfare services for their needs (BBC Wales News, 2008).

The development of a Welsh NHS veterans' service

The Welsh Government (WG) remains committed to improving support and treatment for veterans. This, together with the success of the Welsh Veterans Pilot, led to the creation of a National Task and Finish Group to develop a service specification. The Group met on five occasions between 16 July 2009 and 3 December 2009. The specification has been informed by evidence obtained from the following sources:

- Existing literature regarding the needs of veterans and the provision of services for them.
- Discussions with veterans, their careers and individuals involved in the psychosocial care of veterans.
- Ongoing psychosocial research into the needs of veterans living in Wales.
- The experiences of the six Community Veterans Mental Health Service pilots
- Projects across the United Kingdom, with particular reference to the Veterans Pilot Project based in Wales from 1 October 2010.

Aims

The primary aim of the Veterans' NHS Wales (VNHSW) is to improve the mental health and wellbeing of veterans.

The secondary aim is to achieve this through the development of sustainable, accessible and effective services that meet the needs of veterans with a service-related mental health difficulties who live in Wales.

Outcomes

The key outcomes of the service are:

A. Veterans who experience service-related mental health difficulties are able to access and use services that cater for their needs.

B. Veterans in this service are given a comprehensive assessment that accurately assesses their psychological and social needs.

C. Veterans are signposted or referred to appropriate services for any physical needs that are detected.

D. Veterans and others involved in their care can develop an appropriate care management plan that takes their family and their surroundings into account.

E. Veterans' families are signposted to appropriate services if required.

F. This service has developed local and national networks of services and agencies involved in the care of veterans to promote multi-agency working to improve outcomes for veterans and their families.

G. The service has linked with the military to facilitate early identification and intervention.

H. The service has promoted a recovery model so that veterans can maximise their physical, mental and social wellbeing.

I. Veterans who experience service-related mental health difficulties are provided brief psychosocial interventions if indicated.

J. Veterans who experience 'non-service related' mental health difficulties are signposted to receive appropriate interventions.

K. The service has provided expert advice and support to local services on the assessment and treatment of veterans who experience mental health difficulties to ensure local services, including addictions services, are able to meet the needs of veterans.

L. The service has raised awareness of the needs of veterans and military culture to ensure improved treatment and support across services.

M. The service has identified barriers to veterans accessing appropriate services and attempted to highlight and address these as appropriate.

N. The service has collected data on patterns of referral, routine outcomes and referral on.

Eligibility

Any veteran living in Wales who has served at least one day with the British Military as either a regular service member or as a reservist is eligible to be assessed by VNHSW. Veterans with a 'service-related' injury are eligible to receive an assessment and ongoing treatment from VNHSW. Those with 'non-service related' injuries are signposted to appropriate services for ongoing treatment as indicated.

Access

A centralised open referral system has been adopted whereby veterans can self-refer, be referred by their families (with their consent) or by other agencies or services. Referral can be via the service website (www.veteranswales.co.uk) online referral form or directly to each Local Health Board (LHB) veteran therapist.

The service is designed on a 'hub and spoke service model'. The hub is based in Cardiff, at the University Hospital of Wales provided by the Cardiff and Vale University Health Board (UHB). The other five UHBs responsible for mental health service provision across Wales are the spokes. The UHBs have created local mental health services for veterans, covering the whole of Wales, that deliver the outcomes previously listed.

Staffing

Each UHBs have employed an individual or individuals to undertake the role of a community veterans' therapist (VT). The VTs aim to spend a minimum of 50 per cent of their time delivering psychological treatments to veterans in order to address the gap in current tier three provision.

The VT also skill up others within the mental health service to help provide cover for this service when that individual is away. The VTs are appropriately skilled and trained mental health professionals from nursing, social work and psychology backgrounds. The Cardiff and Vale UHB employed a principal clinician (PC) full-time and a consultant psychiatrist, one session per week for the first three years, to allow the development of the hub and spoke model. Each of the UHB services is supported by a 0.5 whole time equivalent administrator, with an additional 0.5 whole time equivalent administrator based at the hub to undertake all Wales administrative tasks.

Management and professional accountability

The service was initially directed by Professor Jonathan Bisson, an Honorary Consultant Psychiatrist, who was based in Cardiff University Hospital from 2010 to 2013, with support from the PC (the author). All VTs are line managed and professionally managed locally with support from the PC and Director. The VTs receive face-to-face group service supervision every six weeks and telephone supervision from the PC on a monthly basis. The service director is accountable to the WG through the Cardiff and Vale University Health Board.

The original VTs attended a week-long induction programme October 2011, at Dering Lines, Infantry Battle School, Brecon, Wales. The induction week consisted of lectures on military history, military mental health and its research base. The VTs visited the ranges to observe regular army personnel undergoing training under live fire, a visit to the army reserve centre, Cardiff (203 Field Hospital, HQ) for various team building events (command tasks) and to the Brecon military museum.

Staff training

The VTs were appointed due to their proven skills and experience in conducting a full biopsychosocial assessment, developing individual management plans, case management and the provision of brief psychological treatments. An ongoing professional development programme is in place for all the VTs which included three days annual training at the United Kingdom Psychological Trauma Society. All VTs are qualified (or currently working towards becoming trained in) eye movement desensitisation reprocessing (EMDR) to complement their skills in trauma focused cognitive behavioural psychotherapy (CBT). Several VTs are accessing private clinical supervision where there is a lack of expertise within their host UHB, for example, for EMDR and CBT.

Veterans' mental health clinical networks

The UHBs are responsible for health and social care across Wales and responsible for creating and facilitating veterans' mental health clinical networks. These clinical networks are made of key stakeholders which meet regularly to monitor the UHBs progress in offering services to ex-service personnel. These include local veterans and carers, representatives from Health and Social Services, the Royal British Legion (RBL), Combat Stress, Serving Personnel Veterans Agency and other organisations, for example, Citizens Advice Bureau (CAB) and Defence Community Mental Health Services. The creation of clinical networks was recommended in a recent report by the Healthcare Inspectorate Wales to help develop a robust multi-agency approach to the care of veterans and support the VT across Wales (Healthcare Inspectorate Wales, 2012).

Engagement issues

Our experience of engaging ill veterans into a mental health treatment programme remains particularly challenging due to a variety of factors, including stigma, perceived weakness at acknowledging emotional difficulties and the military macho culture. Recent studies have shown that more than 60 per cent of US Iraq veterans screened positive for a mental health problem did not seek treatment (Hoge *et al.*, 2007). Similar findings were reported in a UK study (Iversen *et al.*, 2010), in which only 23 per cent of serving personnel with common mental health problems were receiving any form of medical professional help. Chaplains were much more likely to be supporting these individuals. Those who were receiving medical help were mainly in primary care (79 per cent) and being treated with medication, counselling or psychotherapy. Recent trials in the US and UK with group programmes such as Battlemind (Adler *et al.*, 2009), and Trauma Risk Management (TRiM) respectively, with some evidence that they may improve attitudes to mental-health-seeking behaviours and binge drinking (Greenberg *et al.*, 2010).

What treatments work with veterans?

There is a range of evidence-based treatments for mental health problems that have been shown to be effective in civilian populations, but it is unclear whether they have similar efficacy in serving military and veteran populations, or how well these populations engage with them. Currently, the information is limited to addressing the specific interventions, settings and lengths of treatment that are applicable in the veteran population. Therapies that have some evidence from random controlled trials, completed mostly in the US and Australia, demonstrate that trauma-focused CBT and EMDR therapy does ameliorate post-traumatic stress disorder (PTSD) symptoms (Carlson et al., 1998; Schnurr et al., 2003, 2007; Foa et al., 2009), insomnia (Edinger et al., 2009) and panic disorder co-morbid to PTSD (Teng et al., 2008). Based on a recent systematic review, there is enough evidence for clinical services to treat veterans in a way that is based on the evidence base for certain conditions.

The results from this review suggest that veterans respond to out-patient trauma-focused psychosocial interventions for chronic PTSD on a one-to-one or group basis with the therapist within the same room (Kitchiner et al., 2012). This is consistent with the evidence from meta-analyses of civilian studies (Bisson et al., 2007) and supports a recommendation that trauma-focused interventions should be offered to all veterans with chronic PTSD.

There is also some evidence for dialectical behaviour therapy for treating borderline personality disorder in female veterans, telephone disease management for depression and at risk alcohol abuse, CBT and exercise for Gulf War illness and CBT or panic control treatment for panic disorder co-morbid with PTSD, but replication is required. The lack of efficacy of collaborative psychosocial interventions for veterans with depression suggests that, at present, it is appropriate to offer veterans alternative treatments for depression that have been shown to be effective in civilian populations. However, caution should be exercised until efficacy studies of treatments such as CBT and interpersonal psychological therapy have been conducted on veterans with depression (Kitchiner et al., 2012).

Integrated care pathways

The service model is based on work led by Dr Neil Kitchiner in conjunction with Cardiff University, which developed and tested a specific integrated care pathway (ICP). The ICP is now used across the service and is complemented by an agreed, higher level, Common Care Pathway, which has been agreed by the WG. As part of the ICP, a standardised minimum data set (MDS) is collected on each individual assessed. The MDS includes six self-report clinical measures of anxiety, depression, PTSD, alcohol use and quality of life. These are repeated pre, post-treatment and at one month follow-up. The data are analysed centrally to evaluate the service, facilitate its development and to evaluate the service performance and then presented to the WG. It is recognised that the care pathways will not be identical given the geographical and service differences across Wales. For instance, in west Wales, health and social care is provided by Hywel Dda UHB, where the VT has developed a telephone triage system for veterans, which cuts out unnecessary travel for both therapist and veteran. The veteran is then offered a face-to-face assessment if they meet the inclusion criteria for the service.

Veterans with more complex difficulties are eligible to receive a second opinion assessment with a consultant psychiatrist within their UHB to confirm a diagnosis for access to Armed Forces pensions and pharmacological interventions.

VNHSW service

Management of the VNHSW occurs at local and national levels. Each UHB spoke is fully integrated into its local mental health service and adheres to local policies and procedures. In addition, the VNHSW multi-agency National Steering Group oversees the service and provides strategic input.

Who gets referred?

Based on the first five years' data, the typical veteran assessed is male, aged between 35 and 42 who has served in the army (infantry) with multiple deployments, including several tours of Northern Ireland, Falkland Islands and peacekeeping duties in Bosnia/Kosovo, Iraq and Afghanistan. Since leaving service, he has found it difficult to stay employed, has many and varied social/relationship problems, may have had contact with the criminal justice system and may have been classed as vulnerably housed or homeless at some time. These individuals present with complex presentations which require a varied management plan with referrals and signposting to organisations and veteran charities that can assist with many of the social problems, including debts and require financial advice. They often require pharmacological therapy for common mental health disorders and impulsivity, in tandem with outpatient psychological therapies.

Service evaluation

The following data over the first five years were collected from veterans at their initial assessment and post-treatment. There had been 1,657 referrals (up to end of March 2015). This equates to an average of 331 veterans per annum to the service.

Referrals to VNHSW in 2014 and 2015

In 12 months (2014 to 2015), the service received 542 referrals across all 7 UHBs. By the end of financial year, 339 of these had received an assessment with a VT and 139 of these had begun out-patient psychological treatment. Due to the time between referral, assessment and treatment, these numbers slightly downplay the proportion of veterans that receive assessment and treatment. By looking only at those referrals received in the first half of the year, it is estimated that around 60 per cent to 70 per cent of referrals to the service reach assessment and 30 per cent to 50 per cent of referrals begin some form of psychological treatment from VTs.

Sources of referral

By far the greatest sources of referrals are from primary care services and self-referrals. Together, these account for around half of the referrals received in 2014 and 2015.

Main sources of referral by local health board

Different Health Boards receive referrals from various sources. For example, Betsi Cadwaladr UHB receives a relatively high rate of self-referral, but a low rate from primary care. In contrast, Hywel Dda LHB receives a relatively low rate of self-referral but a high rate from primary care and various voluntary organisations. These differences reveal opportunities for greater engagement with certain referrers, and will be investigated by the service over the next 12 months.

Referral outcomes

There is a great variability in outcome after VNHSW receives a referral. For example, Hywel Dda UHB has a high proportion of their referrals who are not assessed and therefore never enter therapy, compared with Cwm Taf UHB who offer an assessment and treatment to the majority of veterans referred. This is probably a reflection of the VTs having different threshold for entry into the service. This variation will be discussed by the service and steps taken to ensure a consistent and prudent healthcare (Welsh Government, 2015) approach to accessing therapy.

Sign-posting to other services

Following assessment, many veterans are signposted to other NHS departments, veteran organisations or charities for further help with medical, psychological or social support. Cwm Taf UHB signposts its veterans to several agencies compared with Betsi Cadwaladr UHB. The difference in the range of signposting options may reflect geographical differences rather than needs within veterans assessed.

Services signposted

Many veterans assessed required low level psychosocial support to help them engage with other agencies before they could enter into out-patient psychological therapy. Change Step (a peer support charity in Wales) have been able to help with this by offering a 'peer support' intervention and weekly drop in groups, plus further signposting. VTs continue to refer individuals into primary care if the veteran has self-referred to keep their GP informed and request that the GP prescribe various medications for common mental health disorders. Many veterans continue to be unaware that they can claim for 'service-related injuries' (physical/psychological). VNHSW routinely signpost to Veterans UK who can assist them with possible war pension claims

Waiting times for assessment 2014 to 2015

The waiting times for an assessment vary across health boards. With 50 per cent of initial appointments taking place within 36 days of referral and 75 per cent within

58 days of referral. The mean time from referral to first appointment was 42 days. This figure is currently outside of the 28 days' target for a primary care service operating within Wales.

A significant component of these waiting times is often the delay in the opt-in letter being returned by the veteran to the service. Half of those returned took over ten days from information being sent to reach the service. Once the opt-in letter had been returned to the service, VNHSW usually managed to begin the assessment quickly, with 80 per cent of assessments completed within 35 days of the opt-in letter being returned and 90 per cent within 47 days. Veteran therapists typically offer one to three new assessments per week each.

Fifty per cent of first treatment appointments were offered within 42 days of the veteran being assessed and 75 per cent within 113 days. This falls within the 126 days (18 weeks) that the Royal British Legion campaigned for in their 2015 UK government manifesto to meet the government's pledge of parity of esteem between physical and mental problems. This variation in waiting times across the LHBs reflects the services variation in capacity and demand experienced by the service in different regions over the course of the year. The service has increased VTs and administration hours in these LHBs with the highest demand with additional funding from the Welsh Government.

The majority of our patients referred this year live within a close distance to major conurbations and in south and north Wales. There is a small proportion of veterans living remotely in Powys and west Wales. The small numbers living remotely may be a true representation of the veteran population, or that our main out-patient clinics are too far for them to travel too. The latter would be unlikely though as these rural populations are used to travelling long distances to access specialist healthcare.

Branch of service

As in previous years, the majority of our patients are ex-army veterans who have served in infantry regiments and deployed to various theatres of operations.

Veterans who have served between zero and four years are classed as 'Early Service Leavers' (ESL). There were 48 veterans with fewer than 4 years in service, which accounted for 18 per cent of those where the time in service was recorded. A further 52 veterans fell just outside of this category with 5 or 6 years in service. This is important data as ESL may have more complex health and social presentations, which require a multi-agency approach to meet their needs (Buckman *et al.*, 2013).

Employment status

The largest group with 49 per cent describe themselves as unemployed and not fit for work. This was often due to mental and/or physical health problems. This compares with 34 per cent who are working either part-time or full-time and able to maintain employment. The third largest group with 13 per cent are individuals who are medically retired due to ill health, in the majority of cases due to mental health problems.

Primary mental health diagnosis

The majority of our veterans described traumatic stress symptoms to events where they thought they were going to be seriously injured or killed or witnessed others being seriously injured or killed. However, not all veterans with trauma symptoms had experienced exclusively military-related trauma, either pre-enlistment or post-service, for example, working in private security work in overseas; 64 per cent were diagnosed with PTSD, 14 per cent with mixed anxiety and depression and 11 per cent with a depressive episode.

Clinical outcomes of treatment

All veterans who are assessed and at commencement of therapy provide self-report scores via several clinical measures, and again at discharge, to capture any change in reported symptoms. In each chart, those veterans represented by an x in the green corner demonstrated a significant improvement in a particular domain following treatment, for example, a lower score indicates a better state on all instruments (with the exception of the EQ-5D).

The self-report questionnaires routinely used are the impact of events scale revised which captures PTSD symptoms; PHQ-9 used to rate depressive symptoms; AUDIT for measuring alcohol use; GAD-7 for anxiety symptoms; and EQ-5D for measuring the individual's quality of life. The charts demonstrate that many veterans achieve significant improvement in several aspects of mental health following therapy. Some veterans may improve on one measure, even if they do not show improvement on others. There is however, a large number of low self-reported quality of life scores, both before and after treatment based on the EQ-5D, which the service will work to understand what underlies this lack of improvement.

Research activity within the VNHSW

A telephone survey of 207 veterans living in Wales from three different groups found significant differences in the difficulties they experience. A randomly selected group of veterans in contact with Combat Stress had a mean age of 49, 62 per cent were suffering from major depression, 44 per cent had attempted suicide at some point in their life, 20 per cent were drinking at a hazardous level, 27 per cent were probably alcohol dependent and 73 per cent were suffering from PTSD. A group who had been in contact with SPVA had a mean age of 67, 13 per cent had major depression, 6 per cent had attempted suicide, 17 per cent were drinking at a hazardous level, 2 per cent were probably alcohol dependent and 10 per cent were suffering from PTSD. Members of a random group of veterans who were serving in the military in 2003 had a mean age of 38, major depression rate of 4 per cent, 1 per cent had attempted suicide, 37 per cent were drinking at a hazardous level, 6 per cent probably alcohol dependent and 3 per cent were suffering from PTSD. Of the 63 veterans who were diagnosed with PTSD, only one did not have another psychiatric diagnosis. Of the participants who met diagnostic criteria for mental disorder, 46.9 per cent had sought professional help. The main reason not to seek help was a perception that help was not needed. Informal sources of help were more used than professional ones (Wood et al., 2011).

National Centre for Mental Health (Wales)

The VNHSW is actively involved as a key stakeholder with the Wales Mental Health Network (http://ncmh.info/take-part/). The Network aims to recruit 6,000 individuals who have or are suffering from a range of mental health problems including PTSD. Each VT in every UHB provides information on the National Centre for Mental Health research in an attempt to recruit veterans with/without mental health problems into the study. At the time of writing, there have been over 200 individuals recruited into the PTSD registry.

Conclusion

The VNHSW was funded by the Welsh Government in April 2010 following a successful two-year pilot in Cardiff and Vale and Cwm Taf NHS Trusts. Over 1600 veterans have been referred between April 2010 and March 2015. The majority are middle-aged, white males who have been referred by health professionals or veterans' agencies. Data obtained at the screening interview highlights that the veterans seen reported significant problems with their functioning due to a combination of psychosocial factors and mental health disorders, which include a range of anxiety and depressive disorders with co-morbid excessive alcohol misuse/dependency in many individuals. Chronic PTSD with co-morbidity was the primary mental disorder diagnosed in this cohort, with a high proportion describing the onset several decades before presentation. A forensic history was common in the many of those assessed. The majority have received either out-patient therapy from the VNHSW or referral to other NHS services or veterans' charities for treatment and/or support.

The service has established strong links with the veterans' charities and other veterans' agencies within Wales. The service has developed a common pathway which the main veterans' charities and agencies have signed-up to. This establishes VNHSW as central to the assessment and management of veterans with mental health problems who live in.

From our experience, veterans will attend NHS facilities but prefer a veteran-specific service as they view their problems as being unique from the civilian population. Treatment gains are possible with the correct management plan, but are often modest (Kitchiner et al., 2012; Steenkamp et al., 2015).). Targeting their often multitude of social problems in the first instance appears to produce better attendance in outpatient psychological therapy and leads to improved positive outcomes. The formation of a veteran steering group, with a wide membership from the main veteran charities, MOD service personnel and veterans' agency, CAB, prison healthcare, homelessness teams, Combat Stress and local military medical services, will help the new veteran services develop positive practices (Kitchiner *et al.,* 2012).

In the last ten years, there has been a proliferation of charities that have emerged claiming to be able to treat and 'cure' veterans' mental health problems, particularly PTSD (Healing the Wounds, 2009; Wounded Warrior, 2011). They are often staffed by well-meaning ex-service personnel, usually with some medical training from the medical centre. The treatment programmes are, though, often residential focused and use psychological treatments such as neurolinguistic programming (NLP) and emotional freedom techniques (EFT). New veteran services within the NHS need to be mindful of the different charities in their area and have an ability to give accurate information about the treatments they offer and their effectiveness and evidence base whilst attempting to alleviate emotional distress in ex-service personnel.

Veteran mental health services need to collect routine outcome data and work together to share best practices. Continued novel research should also focus on which civilian biopsychosocial treatments are transferable to this deserving and often challenging occupational group and how they can be helped to reintegrate back into the wider community from which they came (Steenkamp *et al.,* 2015).

References

Adler, A.B., Castro, C.A., McGurk, D. (2009). Time-driven Battlemind psychological debriefing: A group-level early intervention in combat. *Military Medicine,* 174, 21–8.

BBC Wales News (2008). Mental health scheme for veterans. Available online at http://news.bbc.co.uk/1/hi/wales/7224874.stm (accessed 20 January 2017).

Bisson, J.I., Andrew, M. (2007). Psychological treatment of post-traumatic stress disorder (PTSD) *Cochrane Database of Systematic Reviews,* 3, CD003388.

Buckman, J.E., Forbes, H.J., Clayton, T., Jones, M., Jones, N., Greenberg, N., Sundin, J., Hull, L., Wessely, S., Fear, N.T. (2013). Early Service leavers: a study of the factors associated with premature separation from the UK Armed Forces and the mental health of those that leave early. *The European Journal of Public Health,* 23, 410–5.

Carlson, J.G., Chemtob, C.M., Rusnak, K., Hadland, N.L. and Muraoka, M.Y. (1998). Eye Movement Desensitization and Reprocessing (EDMR) Treatment for Combat-Related Posttraumatic Stress Disorder. *Journal of Traumatic Stress,* 11: 3.

Edinger, J.D., Olsen, M.K., Stechuchak, K.M., Means, M.K., Lineberger, M.D., Kirby, A., Carney, C.E. (2009). Cognitive behavioural therapy for patients with primary insomnia or insomnia associated predominantly with mixed psychiatric disorders: A randomized clinical trial. *Sleep,* 32, 499–510.

Dent-Brown, K., Ashworth, A., Barkham, M., Connell, J., Gilbody, S., Hardy, G. (2010). *An Evaluation of Six Community Mental Health Pilots for Veterans of the Armed Forces: A Case Study Series.* A Report for the Ministry of Defence. Sheffield: University of Sheffield. Available online at www.sheffield.ac.uk/polopoly_fs/1.120472!/file/Sheffield-evaluation-published-version-15-Dec-2010.pdf (accessed 20 January 2017).

Foa, E.B., Keane, T.M., Friedman, M.J., Cohen, J.A. (2009). *Effective Treatments for PTSD: Practice Guidelines from the International Society for Traumatic Stress Studies.* New York: The Guildford Press.

Greenberg, N., Langston, V., Everitt, B., Iversen, A., Fear, N.T., Jones, N., Wessely, S. (2010). A cluster randomized controlled trial to determine the efficacy of Trauma Risk Management (TRiM) in a military population. *Journal of Traumatic Stress*, 23, 430–6.

Healing the Wounds (2009). Treating PTSD in Wales. Available online at www.healingthewounds.co.uk/ (accessed 20 January 2017).

Healthcare Inspectorate Wales (2012). *Healthcare and the Armed Forces Community in Wales.* Caerphilly: Healthcare Inspectorate Wales.

Hoge, C.W., Terhakopian, A., Castro, C.A., Messer, S.C., Engel, C.C. (2007). Association of posttraumatic stress disorder with somatic symptoms, health care visits, and absenteeism among Iraq war veterans. *The American Journal of Psychiatry*, 164, 150–3.

IAPT (2009). Improving access to psychological therapies. Veterans positive practice guide. London.

IUA/ABI (2004). *Fourth UK Bodily Injury Awards Study*. London: International Underwriters Association and Association of British Insurers.

Iversen, A., van Staden, L., Hacker Hughes, J.H., Browne, T., Greenberg, N., Hotopf, M, Rona, R.J., Wessely, S., Thornicroft, G., Fear, N.T. (2010). Help-seeking and receipt of treatment among UK service personnel. *The British Journal of Psychiatry*, 197, 149–55.

Kitchiner, N., Roberts, N., Wilcox, D., Bisson, J.I. (2012). Systematic review and meta-analyses of psychosocial interventions for veterans of the military. *European Journal of Psychotraumatology*, 3, 19267.

Ministry of Defence (2008). *The Nation's Commitment: Cross-Government Support to our Armed Forces, Their Families and Veterans*. July 2008 CM7424. London: Ministry of Defence.

Schnurr, P.P., Friedman, M.J., Foy, D.W., Shea, M.T., Hsieh, F.Y., Lavori, P.W., Glynn, S.M., Wattenberg, M., Bernardy, N.C. (2003). Randomized trial of trauma-focused group therapy for posttraumatic stress disorder: Results from a department of veterans affairs cooperative study. *Archives of General Psychiatry*, 60, 481–9.

Schnurr, P.P., Friedman, M.J., Engel, C.C., Foa, E.B., Shea M.T. (2007). Cognitive behavioral therapy for posttraumatic stress disorder in women: a randomized controlled trial. *Journal of the American Medical Association*, 297, 820–30.

Steenkamp, M., Litz, B., Hoge, C., Marmar, C. (2015). Psychotherapy for military-related PTSD: A review of randomized clinical trials. *JAMA*, 314, 489–500.

Teng, E.J., Bailey, S.D., Chaison, A.D., Petersen, N.J., Hamilton, J.D., Dunn, N.J. (2008). Treating comorbid panic disorder in veterans with posttraumatic stress disorder. *Journal of Consulting and Clinical Psychology*, 6, 704–10.

Welsh Government (2015). *Prudent Healthcare 2015 – An International Summit*. Cardiff: Welsh Government.

Welsh Health Circular (2008). Priority Treatment and Healthcare for Veterans. Cardiff: Health in Wales.

Wounded Warrior Project (2011). *The Greatest Casualty Is Being Forgotten*. Available online at www.woundedwarriorproject.org/ (accessed20 January 2017).

10

THE SCOTTISH PERSPECTIVE

Lucy Abraham and Charlie Allanson-Oddy

Introduction

In this chapter, we provide an overview of 'The Scottish Perspective', with an emphasis on how this context has influenced the development of the first nation-wide network of holistic NHS services for ex-forces personnel and their families in Scotland.

First, it is appropriate to provide a brief military context for our work to acknowledge the contribution of Scottish soldiers, seamen and airmen over the last 300 years and consider the proud history of the Scottish Regiments of the British Army. It must be noted that the veteran population in Scotland comprises men and women not just from Scotland and the rest of the United Kingdom, but also from the Commonwealth and other countries. We would also like to acknowledge the families of the Scottish armed forces and veterans and the immense contribution they make in supporting loved ones both during deployment and upon their return.

Scottish veteran context

In Scotland, approximately 1,800 men and women complete their military service and settle, many with their families, in Scotland every year (Fraser, 2015). The ex-Service community makeup 10 per cent of the general Scottish population and account for 9 per cent of the total UK ex-Service community. Whilst this is currently a significant proportion of the Scottish population, the number of veterans is expected to fall in the long term. The veteran community in Scotland is forecast by actuarial consultants Punter Southall to decline in size to around 6 per cent of the Scottish adult population by the year 2030. The veteran community is also increasingly elderly. In 2005, 22 per cent were aged over 75, rising to 46 per cent by 2014 (Ashworth *et al.*, 2014). We therefore need to continually respond to this changing profile of veterans in Scotland and design services to appropriately meet their needs.

Support organisations for veterans in Scotland

In order to meet the diverse needs of a changing demographic, the charitable sector has contributed significantly, some since the early twentieth century. Notable charities such as Poppy Scotland, Scottish Veterans Residencies (SVR), the Soldiers, Sailors, Airmen and Families Association (SSAFA) and Combat Stress have long and creditable histories. Veterans Scotland has made great efforts to provide a national overview of the 419 recognised veteran charities in Scotland (Pozo and Walker, 2014). Since its inception, the NHS has also provided substantial support to the veteran community through their mainstream services. This chapter focuses on recent specialist developments within NHS Scotland for veterans and their families that are focused on providing a one-stop shop for all welfare, physical and mental health needs (Figure 10.1).

Veterans F1rst Point: The Lothian service

Veterans F1rst Point (V1P) (Lothian) is a service currently funded by the Mental Health and Protection of Rights Division of the Scottish Government and NHS Lothian. Staff are employed by the NHS and follow NHS policies and procedures. V1P was created in 2009 in response to the self-identified needs of veterans. In 2007, an advisory group made up of veterans with experience of using NHS mental health services was established to design a new model of service provision for this population. From some scribbled notes of an ex-soldier and the aspirations of NHS staff, the vision of V1P was conceived.

The V1P model has three core principles of credibility, accessibility and co-ordination driving its ethos. Credibility comes from our appointment of veterans (or those with experience of military life such as family members) to the post of peer support worker. Our mental health team comprises clinical psychologists,

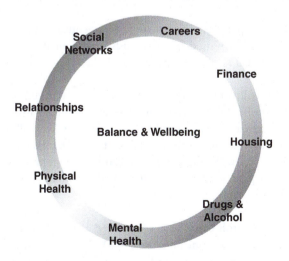

FIGURE 10.1 Balance and wellbeing.

psychological therapists and psychiatrists offering a range of evidence based approaches. Co-ordination is through the caseworker role of the peer support workers who make referrals to the in-house clinical team if appropriate and to partners in the NHS and veteran sector. Four of these partner organisations (Citizens Advice Scotland, Veterans UK, Edinburgh Housing Advice Partnership and Edinburgh Access Practice) provide clinics on a regular basis from our base and many more provide regular talks, training and information to clients and staff. Accessibility for our clients has been improved by our choice of city centre locations, which are relatively anonymous in being off NHS sites and easily accessible by public transport. Throughout the duration of the project, over 50 per cent of clients self-refer, this is facilitated by a 'drop-in' run by a peer support worker from our base between 1pm and 4.30pm each week day. The success of the V1P model was recognised by the Military and Civilian Health Partnership Awards with the service winning four awards over successive years for Care of Veterans (2012), Mental Health (2012), Civilian of the Year (2013) and Health Improvement and Promotion (2014). In 2013, V1P was a winner in the NHS Lothian Celebrating Success awards recognising Partnership in Practice.

Veterans F1rst Point Scotland

In 2010, Murrison's 'Fighting Fit' report advocated the need for services for veterans to be designed differently to reduce the stigma that often deters servicemen and veterans from engaging with conventional mental health provision (Murrison, 2010). The aftercare available as a veteran should be as close to home as possible to maximise engagement. In 2013, at V1P Lothian, one-third of all veterans referred to the service resided outside the Lothian area or were of no fixed abode. Some veterans travelled weekly over 250 miles to attend the V1P service (Lothian), where they felt they would receive a service that could understand and respond appropriately to their needs.

Based on the need for more geographically accessible services in Scotland, combined with the success of the V1P Lothian model, the Scottish Government outlined in Commitment 34 of the Mental Health Strategy 2010–15 that:

> [The Scottish government] will continue to fund the Veterans F1rst Point service and explore roll out of a hub and spoke model on a regional basis, recognising that other services are already in place in some areas. We will collaborate with the NHS and Veterans Scotland in taking this work forward and will also explore with Veterans Scotland how we can encourage more support groups and peer-to-peer activity for veterans with mental health problems.

In line with this commitment, the Scottish Government supported a co-ordinated bid to the Armed Forces Community Covenant Fund in 2013. V1P was awarded the largest donation from the Armed Forces covenant for any individual venture.

A total of £2.4 million was allocated to roll out the V1P model to other areas of Scotland. The initial plan was to develop three additional centres, but due to overwhelming enthusiasm from health boards in Scotland and the dedication of the V1P staff and clients, we have now established a network of eight V1P services across Scotland (Ayrshire and Arran, Borders, Fife, Grampian, Highland, Lanarkshire, Lothian and Tayside) with a supportive research, training and co-ordination hub.

The V1P Scotland Network offers the opportunity for joint training and supervision on an individual and group basis for peer support workers and clinicians working in the sector. In line with the recommendations of the Ashcroft report (2014), the Veterans Scotland team will also help to 'bring together peer-reviewed academic research about veterans and transition [in Scotland], ensuring information is easy to access and identifying gaps for further research'.

Veteran focus group findings (2015)

Despite the changing profile of the veteran population in Scotland, recent veteran focus groups mirror many of the findings of the early focus groups in 2007. Seven health boards (Ayrshire and Arran, Borders, Fife, Forth Valley, Grampian, Highland and Lanarkshire) and 32 veterans were involved in these focus groups (Figure 10.2). The following themes were identified:

Accessibility: Veterans described a theme around wanting smoother access to help and assistance:

> I had to wait about a year for it, but my GP knew what I was suffering from so they kept an eye on me ... every two weeks' [waiting times for specialist therapy, not with Veterans F1rst Point].
> I think geographically it needs to be in a good area, close to all sorts of train routes and bus routes, and that sort of thing.

Co-ordination: Veterans described wanting to have staff support their plans in the short, medium and long term as efficiently as possible:

> Retraining, resettlement ... for me anyway, they're not the kind of courses that work ... so if there was resettlement, somebody was going to learn to drive, a placement maybe with the company, or a company would be prepared to take them on.

Credibility: Veterans described wanting services that understood the experiences and needs of the veteran community:

> It took nearly five weeks to explain how the military worked. How I injured myself, how I was medically discharged ... I just felt like I wasn't getting anywhere at all with him.

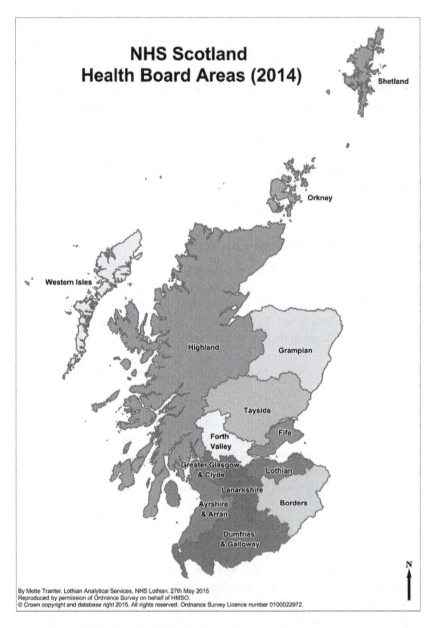

FIGURE 10.2 NHS Scotland Health Board areas (2014).

The Veterans Journey and help-seeking behaviour: Veterans described the stigma associated with seeking help and barriers to approaching services and how families and veteran peers can be helpful:

> People stepping forward and asking for help, they think that other people see that as a weakness and that was my biggest problem. Once I actually asked

for help and I started moving forward and it was like, it was a really big step for me to actually ask for help to start with.

As long as they [families/partners] get the right information to help us then that could be a good supportive thing.

Implications of these themes for development of services

These themes appear to confirm what the Lothian Veterans Group identified, which underpinned the development of V1P (Lothian). They link to themes of the need for more credibility, accessibility and co-ordination of veterans' services. All of which will be offered within the newly formed V1P network.

Helping veterans: Whatever their needs may be

Public definitions of who constitutes a 'veteran' reflect traditional 'warrior' imagery, such as deployment on operations (21 per cent) and combat (18 per cent). Only 2 per cent of the British population have awareness of the Ministry of Defence (MoD) official definition of a 'veteran' as anyone that has served a minimum of one day in the Armed Forces (Hines *et al.*, 2015). Research also indicates that it is the early service leaver (ESL) that is one of the most vulnerable groups. The ESL is also the largest group. In 2009 to 2010, over half of those leaving the military had served fewer than four years (Forces in Mind Trust and The Futures Company, 2013). Lord Ashcroft (2014) recommends that MoD policy is changed so that those personnel who complete basic training are entitled to the full resettlement support package. This would ensure that those most vulnerable are offered more assistance.

Lord Ashcroft (2014) however also recommends that we 're-examine the definition of the term "veteran" and refine the criteria to produce an acceptable qualification with greater credibility and exclusivity'. At V1P, we accept the current definition, despite its limitations, because whilst we are a veteran's service we are also an NHS organisation. As such, we work to the ideal that 'good healthcare should be available to all, regardless of wealth, that it meet the needs of everyone, that it be free at the point of delivery and that it be based on clinical need, not ability to pay'. Therefore, if a veteran who failed to complete basic training due to injury approaches our service, we will welcome them in the same way as any other veteran. Males generally in the 40 to 50 age range, and even more specifically, the veteran group, are less likely to approach medical establishments for assistance. The NHS wants to reduce stigma as a barrier to engagement in care. If a 'veteran' feels more comfortable approaching a veteran service than a mainstream establishment then we will help at point of need.

As a service model, we have moved away from the historic perception of the 'worthy soldier'. Those without a full and decorated military history are arguably least likely to engage with services if they view the cause of their injury as unworthy of support. Therefore, rather than transfer veterans to other local services V1P responds to veteran needs whatever they may be, regardless of where, or for how long they have served. In accordance with the MoD official definition of veteran, anyone who has served their country for a day or more is eligible for the V1P service.

What are the needs of our veterans?

Most veterans transition well into civilian life and become valuable members of the workforce. However, in 2014 to 2015, V1P (Lothian) conducted 187 new registrations and of these:

- 80% described their living situation as unstable
- 45% had described themselves as being homeless at some point in their lives
- 25% of referrals had relationship difficulties and were currently separated or divorced
- 81% requested a clinical assessment for mental health concerns

These statistics suggest that we need to do more for vulnerable soldiers in transition. As a service, we work closely with the Personnel Recovery Unit (PRU) and recently began attending pre-discharge meetings to help in the planning for the resettlement of wounded, injured and sick (WIS) personnel.

Peer support

The Peer Support Team leads many aspects of the service and their knowledge and skills are vital. Every veteran or family member is allocated to a peer support worker's caseload following referral and invited for what we call a 'registration'. This is an overview of need and the initial development of a care plan across welfare (housing, finance, employment, social relations and activities), physical and mental health. We liaise with military services to confirm veteran status and request service documents for those accessing the clinical team. Support comes through individual appointments, a daily drop-in service and a range of social activities including music, gardening and walking groups. We have good links into the specialist veteran provision available through the aforementioned charities. As well as our colleagues in the statutory and third sectors, V1P has established links with MoD Welfare Services and the PRU, allowing earlier identification and more seamless integration of support when service personnel leave the military. Prison 'in-reach' is provided to local Edinburgh and Addiewell prisons to help with 'secondary transition'. By working on both welfare and mental health issues, service users can receive holistic support on the major aspects of their lives.

The current service team, when asked to provide an overview of their role, its challenges and opportunities, cited:

- The potential for role-modelling transition and appearing as a bridge to civilian life

- Close involvement with the clinical team means they are knowledgeable about and well equipped to work with a range of mental health needs
- Our stance of any veteran, any need, allows us to work with the small population who can be denied access to other agencies due to their current risk to self or others and their forensic history
- Clients (who are not as the media portrays) who need boundaries and appropriate role models
- A wide range of group activities is important in order to engage with those who find social situations difficult or for whom psychological therapy is not appropriate
- Close links to the military (for instance, access to military documents) are helpful

Housing

Access to veterans housing is good in Scotland, although social housing is vastly oversubscribed. Unfortunately, those veterans with housing tend to reside in Lothian's most deprived areas, suggesting that those leaving the military are likely to enter a more deprived lifestyle than their age-matched civilian peers. It remains encouraging however that the V1P model is managing to engage those with more chaotic and unstable lifestyles.

With regard to housing advice, one of the significant challenges for peer support workers is helping veterans to understand the housing legislation in each council area, as outlined by the Veterans Commissioner:

> Housing is a devolved matter in Scotland, which means there is a markedly different system of legislation, policy and service provision than found in the rest of the UK. Under a concordat between the Scottish Government and its thirty-two Local Authorities, Scottish Ministers are responsible for setting the direction of policy and over-arching outcomes that the public sector in Scotland is expected to achieve. Each Council has responsibility for service design, resourcing and delivery. Adding to this complexity is the fact that many Local Authorities own and manage the allocation of their own housing stock but others, such as Glasgow, have transferred all of their housing to associations or Registered Social Landlords (RSLs). As a result of these disparities, Service Leavers and their families are immediately faced with the challenge of understanding how the local 'system' works in their area (as opposed to the rest of the UK), how they should interact with their Local Authority (or housing association) and what sort of response they can expect. The problem for many is that each Council has quite different ways of conducting its business and often uses a range of criteria for allocating houses. Where housing stock has been transferred, each housing association may well have its own allocation policy and application process – all potentially adding further confusion and complexity.

As well as these organisational differences in Scotland there are also distinctive legislative and regulatory frameworks which can muddy the waters for Service Leavers whose understanding – if any – is more likely to be based on the system found in England. Some of these differences can offer benefits and opportunities, which may be significant and need to be highlighted to any Service Leavers choosing to settle in Scotland. Notwithstanding, there is also is a clear and immediate requirement to ensure all personnel, wherever they are based, are aware of the different frameworks that exist. This includes the impact of homeless legislation and the availability of shared equity schemes operating in Scotland. Ability to access these opportunities will depend on the availability, accuracy and relevance of the information provided to those going through the transition process.

(*Eric Fraser, Transition Review*)

Finance

One of the most significant concerns for veterans approaching V1P are financial difficulties. The Scottish charitable sector offers a range of support to veterans and their families. The Armed Services Advice Project (ASAP) is a Citizen Advice Scotland project initiative funded by Poppy Scotland and offers advice specifically to ex-military personnel. In Lothian, we have had a dedicated Citizen Advice Bureau representative who works closely with partners and staff in-house. The following offers an anonymised case example of a bereaved widow.

Sophie was referred to the CAB clinic at Veterans F1rst Point by her Peer Support Worker due to worries about debts. Sophie's husband served in the British Army but passed away due to cancer. Since his death, she was struggling to manage financially – particularly after the reduction in her benefits since her son left school. She gets her late husband's pension which was arranged through Veterans UK. In addition, she receives minimum fortnightly benefits and was having money deducted from her but wasn't sure why. Her rented property is damp and she has some rent arrears after withholding the rent as a protest for non-attendance to repairs. She had agreed a small repayment plan with her landlord but stopped paying this as she says she could no longer afford it.

Pauline explained that her late husband's pension will be taken into account when calculating benefits and agreed to find out what the deductions were for. Pauline did a benefit check and confirmed she would be entitled to more money after taking the pension into account and before any debt repayments. The importance of making payments towards rent arrears to avoid eviction was emphasised. Pauline agreed to contact the benefit debt management to establish what the deductions from benefit were for and to see if the deduction can be reduced. She asked Sophie to complete expenditure forms to submit with a reduced offer.

After Sophie had gone, CAB contacted her landlord who explained the rent statement and confirmed the arrears were not as much as the client thought. Pauline negotiated a reduced payment plan towards arrears. She then wrote to DWP debt management, enclosing the client's financial statement to request reduction of benefit deductions. They later confirmed that the deductions were for arrears of council tax and an overpayment of JSA in April-July 2014 and agreed to reduce the deductions.

Pauline agreed to discuss with the client's peer support worker as there was the possibility of SSAFA helping out with debts. She discussed the case with the PSW, who spoke with Sophie which led to disclosure of more debt. An application had been made to SSAFA for household items from Argos and a further application would be made to SSAFA for help with debts later.

CAB wrote to the client to advise her that she had managed to reduce the deductions from her benefits and advised her to discuss with her landlord how she could make payments towards rent arrears. CAB agreed to see her at a further appointment for a review.

Employment

At V1P, we are continually listening to the needs of veterans in Scotland and responding to their developing needs. The MoD Transition Team means that the majority of recent service leavers do not require assistance finding employment and are regarded as valuable additions to their new civilian teams. However, as a service treating those with more complex social or health backgrounds, the employment search can be more difficult.

Only one-third of veterans registering at V1P Lothian have paid employment of any kind. More encouragingly, over 90 per cent have had some form of civilian employment since discharge but have not been able to sustain this. These figures suggest that our client group requires more assistance in finding, securing and retaining employment opportunities.

Many charitable services have been providing exemplary services for veterans in Scotland. We are a regular referrer to 'Employ-Able', a joint initiative between Poppy Scotland and Scottish Association for Mental Health (SAMH). However, research also suggests that providing advice in one place through an integrated service for healthcare and employment support has been found to be more efficient and delivers successful outcomes (Leopper, 2006).

According to the literature, there is a very positive impact of supporting prison leavers into employment, such as offering hope of recovery and re-entry into society (Hammond, 2007), providing ex-prisoners with a valued role in society, an increase in self-belief and self-efficacy (Forste, 2011) and an increased motivation to better manage health conditions (Tschopp, 2011). Arguably the same principles apply to those service personnel transitioning from the military into the civilian community.

V1P (Lothian) are trialling the individual placement support (IPS) model within the team between February 2016 and February 2017. IPS is a vocational rehabilitation intervention for people with severe mental disabilities. IPS draws from components and philosophies of several other models. Employment specialists now form part of the team, provide services both in the centre and in the community. IPS emphasises client preferences, rapid job finding, continuous assessment, competitive employment, integrated work settings and follow-along individualised supports.

Mental health

The mental health team at V1P Lothian includes psychiatry, clinical psychology and psychological therapists. This range of expertise offers flexibility in terms of assessment and treatment approaches. Individual and group psychological therapy approaches offered include cognitive behavioural therapy (CBT), acceptance and commitment therapy (ACT), cognitive analytic therapy (CAT) and compassion focused therapy, as well as interpersonal therapy (IPT). We also offer specialised approaches to treating trauma (both post-traumatic stress disorder [PTSD] and complex PTSD), including all of those already cited with the addition of trauma focused CBT (including prolonged exposure) and eye movement desensitisation and reprocessing (EMDR). We are able to offer long-term flexible approaches that can promote engagement, recovery and include those whose lifelong experience has often been harsh.

It is important to note that the system, based approach employed in the clinical team is service-wide and that the range of supports through peer support are crucial to providing help. A key part of the clinician's role is disseminating knowledge of psychological theory and learning from peers about the military experience of their clients. The team has regular formulation sessions to discuss the factors leading to the client's current difficulties and develop a detailed treatment plan. Discussing clients in this way enables the team to begin to predict issues within the therapeutic relationship rather than simply exploring them retrospectively after difficulties have arisen (Dunn and Parry, 1997). The reformulation also helps develop the team approach rather than individual workers acting independently (Ryle and Kerr, 2002).

Two brief case studies may help illustrate this:

Jack

Jack was a 22-year-old man who was referred by his general practitioner (GP) to V1P in November 2014. His GP was concerned about depressive symptoms, and described him as a bit 'lost' since leaving military service three months previously. His employment and relationships were affected by his low mood.

Jack had five years' service with a Scottish regiment as a private soldier including two tours of Afghanistan and chose 'Premature Voluntary Release'.

Jack did not attend his first offer of a registration but attended the next available appointment and was seen for clinical assessment within the month. He was diagnosed with an adjustment disorder and offered a course of CBT (an approach with a good evidence base for working with anger (Saini, 2009) to address, in the first instance, anger outbursts that had resulted in several court appearances for assaults. Anger is a common symptom among military populations (Forbes *et al.*, 2008; Elbogen *et al.*, 2012) and is a frequent component of mental health disorders, often comorbid with other diagnoses (Rona *et al.*, 2015). These co-existing problems increase risk of offending and violence. In Jack's case, the presentation of anger was with mild depressive symptoms that were treated as a secondary concern.

At the beginning of March, he attended drop-in in crisis having been suspended from work and having split up with his girlfriend. He reported nightmares which had not been part of his experience before and he was waking up from these. He was seen jointly by his peer support worker and assessing clinician who advised contact with his GP. It was agreed that he would return to his mother's as a place of safety and he was offered a follow-up appointment the next day.

On attending the next day, Jack explained that his GP had signed him off work and mentioned PTSD to him. This was presumably after disclosure of nightmares about military service. He was referred for accommodation with Scottish Veterans Residencies (SVR) and encouraged to attend his first session of CBT the following week. At the initial therapy session, he reported having been dismissed from work and talked of his anxiety and a concern over his difficulty controlling his levels of aggression. This aggression had unfortunately led to community service and another pending court case. At the second therapy session, the therapist discussed his angry responses in the context of a formulation that included his early life experiences and childhood development in relation to his parents' personalities. The mixture of anxiety from his mother and anger from father was obvious to him. His recent anger was out of character and represented a frustration in adjusting to his role in a civilian workforce and some change in definition from soldier to civvy.

By the third therapy session, he was in SVR accommodation and using breathing relaxation and 'worry time' to manage his anxiety and agitation. The nightmares had stopped and he was discussing training and employment so we referred him to a Poppy Scotland SAMH project called 'Employ-able' which specialises in helping veterans into training and employment.

His last session found him back to a fitness regime and considering moving back in with his girlfriend with whom he had a holiday planned. He described his previously disturbing images as 'just a memory'.

Reflections on Jack's case

This case highlights a number of the strengths of the service model with its system-based approach and quick response to crisis. Our partnerships within the veteran sector are also crucial to providing stability. It also mentions the difficulty faced by some GPs – and indeed other clinicians and professionals in general – in recognising trauma symptoms that can often be manifestations of a more general stress. During the last year, of the 187 veterans registered with V1P Lothian, 60 per cent explained that they had previously received a diagnosis of PTSD, mainly from their GP (44 per cent). PTSD has, in recent years, become the most common diagnosis at V1P

Lothian, but our figures would suggest rates are much lower than this (19 per cent). This suggests some confusion of the nature of the veteran's mental health condition for both professionals and veterans themselves.

Donald

Donald was referred to V1P by his GP. He presented with heavy alcohol use and he was self-isolating due to a lack of trust in his relationships. He also had paranoia and was suspicious of others. Recently, his paranoia had led to some violent altercations with short custodial sentences.

He was assessed initially and did not feel ready to engage in clinical work due to his belief that the accommodation was the priority issue. He viewed his paranoia about his neighbours as justified and there was potentially some degree of truth in this given the neighbourhood in which he lived. At formulation, the team agreed for the peer support worker to explore accommodation options prior to commencing therapy. They would also increase social activities and networks that did not involve alcohol, which he was using due to a strong social pressure.

Donald commenced therapy once these issues had been resolved. At this point, he had been allocated alternative accommodation and had developed a sound and meaningful relationship with his peer support worker. He engaged in regular hill walks, art and music activities. Despite these improvements, the anger, anxiety and paranoia persisted. Due to the nature of his interpersonal difficulties with others, he was allocated to a therapist for 16 sessions of CAT to focus on anger, relationships and development of self after his divorce. CAT has a sound evidence base particularly for interpersonal difficulties and complex trauma (Brockman *et al.*, 1987).

He disclosed, in therapy, that he had suffered significant early abuse. As a result, he had internalised specific roles for himself as 'weak' and 'scum'. He had worked hard to overcome this with his military career and marriage. After his discharge from the military, and his recent divorce, he had reverted to these pre-existing roles. He was trying to prove himself as worthy through violent altercations and had learnt that relationships were not to be trusted. Therapy helped him to identify the roles and procedures that he had reverted to in his life. He used alcohol to give him courage for social interactions and to numb the emotional pain. His peer worker and therapist modelled a trusting relationship for him that helped him move on.

Donald displayed significant improvements in the CORE-OM (a well validated 34-item generic measure of psychological distress) and he was engaging in better relationships both at V1P and with partner organisations he was referred on to for training and work opportunities. He was better able to respond to conflict assertively rather than by using violence and he had entirely given up alcohol.

Reflections on Donald's case

Donald's case highlights the service's strengths in terms of being able to stage and time interventions to meet the individuals' needs. It is this balance within the team of peer support and clinicians that allows that to happen. The relationship with Donald's peer support worker was key for his engagement in therapy and the success of our work with him. In the last 12 months in V1P Lothian, over 90 per cent of veterans attended their clinical assessment. We feel that this is testament to the relationship and support they receive throughout their journey from peer support workers.

Donald is not alone in his difficulties with alcohol and in this case, as with many others, we had close links with the local alcohol problem service. A number of UK studies have shown that serving personnel drink more than civilians (Fear *et al.*, 2007; Jones and Fear, 2011), but few studies have examined the long-term risks to veterans' health. The Scottish Veterans Health Study, a retrospective cohort study of 57,000 veterans who served between 1960 and 2012 and 173,000 people with no record of service, matched for age, sex and area of residence, conducted at the University of Glasgow, has provided an insight into long-term alcohol-related outcomes (Bergman *et al.*, 2015). The study showed that overall, veterans were at lower risk of alcoholic liver disease or alcohol-related death than non-veterans, after taking deprivation into account, although the risk was increased in veterans born between 1945 and 1949, especially if they had been older when they joined the Armed Forces and if they had entered service at a time of high-operational activity, as in the early 1970s.

This pattern was not seen, however, in more recent veterans. Those who left prematurely (ESLs) were also at increased risk, but only if they had entered trained service; there was no increase in risk for people who left before completing basic training, and those who had served for longest were similarly at no greater risk than non-veterans. Despite documented high levels of alcohol consumption in service, it is perhaps the most vulnerable who are predominantly at risk of heavy drinking that persists for long enough to cause long-term harm. Therefore, we would hope that Donald will not have long-term consequences of his significant alcohol use.

Conclusion

The veteran population is significant to the wider Scottish perspective and many veterans and their families are integrated into civilian life. For some, challenges remain, as they will for future veterans. A great deal has been done by the charitable sector, the NHS, the Veterans Commissioner and Veterans Scotland to improve the confusing network of over 400 support organisations available to veterans and their families. Unfortunately, as the recent focus groups illustrate, we all too often hear veterans describing that they have been bounced between services because their difficulties do not meet referral criteria. It is also common to hear that clinicians do not have confidence in treating the complex needs of this client group and that often veterans are unable to engage in mental healthcare and treatment because of other welfare difficulties in their lives.

In this chapter, we celebrate a new model for services that develops meaningful and lasting relationships with clients, works with partners to improve care and treats the individual rather than simply the diagnosis. We acknowledge the help of all our partners in this. We hope that the V1P network, which launched in March 2016, will help to provide improved co-ordination of care, better training for staff regarding the needs of the veteran population and a better understanding of the client group. We would like to thank all the V1P team for their input into this chapter which, like all our work together, was a collaborative team effort.

References

Ashcroft, M. (2014). *The Veterans' Transition Review*. London: Biteback Publishing.

Ashworth, J., Hudson, M., Malam, S. (2014). Health and welfare of the ex-Service community in Scotland 2014. *A Poppy Scotland Supplement to the Royal British Legion Report. A UK Household Survey of the Ex-Service Community 2014*. Edinburgh: Poppyscotland. Available online at www.britishlegion.org.uk/media/2274/poppyscotland-household-survey-report-final.pdf (accessed 20 January 207).

Bergman, B.P., Mackay, D.F., Pell, J.P. (2015). Long-term consequences of alcohol misuse in Scottish military veterans. *Occupational and Environmental Medicine*, 72, 28–32.

Brockman, B., Poynton, A., Ryle, A., Watson, J.P. (1987). Effectiveness of time-limited therapy carried out by trainees. *British Journal of Psychiatry*, 151, 602–10.

Dunn, M., Parry, G. (1997). A reformulated care plan approach to caring for people with borderline personality disorder in a community mental health service setting. *Clinical Psychology Forum*, 104, 19–22.

Elbogen, E.B., Johnson, S.C., Newton, V.M., Straits-Troster, K., Vasterling, J.J., Wagner, H.R., Beckham, J.C. (2012). Criminal justice involvement, trauma, and negative affect in Iraq and Afghanistan war era veterans. *Journal of Consulting and Clinical Psychology*, 80, 1097–102.

Fear, N.T., Iversen, A., Meltzer, H., Workman, L., Hull, L., Greenberg, N., Barker, C., Browne, T., Earnshaw, M., Horn, O., Jones, M., Murphy, D., Rona, R., Hotopf, M., Wessely, S. (2007). Patterns of drinking in the UK Armed Forces. *Addiction*, 102, 1749–59.

Forbes, D., Parslow, R., Creamer, M., Allen, N., McHugh, T., Hopwood, M. (2008). Mechanisms of anger and treatment outcome in combat veterans with posttraumatic stress disorder. *Journal of Traumatic Stress*, 21, 142–9.

Forces in Mind Trust and The Futures Company (2013). *The Transition Mapping Study. Understanding the Transition Process for Service Personnel Returning to Civilian Life*. Available online at www.fim-trust.org/wp-content/uploads/2015/01/20130810-TMS-Report.pdf (accessed 6 October 2015).

Forste, R., Clarke, L., Bahr, S. (2011). Staying out of trouble: Intentions of young male offenders. *International Journal of Offender Therapy and Comparative Criminology*, 55, 430–44.

Fraser, E. (2015). *Scottish Veterans Commissioner: Transition in Scotland Report*. Edinburgh: Scottish Government. Available online at www.gov.scot/Resource/0047/00474235.pdf (accessed 6 October 2015).

Hammond, J. (2007). Criminal justice mental health and employment. *A Life in the Day*, 11, 16–18.

Hines, L.A., Gribble, R., Wessely, S., Dandeker, C., Fear, N.T. (2015). Are the Armed Forces understood and supported by the public? A View from the United Kingdom. *Armed Forces and Society*, 41, 688–713.

Jones, E., Fear, N.T. (2011). Alcohol use and misuse within the military: A review. *International Review of Psychiatry*, 23, 166–72.

Leopper, R. (2006). Integrating health care into the one-stop system for workforce development as a safety net for ex-offenders. *American Journal of Public Health*, 96, 1147.

Murrison, A. (2010). *Fighting Fit: A Mental Health Plan for Servicemen and Veterans*. London: Ministry of Defence. Available online at www.gov.uk/government/uploads/system/uploads/attachment_data/file/27375/20101006_mental_health_Report.pdf (accessed 8 May 2013).

Pozo, A., Walker, C (2014). *UK Armed Forces Charities: An Overview and Analysis*. London: Directory of Social Change.

Rona, R.J., Jones, M., Hull, L., MacManus, D., Fear, N.T., Wessely, S. (2015). Anger in the UK Armed Forces: Strong association with mental health, childhood antisocial behaviour, and combat role. *The Journal of Nervous and Mental Disease*, 203, 15–22.

Ryle, A. and Kerr, I.B. (2002). The 'difficult' patient and contextual reformulation. In Ryle, A., Kerr, I.B. (eds.), *Introducing Cognitive Analytic Therapy. Principles and Practice*. Wiley: Chichester, pp. 202–13.

Saini, M. (2009). A meta-analysis of the psychological treatment of anger: Developing guidelines for evidence-based practice. *The Journal of the American Academy of Psychiatry and the Law*, 37, 473–88.

Tschopp, M.K., Perkins, D.V., Wood, H., Leczycki, A., Oyer, L. (2011). Employment considerations for individuals with psychiatric disabilities and criminal histories: Consumer perspectives. *Journal of Vocational Rehabilitation*, 35, 129–41.

11

THE ROLE OF THE THIRD SECTOR CHARITY COMBAT STRESS

An Update

Walter Busuttil

Introduction

Combat Stress is the leading British national third sector charity specialising in veterans' mental health. It works in strategic partnership with the Department of Health, Ministry of Defence, The Royal British Legion (TRBL) and Help for Heroes. Combat Stress also works closely with many other military charities.

Combat Stress is a service provider delivering mental healthcare collaboratively with the NHS and other veterans' charities in a day to day basis. Combat Stress attracts help-seeking veterans, who are the neediest in terms of mental illness. They most commonly suffer from post-traumatic stress disorder (PTSD), which is present with co-morbid illness such as depression and alcohol misuse disorders. Clinical services provided are based in the community and in three residential centres across the United Kingdom, and they are designed to maximise access and engagement into treatment. This chapter will describe these clinical services delivered by multidisciplinary clinicians.

Combat Stress: The charity and service provider

From 1919, Combat Stress has helped over 120,000 veterans suffering from mental health illness. Combat Stress sees veterans who have served in all wars from, and including, the Second World War. The oldest veteran accessing services is aged 97 and the youngest is 19 years-old.

Combat Stress operates three residential treatment centres with 87 beds, allowing residential intervention programmes to be delivered. It also operates 15 community services across the United Kingdom and outpatient services. It is registered with the Care Quality Commission and its equivalent in the devolved governments and operates within a Clinical Governance Framework.

The need

Patterns of referral to Combat Stress over the past 20 years have been the subject of a recent study (Murphy *et al.*, 2015a). Numbers coming forward for help have increased steadily over the past 20 years. A fourfold increase in the number of referrals received each year over the duration of the study period was observed. Over the study period, the time it took for participants to seek help after they left the military reduced by a half. In the past eight years, there has been an acceleration in numbers coming forward for help. This is thought to be due to the wars in Afghanistan and Iraq, which have highlighted the plight of veterans suffering from mental health disorders. In March 2015, there were 5,954 active veterans receiving help from Combat Stress compared with 5,473 in March 2014. This represented a 9 per cent increase in numbers. During that year, Combat Stress discharged 1,168 veterans after intervention. In the financial year 2014 to 2015, there was a 26 per cent increase in new referrals. This was the largest increase recorded for Combat Stress, up to 2,328 from 1,854.

In the financial year 2015 to 2016, the numbers in new referrals rose to 2472, or an increase of a further 6 per cent over the previous year. These large increases in veterans coming forward for help was mainly accounted for, once more, by veterans who served in Iraq and Afghanistan, although other veteran era groups such as those who served in Northern Ireland, the Balkans and/or the First Gulf War, for example, are still coming forward for the first time. Veterans who served in Northern Ireland remain the largest group accessing care. Until March 2014, this group was followed by those who served in the Balkans and the First Gulf War. However, the Iraq group overtook the Balkans and then in November 2014, Afghanistan veterans reached the third commonest operational group. During the period, April 2014 to April 2015, the increase in new Afghanistan veterans asking for help grew by 57 per cent on the previous year (Murphy *et al.*, 2015a).

The recent sharp increase in the overall numbers of veterans seeking support for mental health difficulties in recent years of 26 per cent over the previous year is thought to reflect a 'period effect', with individuals more willing to seek help sooner now than in the past. For example, veterans from Iraq and Afghanistan are seeking help more quickly than veterans from previous conflicts. The study findings suggest that there will continue to be an increase in the numbers of veterans seeking support for mental health difficulties over the coming years (Murphy *et al.*, 2015a).

Overall, the average time lag for veterans, from the time when they leave the military to the time when they access help from Combat Stress, has been reducing from an average of 14 years in 2007 to 13.2 years in 2015. The evidence is that veterans from Afghanistan and Iraq wars present earlier than expected, as compared with veterans from earlier conflicts. Those from Afghanistan and Iraq are presenting at an average of 2.2 and 4.8 years respectively after leaving the military, in contrast to an average of 13.2 years for those veterans involved in all other conflicts and wars (van Hoorn *et al.*, 2013; Murphy *et al.*, 2015a).

This may reflect better education in the military about mental health matters, the effect of pre- and post-deployment mental health training, the introduction of a 'trauma risk management' process (TRiM) within the military since 2005 and better awareness of family members of mental health issues linked to military service, as well as better knowledge and media promotion of the existence of the charity, Combat Stress, and the clinical and welfare services on offer (van Hoorn *et al.*, 2013).

Causes for delayed presentation include issues concerning stigma and the belief that the individual does not think they are ill and do not need help to solve their own problems. Many veterans accessing help from Combat Stress reported that they knew that they had problems while serving in the military, but that they felt unable to go for help because of fear of loss of their career, fear of ridicule and because they had tried to solve their own problems themselves – which is in keeping with the military culture (Scheiner, 2008; Murphy and Busuttil, 2014).

In recent years, Combat Stress has led the way with educational and media campaigns to try to reduce stigma surrounding veterans' mental illness. This was carried out through media campaigns (2012 to 2013), and advising and helping to set up and write e-learning packages posted on the Royal College of Psychiatrists' website and a separate one for the Royal College of General Practitioners' website, as well as many contributions to academic and other lower-key conferences and academic and veteran service user publications (Neville and Hacker Hughes, 2014; Murphy and Busuttil, 2014).

Those accessing help have also reduced in average age over the past years. In 2007, the average age of the veteran was 60 years, with many veterans having served in the Second World War. Currently, the average age of a veteran is 42.8 years (down from 44 years in 2008); 84 per cent of these are ex-Army, 7 per cent are ex-Royal Air Force, 6 per cent are ex-Royal Navy and 3 per cent are ex-Royal Marines. Female veterans account for around 3 per cent of the total. The under 65-year-old group accounts for 89 per cent of the population. Of these, 48 per cent are employed, 50 per cent are unemployed and 2 per cent are retired.

Clinical presentation

Combat Stress attracts a help-seeking population. Clinical (n = 604) and psychometric (n = 704) audits of new patients conducted between 2005 and 2009 demonstrated that 92 per cent were exposed to multiple military-related psychological traumas; with 75 per cent qualifying for a primary diagnosis of PTSD; with high co-morbid presentations, with 62 per cent also presenting with depression and 69 per cent with alcohol disorders; 52 per cent having other underlying issues, including exposure to childhood trauma, neglect and poor care giving, histories of isolation, social exclusion, social withdrawal, unemployment (with multiple episodes of unemployment being common), inadequate housing, multiple house moves, periods of homelessness, episodes of being in prison or in the criminal justice system and multiple marriages and relationships. Many frequently present with behavioural disorders manifested by anger and outbursts. These internal audits (Busuttil, 2009, 2010) have been verified independently (Welsh Affairs Committee, 2011; Wood *et al.*, 2011). The characteristics of veterans accessing NHS Veterans' networks and

TABLE 11.1 Mental health profile of new clinical referrals to Combat Stress, 2014

Health outcome	% (n = 425)
Post-traumatic stress disorder	79%
Depression	88%
Anxiety	79%
Anger problems	46%
Illicit drug misuse	44%
Functional impairment	13%
• Significant	25%
• Severe	64%

the mental health pilot sites are very similar indeed (Dent-Brown *et al.*, 2010). The Combat Stress clinical audits demonstrated that 80 per cent of new clinical cases have tried to access help through the NHS, but that for some reason, this help has either been inadequate, or not been delivered or the individual has failed to engage (Busuttil, 2009, 2010). The US veteran literature demonstrates that poor engagement rates in treatment, as well as poor completion of treatment rates, are a real risk in this hard to reach and difficult to treat population (Hoge *et al.*, 2006; Rosenheck and Fontana, 2007). The most recent Combat Stress audits, conducted in 2014, demonstrate similar levels of mental illness as well as compromised work and social function in new patients (Table 11.1).

Treatment philosophy

Combat Stress has adopted an evidence-based phasic treatment strategy with initial preparation which helps to ensure engagement into treatment services and the addressing of welfare needs and benefits; stabilisation and safety with appropriate assessment, appropriate prescription of psychotropic medication; and, if required, access to psychoeducation and skills training groups; followed by trauma focused psychotherapy which includes trauma focused-cognitive behaviour therapy (TF-CBT) and/or eye movement desensitisation and reprocessing (EMDR); a rehabilitation phase, with reintegration into society, followed by relapse prevention and maintenance. Treatment is delivered in a stepped-care model allowing those who are less severely unwell to be treated using less intense interventions with those who need most care receiving the most intensive interventions (Foa *et al.*, 2009; Herman, 1992; NICE, 2005; Busuttil 2012).

Services

Combat Stress has developed a repertoire of clinical services which include a national helpline, community and outreach, a community substance misuse case management service and outpatient, residential and rehabilitation services. Combat Stress is also formally linked with the King's Centre for Military Health for research purposes.

Combat Stress employs an average of 300 staff. Clinicians include consultant psychiatrists, psychologists, cognitive behaviour therapists, art therapists, occupational therapists, registered mental health nurses, community psychiatric nurses, welfare officers, nursing assistants and clinical governance administrators. The organisation has a clinical governance structure and is fully compliant with clinical service provider regulations.

Access and engagement

Self-referral is the most common source of referral. Referral sources are given in Table 11.2. As can be seen, self-referral accounts for 52 per cent of the total, with a further 3 per cent being referred by family members. It is usually the wife or partner of a male veteran who instigates the self-referral. Many veterans ask for help when they are in a crisis and at risk of losing their relationship, or after they have lost this. A further 4 per cent are referred through the Combat Stress website. The Combat Stress helpline is also a source of referrals, with 17 per cent of referrals being made through this route. Over the past 8 years, referrals from the medical profession have increased from 0 per cent to a total of 10 per cent (4 per cent from general practitioners [GPs] or consultant psychiatrists and 6 per cent from community mental health teams). Other military veteran-related organisations referred significant numbers in 2014 to 2015 with Soldiers Sailors and Airmen's Families Association (SSAFA) accounting for 3 per cent, TRBL (2 per cent), service welfare organisations (4 per cent) and war pensions welfare services (4 per cent). Of these initial referrals, an average of 59 per cent of enquires for help and information about the services offered convert to active cases which required intervention (Murphy *et al.*, 2015a).

Historically, referrals have been handled by the community team welfare desk officers who then used to process the administrative pathway into the service. This included contacting the GP and obtaining clinical records and referral information from the GP as required. A recent restructuring of the access to Combat Stress has seen the introduction of triage mental health nurses who are the initial point of contact. This is helping to speed up and prioritise referrals depending on clinical need and reduce waiting times. The GP is kept informed of their patient accessing care and is communicated with throughout the whole of the episode of care.

Table 11.2 Referral sources, 2014–2015

Self	52%
Relatives	3%
Combat Stress helpline	19%
Combat Stress website	3%
General practitioner and community mental health services	10%
War Pensions Agency (SPVA)	4%
Other military charities	9%

National helpline

The Combat Stress National Helpline was set up in 2012 and has historically received 800 calls a month. During 2014/2015, the number of contacts increased by 37 per cent to 11,807, including 2,347 new users to the service. The helpline is run in collaboration by the charity Rethink. Staff are trained in mental health. Callers are given support and advice and, in some cases, brief counselling and are signposted to clinical services as required. This helpline is available to the whole of the military community including serving personnel and their families as well as veterans and their families. One-quarter of those who call are serving personnel or their family members.

Community, outreach and outpatient services

Outpatient services offered by Combat Stress were set up in 2013. These operate in the treatment centres, primarily from purpose-designed outpatient suites. Clinics currently provide assessment and follow-up and review by psychiatrists and psychologists. Clinics are mainly geared to preparing and stabilising patients to access specialised group treatment interventions. Some patients are also followed up for prolonged periods.

Recently, clinics have also been run within the community to improve access for veterans. Clinics are now run regularly in Manchester, Exeter, Colchester, Glasgow and other cities and towns. More recently, these clinics have been running from the newly set up 'Pop In Centres' operated by our strategic partners, TRBL, and run in the high street. Total number of consultant psychiatrists' outpatient appointments attended by veterans in 2014 to 2015 was 2,342, with 808 joint psychiatric and psychological assessments performed.

Combat Stress initially set up community and outreach services in 2010 to compliment the welfare that was offered by 14 ex-military (regional) welfare officers. Currently, 15 community and outreach teams exist across Britain and Ireland. In each team, a regional welfare officer (RWO), who is an ex-military officer, has historically been the first point of contact. The military background of the welfare officer offers the veterans a sense of familiarity and this is thought to help break down the barriers of stigma and increase engagement of the veteran in to the service. The team includes community psychiatric nurses and occupational therapists who work with psychiatrists and psychologists who are based in the treatment centres but who also carry out outpatient community clinics.

The service has recently been restructured with the aim of improving access and engagement, service delivery and increasing the variety of interventions available. Interventions aim to improve function, reduce symptoms and to encourage veterans to take more personal responsibility and resilience.

With the new triage nurses in post, first point of contact will be the most appropriate clinician either in the community or outpatients. If the presenting issues are not clinical then the RWO will be the first point of contact. Therefore, all new veterans to the service will continue to be assessed for their clinical and welfare needs as a routine but that prioritisation of when, and by who, will occur at Triage. Each team receives support from an administrative officer who is the point of contact for the veteran, organises clinics and appointments and who also gives telephone advice about welfare issues.

A comprehensive mapping exercise documenting where veterans reside informed the location of the clinical hubs and spoke services. The restructuring of the outreach and community service coincided with the moving of psychiatric and psychology and psychotherapy outpatient clinics to the community. The community services and outpatient clinics are now situated in more accessible hub and spoke locations. This was done in collaboration with TRBL, as these clinics are operating from TRBL 'Pop In Centres' located in easily accessible places in the high street of many towns and cities.

The practice of visiting veterans at home is the domain of the RWO. This enables a welfare assessment to be performed in a meaningful way. Some clinical assessment and treatment is also delivered in the veterans' home. Historically, this practice has been difficult and time consuming. Until recently, a significant amount of clinical intervention was being delivered within the veterans' homes. Some group work was performed in premises loaned or hired through local arrangements. It is envisaged that the provision of services within fixed clinic bases increases access and the numbers receiving help and treatment. For those who are unable to travel to the hub and spoke clinics which have been set up, home visits may remain an option. For others, telemedicine projects are currently being explored. This is especially for those who have been seen face to face for some time, who know their therapist or mental health worker well enough and are stable enough to use this medium. The community service is now a clinic-based service to be used by clinicians primarily and outreach in the veterans' home is reserved for the RWOs, as well as for those veterans who are ill enough to warrant a home visit by clinical staff. This is in keeping with best practice in the USA for veterans' mental health (Brooks *et al.*, 2012). This pattern of work will depend on geography as well as need and will be available within cities as well as within rural areas. For those who live in remote areas and those who are so unwell that they cannot access the high street, other provision will be made including: home visits, admission to treatment centres; or the employment of local community sessional workers; or even in the future, the development and use of telemedicine (Brooks *et al.*, 2013; VHRA, 2011).

This development of clinics in TRBL buildings also allows the possibility of setting up a similar practice with the NHS with joint clinics running in NHS premises in the future.

Community services now offer assessment and one-to-one interventions. Group interventions include psychoeducation groups and, increasingly, skills training groups as well as 'one stop shop drop in days' where other ex-service charities are present. This system allows the veteran to access not only mental health interventions but also to be advised about their war pensions, welfare, housing and other needs. These group days also help with mentoring and retraining in partnership with other veterans' charities. Carers groups are also held in the community.

These deliver psychoeducation and support. Peer groups based on veterans' peer support groups, which have been running for some time in Holland and Canada (Weingarten, 2012; Richardson et al., 2008), are also being set up. Individual Trauma Focused therapies are delivered in outpatients where appropriate.

Alcohol and illicit drug case management programme

As has been seen from the clinical audits presented, co-morbid presentations are the norm in this help-seeking veteran population. Many veterans who are alcohol or drug dependent have underlying mental health disorders. Alcohol and drugs are commonly used to 'self-medicate' to reduce symptoms of PTSD such as emotional numbing, using 'uppers such as cocaine' or avoiding things such as using alcohol or cannabis (Busuttil, 2014).

Veterans who develop dependence disorders find it very difficult to receive successful treatment for any underlying mental health condition (Klein et al., 2013). For example, treatment for PTSD will usually include completing effective trauma focused therapy and for appropriate medications that may need have prescribed to work (Busuttil, 2014).

Depending on clinical assessment and need, they may be reviewed in Combat Stress consultant psychiatrist led outpatients' clinics where they will get help to reduce their intake gradually; alternatively, they may be referred to a detoxification programme delivered by the NHS or other statutory provider. The problem in the past was that many were not then returning to have their underlying mental health illness treated once they had had a detoxification, and hence, they did not engage with services designed to treat their underlying mental health disorders. Combat Stress recognised this as an increasing problem. As a result, Combat Stress has rolled out pilot services which are designed to case manage those who are addicted to alcohol or illicit substances. These Substance Misuse Case Management Services work in conjunction with statutory substance misuse services. They are run by addiction specialist nurses employed by Combat Stress. The nurses' case manage the individual into an appropriate detoxification service, and when this has been carried out, they are case managed assertively back into an appropriate clinical service for treatment of any underlying mental health disorder. This will then ensure that psychiatric assessment of any underlying mental health disorders and assertive engagement in the most appropriate mental health clinical service both statutory and those run by Combat Stress actually occurs. The pilots are being run in Wiltshire, Glasgow and Forth Valley, with services opening in Manchester and Portsmouth soon. Since this service started, many veterans have been able to engage with mental health services for the first time, after having been locked into addiction services in a revolving door for many years.

Residential programmes

Residential services provided by Combat Stress are delivered in three treatment centres: Hollybush House located in Ayrshire in Scotland, Audley Court in Newport in Shropshire and Tyrwhitt House based in Leatherhead. These residential centres are designed in a manner that is sensitive to military culture. There are defined living and work areas with rooms to relax and eat in, and group rooms and individual consulting rooms; each centre has an occupational therapy centre and art therapy work rooms. The treatment centres also host bespoke outpatient suites. There is an allowance for overnight assessment accommodation and multidisciplinary assessment for those who need it clinically, as well as offering overnight accommodation for those who live remotely geographically. Each centre is staffed by multidisciplinary teams including, psychiatrists, psychologists, occupational therapists, cognitive behaviour therapists, art psychotherapists and registered mental nurses and nursing assistants. A variety of treatment programmes are offered.

Short psychoeducation programmes, each lasting two weeks, are delivered at the treatment centres. These include a stabilisation programme that focuses on emotional regulation combining one-to-one therapy with psychoeducation group sessions using cognitive skills training. This programme is aimed at preparing the veteran for further treatment. An anger management programme designed to address anger generated through having been in combat is also on offer. This utilises cognitive behaviour therapy, mindfulness and distress tolerance skills training on a one-to-one and group therapy format. The transdiagnostic programme can be assessed by veterans with any diagnosis at any time along the clinical recovery pathway. This is a CBT skills focused group work programme again linked to individual therapy sessions. Symptom management is the main goal of this programme with the aim of enabling veterans to learn how to find alternative ways of coping with a variety of problems. This is a flexible programme allowing admission depending on need of between one and two weeks.

Two further short programmes are expected to be trialled shortly. These are both psychoeducation groups, for PTSD present with alcohol and illicit drug disorders, and PTSD present with chronic pain.

Individual therapy is also delivered on a case-by-case basis in outpatients and in a residential setting and a new project will also develop this further to be delivered by means of telemedicine, which will be especially useful for those living in remote areas (Brooks *et al.*, 2012, 2013).

Combat Stress runs a national residential Intensive Treatment Programme (ITP) for those veterans who are the most unwell. Combat Stress was awarded National Specialised Commissioning funds from NHS England in 2001 to deliver the ITP. The assessment of need audits referred to earlier identified that some 300 new veterans would require this intensive programme each year and led to the calculation that 224 would require it from England and 32 for each of the devolved governments. NHS Scotland also funds 32 places for veterans who live in Scotland. Northern Ireland and Wales have no funding arrangement in place and charity funds those who require this programme.

This programme caters for those veterans who have complicated clinical presentations and who have a primarily diagnosis of PTSD, which is present with co-morbid depression and a past or present history of alcohol and illicit drug disorders. The essential components of the programme are group psychoeducation and group skills training, and individual trauma focused cognitive behaviour therapy. Some 20, 90 minute sessions of this individual therapy are delivered. The format comprises eight patients, two therapists per session and closed groups. The programme is standardised across the treatment centres by means of staff training, manuals for both therapists and veterans. The programme runs between 9am and 5pm, five days per week. Homework is given and out of hours' work is guided by the occupational wellbeing programme. Family days are included in the programme schedule which allows psychoeducation of the close family.

There are strict inclusion and exclusion criteria: for example, patients must be able to undergo therapy and must not be drinking alcohol while on the programme. Dissociation, depression, self-harm and suicidality must be under control – usually these factors are stabilised beforehand in outpatients and the prescription of appropriate medication and removal of inappropriate medications accumulated over the years. Many are also stabilised by attending the shorter programmes beforehand, depending on their needs. There is also a stringent assessment protocol with each patient assessed by a psychiatrist and a psychologist and a multidisciplinary panel then deciding on these findings before a place is awarded on the programme. Those not quite making admission criteria are usually stabilised further in outpatients, or in the community or after attending further preparatory programmes as required. They are then put forward once more after they have progressed.

The evidence base for the programme is based on Australian Veterans Clinical Services, where 4,000 Vietnam War veterans suffering from complicated presentations of PTSD have been treated since the late 1990s using similar programmes (Creamer et al., 1999; Forbes et al., 2008). The programme has been running since September 2011, initially in Leatherhead. In September 2012, the programme was expanded to all treatment centres. The Australian outcomes by and large demonstrated a rule of thirds with one-third doing well at one-year follow-up and needing little help, one-third getting better and needing some help and one-third not doing so well and needing more help but less help overall compared with their initial presentation (Creamer et al., 1999; Forbes et al., 2008; Forbes and Creamer, 2003).

Combat Stress started to deliver the ITP programme at Tyrwhitt House in Leatherhead in September 2011. In September 2012, it was expanded to all our treatment centres. The outcomes of the Combat Stress intensive programme have been good with initial yearly clinical audits demonstrating a good uptake, low drop out of 15 per cent and objective and subjective psychometric measures demonstrating improved PTSD, depression, anxiety, anger, alcohol and dissociation. Function also improved (Busuttil and Hinton 2013).

A naturalistic outcome study has been published (Murphy *et al.*, 2015b). This followed up 246 successive veterans who accessed the ITP between late 2012 and early 2014 and who were followed up at six weeks and six months. The study demonstrated very high-engagement and high-completion rates (94 per cent), much higher than comparable US programmes, which demonstrated dropout rates of 22 per cent to 46 per cent. There was no difference detected in baseline outcomes between completers and non-completers. There was a high-response rate of 80 per cent responders at 6 months, with no evidence of differences between those who were followed up at 6 months and those lost to follow up. There were highly significant reductions in PTSD scores following treatment, on both clinician-completed measures and self-reported measures, with 87 per cent of participants reporting a reduction in PTSD symptoms, which was maintained over a 6-month follow-up period. This is in contrast to equivalent US studies, with a 49 per cent reduction in PTSD symptoms. Similar improvements in anxiety, depression, alcohol misuse and anger scores were demonstrated, with highly significant improvements in functional impairment which continued to improve between six weeks and six months' follow-up. The effect of chronicity was not a barrier to improvement with similar outcomes for those with very chronic illness versus those who suffered relatively low chronicity.

A separate study revealed that explored the relationships between baseline health and PTSD and functioning outcomes in veterans treated for PTSD using the ITP demonstrated that higher levels of baseline anxiety and dissociation were associated with worse post-treatment PTSD outcomes (Murphy and Busuttil, 2015). This suggests the importance of treating these difficulties in UK veterans before intervening for symptoms of PTSD. Another finding of this study was that hazardous drinking was not a predictor of poorer outcome. Other studies will be published soon including one-year follow-up outcomes, as well as a study that has explored the mental health needs of partners of those attending the ITP.

Wellbeing and recovery and social reintegration programme

As part of setting up the ITP, an occupational therapy (OT) led wellbeing programme was devised. This was initially designed to run at weekends and out of the hours of between 9am and 5pm for patients attending the ITP six-week programme. The initial thinking was that it allowed the individual to remain engaged, encouraged participation in OT led activities, including ensuring that essential skills such as shopping and cooking were in place, as well as allowing participation in OT exercises in the Combat Stress Activities Centres at the treatment centres. In addition, many patients are set 'homework tasks' during the six-week programme, and the wellbeing programme was designed to facilitate these behaviourally based tasks. For example, some patients require practice sessions of exposure therapy to difficult situations such as being in a crowd on a Saturday morning in a shopping centre.

Access to this wellbeing programme was initially only aimed at those attending the intensive six-week programme. It proved to be very popular and it was enhanced and expanded to allow participation of more patients including a subset of patients who had been attending the treatment centres for many years and who had not engaged in meaningful psychotherapy for various reasons, with a consequent lack of clinical and functional improvement.

As a result, a treatment pathway was developed for these patients that commences with a community OT intervention, a treatment centre-based wellbeing programme and is completed in a Breakaway Centre. A Breakaway Centre is a four-star hotel run by TRBL near the seaside. They are usually used for impoverished veterans and their families to go on holiday. TRBL has allowed Combat Stress to use these centres off peak season. An OT and registered mental health nurse led programme is run for veterans and their partners. This ten-day programme uses behavioural activation techniques and is a recovery and maintenance therapeutic intervention, allowing patients to further expose themselves to difficult situations, away from the treatment centre, with less staff support than otherwise. Therapeutic tools used include OT, skills training and symptom management. Veterans are encouraged to take personal responsibility for their own symptoms and situation. A clinical audit conducted between 2012 and 2014 on successive attendees (293 veterans and 47 of their spouses or partners [n=340]) demonstrated improved personal responsibility for their illness improved function: movement away from the sick role as demonstrated by psychometric measurement and clinical observation and adaptive functioning. A university-based outcome study relating to this programme is underway.

Research

In 2014, Combat Stress appointed a lecturer in psychology to a formal post at the Kings Centre for Military Health. This has allowed a proliferation of research projects all aimed at learning more about the needs of the help seeking veterans attending Combat Stress and aimed at further service development. Publications can be found on the KCMHR publications website.

Study projects in progress but not already mentioned in the chapter include treatment effects of all aspects of the treatment pathways: prevalence and effects of traumatic brain injury, a telemedicine study into a telephone-based cognitive processing therapy to veterans with PTSD and post-traumatic growth studies.

Several international collaborations are in place with academic departments, as well as with other clinical services and providers for veterans' mental health most notably in the USA, Canada and Australia and the Netherlands.

Conclusion

In the past few years, there has been an increase in demand for clinical service overall, especially generated through the wars in Iraq and Afghanistan. It is clear that the younger veterans are presenting earlier, and this probably reflects more sophisticated education by the military and better uptake by the service person and family.

A variety of clinical services are now being offered, however, much more work needs to be completed to ensure there is a coherent clinical pathway between statutory, voluntary and any other qualified providers in the support of veterans' mental health.

References

Brooks, E., Novins, D.K., Thomas, D., Jiang, L., Nagamato, H.T., Dailey, N., Bair, B., Shore, J. (2012). Personal characteristics affecting veterans' use of services for posttraumatic stress disorder. *Psychiatric Services*, 2012, 63, 862–7.

Brooks, E., Novins, D.K., Noe, T., Bair, B., Dailey, N., Lowe, J W.J., Richardson B., Hawthorne, K., Shore, J.H. (2013). Reaching rural communities with culturally appropriate care: A model for adapting remote monitoring to American Indian veterans with posttraumatic stress disorder. *Telemedicine and e-Health*, 19, 272–7.

Busuttil, W. (2009). *Psychometric Data Analyses and Clinical Audit Data for Combat Stress 2005–2009*. Internal publication. Leatherhead: Combat Stress.

Busuttil W. (2010). Veterans' mental health: The role of the third sector charity Combat Stress: Expanding community outreach services and bespoke residential treatment programmes. BACP, Spring, 2–9.

Busuttil, W. (2012). Military veterans' mental health – the long term post trauma support needs. In Hughes, R., Kinder, A., Cooper, C.L. (eds.), *International Handbook of Workplace Trauma Support*. Oxford: Wiley-Blackwell, pp. 458–74.

Busuttil, W. (2014). Trauma related substance misuse. In Hunter, B. (ed.), *Attorney's Guide to Defending Veterans in Criminal Court*. Minneapolis: National Veterans Foundation.

Busuttil, W., Hinton, M. (2013). *PTSD Intensive Rehabilitation Programme with Combat Stress Shellshock, Almost a Century of Military Mental Health*. London: Royal Society of Medicine.

Creamer, M., Morris, P., Biddle, D., Elliott, P. (1999). Treatment outcome in Australian veterans with combat-related posttraumatic stress disorder: A cause for cautious optimism? *Journal of Traumatic Stress*, 12, 545–58.

Dent-Brown, K., Ashworth, A., Barkham, M., Connell, J., Gilbody, S., Hardy, G. (2010). *An Evaluation of Six Community Mental Health Pilots for Veterans of the Armed Forces: A Case Study Series*. A Report for the Ministry of Defence. Sheffield: University of Sheffield. Available online at www.sheffield.ac.uk/polopoly_fs/1.120472!/file/Sheffield-evaluation-published-version-15-Dec-2010.pdf (accessed 20 January 2017).

Foa, E.B., Keane, T.M., Friedman, M.J. (eds.) (2009). *Effective Treatments for PTSD: Practice Guidelines from the International Society for Traumatic Stress Studies*, 2nd Edn. New York: Guilford Press.

Forbes, D., Creamer M. (2003). The treatment of chronic posttraumatic stress disorder. In Kearney, G.E., Creamer, M., Marshall, R., Goyne, A. (eds.), *Military Stress and Performance:*

The Australian Defence Force Experience. Canberra: Paul & Co Pub Consortium: Defence Science and Technology Organisation, pp. 206–18.

Forbes, D., Lewis, V., Parslow, R., Hawthorne, G., Creamer, M. (2008). Naturalistic comparison of models of programmatic interventions for combat-related post-traumatic stress disorder. *Australian and New Zealand Journal of Psychiatry*, 42, 1051–9.

Herman, J. (1992). *Trauma and Recovery. The Aftermath of Violence – From Domestic Abuse to Political Terror*. New York: Basic Books.

Hoge, C.W., Auchterlonie, J.L., Milliken, C.S. (2006). Mental health problems, use of mental health services, and attrition from military service after returning from deployment to Iraq or Afghanistan. *Journal of the American Medical Association*, 295, 1023–32.

Klein, S., Alexander, D., Busuttil, W. (2013). *Scoping Review: A Needs-Based Assessment and Epidemiological Community-Based Survey of Ex-Service Personnel and their Families in Scotland*. Aberdeen: Robert Gordon University. Available online at www.scotland.gov. uk/Resource/0041/00417172.pdf (accessed 20 January 2017).

Murphy, D., Busuttil, W. (2014). PTSD, stigma and barriers to help-seeking within the UK Armed Forces. *Journal of the Royal Army Medical Corps*, 161, 322–6.

Murphy, D., Busuttil, W. (2015). Exploring outcome predictors in UK veterans treated for PTSD. *Psychology Research*, 5, 441–51.

Murphy, D., Weijers, B., Palmer, E., Busuttil, W. (2015a). Exploring patterns in referrals to Combat Stress for UK veterans with mental health difficulties between 1994 and 2014. *International Journal of Emergency Mental Health and Human Resilience*, 17, 652–8.

Murphy, D., Hodgman, G., Carson, C., Spencer-Harper, L., Hinton, M., Wessely, S., Busuttil. W. (2015b). Mental health and functional impairment outcomes following a 6-week intensive treatment programme for UK military veterans with post traumatic stress disorder (PTSD): A naturalistic study to explore dropout and health outcomes at follow-up. *BMJ Open*, 5, e007051.

Neville, M., Hacker Hughes, J. (2014). Battle against stigma. Neville, M., Hacker Hughes, J. (eds.), *Bringing War Home*, Vol. 2. London: Wellcome Trust, pp. 66–79.

NICE (2005). *Post-Traumatic Stress Disorder (PTSD): The Management of PTSD in Adults and Children in Primary and Secondary Care*, NICE Guideline GC26. London: NICE.

Richardson, D., Dante, K., Grenier, S., English, A., Sharpe. J. (2008). Operational stress injury social support: A Canadian innovation in professional peer support. *Canadian Military Journal*, 9, 57–64.

Rosenheck, R.A., Fontana, A.F. (2007). Recent trends in VA treatment of post-traumatic stress disorder and other mental disorders. *Health Affairs*, 26, 1720–7.

Scheiner, N.S. (2008). *Not 'At Ease': UK Veterans' Perceptions of the Level of Understanding of their Psychological Difficulties Shown by the National Health Service*. Doctoral Thesis. London: City University London, Department of Psychology and Combat Stress.

VHRA (2011). *VRHA Veterans' Health Policy Brief 2011*. Blacksburg: Virginia Tech Institute for Policy and Governance.

van Hoorn, LA., Jones, N., Busuttil, W., Fear, N.T., Wessely, S., Jones, E. Hunt, E., Greenberg, N. (2013). Iraq and Afghanistan veteran presentations to Combat Stress, since 2003. *Occupational Psychiatry*, 63, 238–41.

Weingarten, R. (2012). The development of peer support in the Netherlands, Brazil and Israel. *Psychiatric Rehabilitation Journal*, 35, 476–7.

Welsh Affairs Committee (2011). *Written Evidence from All Wales Veterans' Health and Wellbeing Service*. London: Welsh Affairs Committee. Available online at www.publications.parliament.uk/pa/cm201213/cmselect/cmwelaf/131/131we03.htm (accessed 17 January 2017).

Wood, S., Jones, C., Morrison, S., Kitchner, N., Dustan, F., Fear, NT., Bisson, J. (2011). *Mental Health, Social Adjustment, Perception of Health and Service Utilisation of Three Groups of Military Veterans Living ln Wales: A Cross-Sectional Survey*. Unpublished study. Cardiff: Cardiff University.

12

VETERAN PSYCHOLOGICAL HEALTH AND SOCIAL CARE

A Dutch Perspective

Jacco Duel, Martin Elands and Coen van den Berg

We honour our dead, care for our wounded and support our veterans.[1]

Introduction

In the first half of the twentieth century, the military veteran was a rare phenomenon in Dutch society as the Netherlands did not participate in the First World War due to its neutrality. Whereas in the surrounding countries, millions of veterans returned home from the battlefields, Dutch society numbered only a few thousand veterans in the period between both world wars. These veterans were soldiers who had fought in the Royal Netherlands East Indies Army in the then Dutch colony and who were repatriated to the Netherlands (Elands, 2000).

This situation changed rapidly with the outbreak of the Second World War in which the Netherlands deployed soldiers in Europe and Asia. Moreover, following that war, the Royal Netherlands Armed Forces were engaged in a large-scale war of decolonisation in Indonesia and – especially since 1979 – in more than 100 military peace operations to promote the (inter)national rule of law and stability. Since 1940, over 670,000 men and women have served the Royal Netherlands Armed Forces during wars or peace operations (Veteraneninstituut, 2014). These men and women are regarded as veterans by Dutch law.[2] Today, about 117,500 of these veterans are alive and approximately 30,000 of them are still on active service as military personnel.[3]

It is well known that taking part in military missions may have both positive and negative consequences for the health and wellbeing of veterans and their close relatives.[4] For those veterans or close relatives that need support due to deployments, there is a comprehensive system of veterans' care in the Netherlands. The aim of this chapter is to present that system as it is today. In that, we focus on veterans once they have left the Armed Forces.[5] We define care rather broadly. Besides (health) care *per se*, we also regard measures that contribute to the acknowledgement and appreciation within society of the veteran's efforts and personal sacrifices as care. The idea behind this is that when veterans feel respected and appreciated for their military contribution during war or peace missions, this will enhance their wellbeing.

The outline of this chapter is as follows. First, we will present the Dutch context. Several major developments in the care of veterans during the last seventy years will be mentioned ending with the Veterans Law (Veteranenwet) that came into effect in 2014 and which provides for a legal framework of veterans' care. Moreover, we will pay some attention to healthcare in Dutch society in general. Next, we will describe the activities and services that are provided by the government and other institutions and which are aimed at enhancing the wellbeing of veterans. In addition, we will describe the role of the Veterans Institute (Veteraneninstituut) in the care of veterans. After that, we will describe the National Veterans Healthcare System (Landelijk Zorgsysteem voor Veteranen). We will present the organisations, both military and public, that together form this healthcare system. We will conclude this chapter by shortly mentioning several issues that, we think, will affect the care for veterans in the near future.

The Dutch context

Following the Second World War until the mid-1980s, there was hardly, if any, care specifically aimed at veterans that was initiated or provided by the government. Besides medical care for physically wounded personnel and disability pensions, veterans and their relatives were more or less left on their own and to private initiatives if they needed aftercare because of their deployment. An important private initiative was the founding of the Association for Military War and Service Victims (Bond voor Nederlandse Militaire Oorlogs- en dienstslachtoffers) in 1945.[6] This association took care of its members' needs by providing information, social work, legal advice and organising activities. Moreover, several veterans' unions were formed that provided support for their members. The activities of the several unions differed somewhat, but mainly they were aimed at providing the opportunity for its members to meet each other, to help them when in need and to attend for the collective interest of its members.

So, time progressed and a substantial number of veterans struggled with their pasts until the 1980s when the tide changed. The reasons for that change are complex and a detailed explanation is beyond the scope of this chapter.[7] However, the almost 150,000 veterans of the war of decolonisation in the former Netherlands East Indies (1945 to 1949) played an important role in this change. When returning home from their deployment, there was hardly any attention in society to their experiences and needs. The nation was busy rebuilding society following the Second World War. Moreover, the lost colonial war was a controversial one (Algra *et al.*, 2007; Elands, 2000; Scagliola, 2002), which made it even more difficult to discuss it or one's role in it. The overall sense within Dutch society was that these veterans should bury their past, get a job, raise a family and just move on. Which they did.

In the 1980s, however, most of these veterans reached the age of retirement. In that phase of life, they were more prone to look back on their mission in which most were deployed as conscripts for two years or more. This was fuelled as several reports of incidents of excessive violence, and even incidents of war crimes, committed by Dutch soldiers in the former East Indies, attracted the interest of Dutch society by that time. After decades of silence and neglect of their efforts and sacrifices in service of their country, these veterans were suddenly confronted with pervasive negative attention and criticism which was a big disappointment for them. Moreover, within this group, there was a considerable number of veterans who suffered from mental health complaints or who struggled with financial issues as a legacy of the mission in which they had participated decades ago and for which there had still been no positive attention from society or the government. For this group of Netherlands East Indies veterans, enough was enough. It was time to raise their voices and utter their dissatisfaction and needs. One of the results of raising their voices was the instalment of a trusted representative for the Netherlands East Indies veterans by the Minister of Defence in 1987. This representative was tasked, among other things, to investigate the issues raised by the veterans (Van der Mei, 1989). Moreover, in 1989, several veterans' unions joined forces into a Veterans Platform (Veteranen Platform) and, united, they were more able to act as a strong partner towards the government and society in attending to the collective interest of the 50,000 veterans that were directly represented by the platform and the other 250,000 veterans at that time.[8]

The trusted representative reported his findings in 1989 (Van der Mei, 1989) and the government acted quickly in reaction to the report. In 1990, the Dutch government issued its first policy letter concerning care for veterans.[9] The government took the position that veterans deserve respect and appreciation from the government and society for their contribution and sacrifices in service of their country. Moreover, the government recognised that taking part in military operations may have its consequences for personnel involved and their close relatives and that the government had an obligation to care for them. In that policy letter, the government announced many initiatives that were intended to contribute to the respect for, and appreciation of, veterans and to enhance their wellbeing when in need for care because of their deployment. Therefore, this policy letter can be seen as a turning point in the care of veterans. Following this policy letter, several other veteran policy letters were issued throughout the years, until 2005. Since that time, every year the Minister of Defence writes a veteran policy letter to the chairman of the House of Representatives and discusses policy issues with members of parliament.

Together, these policy letters formalized numerous initiatives such as the introduction of a Wounded Insignia for veterans who had been physically or mentally wounded (1990),[10] several financial compensations or benefits throughout the years,[11] the foundation of the Veterans Services Association (1992), which evolved into the Veterans Institute (2000), the start of the annual Netherlands Veterans Day[12] (Nederlandse Veteranendag) in 2005, the usage of the Veterans Registration System (2006)[13], the foundation of a National Veterans Healthcare System (2007)[14] and the Veterans Law (2012), which came into effect on the tenth Netherlands Veterans Day in 2014. We shall return to most of these initiatives in the remainder of this chapter, together with considering other initiatives.

Besides these developments that are directly related to the care for veterans in the broader sense, one other aspect concerning the care for veterans in the Netherlands deserves attention. That is the public healthcare system. Everybody who lives or works in the Netherlands is obliged to have standard health insurance.[15] This insurance covers the cost of, for example, consulting a general practitioner, hospital treatment and prescription medicine. In general, the standard health insurance covers more curative care as compared with most other European countries and few other countries than the Netherlands provide the amount of long-term care covered by this insurance (Van Ewijk et al., 2013). Therefore, healthcare is relatively easily accessible for those with a low income or for those with high healthcare costs (Van Ewijk et al., 2013). Besides this financial accessibility, the system is also easy accessible physically in that there are ample healthcare providers and institutions (e.g. general practitioners, hospitals) spread around the country (Van den Berg et al., 2014). Moreover, waiting lists are not a real issue for most institutions and treatments (Van den Berg et al., 2014). Finally, in general, the healthcare system in the Netherlands is of good quality and performs above average as compared with other Western countries (Van den Berg et al., 2014). So, veterans who are in need of care, whether this need is deployment related or not, can always fall back on a public system of care that is nearby, relatively cheap and of good quality.

Besides this system of public healthcare, the care specifically aimed at veterans, in the broadest sense, has developed tremendously in the last decades. From hardly no care, besides medical care for physically wounded personnel and some private initiatives, to a comprehensive healthcare system specifically targeted at veterans. Moreover, this system is firmly grounded in the Veterans Law. In the next section of this chapter, we will outline, in a broad way, the services and care that are provided to veterans and their close relatives.

Services and care for Veterans[16]

Military personnel who have taken part in a war or military mission to promote the (inter)national rule of law and stability are recognised as veterans. To mark the transition to that status, the veteran will be issued insignia and an identification card following their first deployment.[17,18] When the veteran leaves the Armed Forces, these two tokens can be used to identify himself towards other veterans and society. Moreover, the identification card comes with several benefits for veterans who have left the Armed Forces. Monthly, they receive the magazine, *Checkpoint*, with human interest stories about veterans, their missions and activities and news related to veterans or the military. They may apply for benefits that are advertised in the magazine (e.g. free music concerts or reduced entry fees for events or museums). They may also apply for a limited number of free train tickets to visit events that are organised for veterans or to commemorate comrades who were killed in action.

These events for veterans are, for example, the yearly Netherlands Veterans Day, local or regional veterans' days, veterans' days organised per branch of the Armed Forces or reunions. In the Netherlands, there are over 500 registered veteran reunion organisations that are grouped around a specific unit, mission, branch of service or functional background, among other aspects. Each year, these registered organisations may apply for conveniences provided by the government, such as the free use of (semi)military facilities, and discounts on foods and beverages that are provided at those facilities.

All these tokens and services are expressions of the respect and gratitude for veterans by the government and, indirectly, by society. However, there are several events that attract people to actively support the veterans as well. Most notably among these events is the Netherlands Veterans Day. Each year, on the last Saturday of June,[19] Dutch society honours its veterans in The Hague. There are several activities on Veterans Day, such as a gathering with the King, members of government and parliament and a representation of veterans and other distinguished guests in the Hall of Knights (De Ridderzaal), a medal parade at the Inner Court (Het Binnenhof),[20] a parade of veterans before the King and all kinds of activities in the city centre of The Hague. Annually, this event is visited by about 90,000 people. Moreover, the day is subject to nationwide media coverage by television and radio. In addition to this nationwide Veterans Day, about 70 per cent of the municipalities organise a local or regional Veterans Day. Likewise, all service branches of the Armed Forces organise a yearly Veterans Day.

Other veterans-related events are, to mention just a few, yearly commemorations such as the national commemoration of all Dutch victims of war and peace operations on 4 May[21] (Nationale Herdenking) and the commemoration of all victims of peace operations at the National Monument for Peace Operations in Roermond.[22] Moreover, there are over 3,500 war monuments in the Netherlands that reminds society of the Second World War, war situations or peace operations since then and of those who acted in them.[23]

Finally, there are two initiatives worth mentioning that aim at providing more knowledge within society about veterans and their contributions to the nation and which are intended to enhance the respect for veterans and acknowledgement of their efforts and sacrifices. The first is the educational programme 'Veterans in the classroom'. Each year, several hundred veterans talk about their experiences in school classes as visiting lecturers. In the school year, 2013 to 2014, almost 400 primary and secondary schools participated in this project and almost 1,100 lectures were given. In total, over 23,000 pupils were reached and informed (Veteranennota 2014–2015, 2015) in this way. The second is 'Speed dating with veterans'. Every year, there are 14 Liberation Festivals (Bevrijdingsfestivals) throughout the country, on 5 May, the day that the Second World War officially ended in the (European part of the) Kingdom of the Netherlands. One feature on these festivals is the ability for people to meet and greet with veterans who will share their experiences. The aim is to inform society in general about their contribution for the freedom of the Netherlands and international peace and stability.

Now, how does society look towards its veterans? Do all these activities and initiatives pay off? In general, society holds a positive view of veterans, regarding them as conscientious, helpful, courageous and brave. This view of veterans within society has been stable in recent years (Duel, 2015). About 75 per cent of the Dutch population believe that veterans deserve outright appreciation for their contributions in service of the country (Veteranennota 2014–2015, 2015). Moreover, about 90 per cent of the Dutch population believe that veterans deserve optimal healthcare when in need because of their deployment (Veteranennota 2014–2015, 2015). Both findings have remained stable in recent years (Veteranennota 2014–2015, 2015).

The other side of the coin is the opinion of the veterans. In general, over 70 per cent of the veterans are satisfied with the governmental veterans' policy (Duel and De Reuver, 2014). Not all aspects of that policy are of the same importance to veterans, however. They attach great importance to commemorations (94 per cent), receiving appreciation (88 per cent), after care (88 per cent) and services provided by the Veterans Institute (84 per cent; Duel and De Reuver, 2014) whereas aspects such as local veterans days or veterans days per branch of service are considered to be of lesser importance.

More intriguing, however, is that most veterans do not feel appreciated. Fewer than one-half of the respondents (49 per cent) feel appreciated by the government (Duel and De Reuver, 2014) and even fewer veterans feel appreciated by the media, society and by those in their direct environment (respectively 37 per cent, 29 per cent and 45 per cent; Duel and De Reuver, 2014). Throughout recent years, there is a group of veterans who feel a lack of appreciation from the government, the media, society or their direct environment (Duel and De Reuver, 2014).

So, there are lots of services, initiatives and activities aimed at providing care for veterans in the broadest sense. As shown by the results of research on public opinion regarding veterans, these veterans are appreciated by society for their contributions in the service of the country. In general, society holds a positive view about veterans and there is a general view within society that those who are in need of care because of their deployment deserve optimal care. Veterans themselves hold a positive view of the governmental veterans' policy but are less outspoken about the appreciation that they perceive from several groups within society. However, the reasons for this discrepancy are not clear.[24]

In the next part of this chapter we will focus on the Veterans Institute. This institute plays an important role in delivering most services just mentioned to veterans, their relatives and society in general. In this, the Institute is a major partner for the government in enhancing the respect for veterans and acknowledgement of their contributions.

The Veterans Institute

The precursor of the Veterans Institute emerged following the first policy brief on veterans' care, in 1990. From the beginning, the Institute has been a private

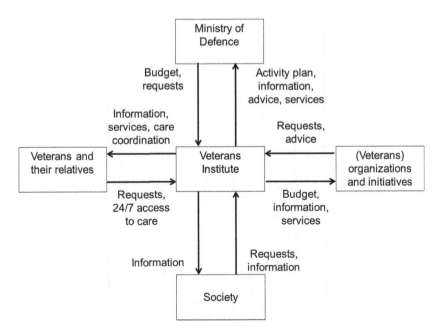

FIGURE 12.1 The Veterans Institute's Organisations.

organisation (foundation) in order that veterans could regard the institute as 'their own'. In general, the tasks that were assigned to the Institute then, are more or less comparable with the tasks of the Institute today, albeit that the amount of services and activities has grown over the years.

Nowadays, the Veterans Institute is located in Doorn, which is in the centre of the Netherlands. Together with the Veterans Platform, the Association for Military War and Service Victims, the management of the National Veterans Healthcare System and the Institute for Social Work for uniformed services – The Base (De Basis) – is housed in one building which facilitates the cooperation between these partners. The Veterans Institute aims its activities at four distinct target groups (see Figure 12.1).

Although the Veterans Institute is a civil organisation, it is closely linked to the Ministry of Defence as it acts on its behalf. Within the Ministry of Defence, there is a specific department for veterans' affairs, besides other departments such as the Personnel Directory, which also addresses veterans' issues. This department for veterans' affairs[25] is involved in providing the budget for the Veterans Institute. The budget is based on an activity plan that is drawn up in close cooperation between the Ministry of Defence and the Institute. In exchange for the budget, the Institute delivers a wide array of services (see Table 12.1 for an overview – Not exhaustive).

Most of these services have already been mentioned. In general, most services relate to the gathering and dissemination of information to all kinds of audiences regarding military missions, how these missions affected, or still affect, veterans and their relatives, how veterans appreciate the various aspects of the governmental

TABLE 12.1 Activities performed by the Veterans Institute

For the Ministry of Defence	For (veterans) organisations and activities	For society (in general)	For veterans and their close relatives
Providing policy advice/information	Publicity campaigns for initiatives	Organising the yearly Veterans Lecture	Providing Veteran Insignias
Performing or supporting research projects	Help with organisation of events	Organising or facilitating symposia	Providing Veteran Identification cards
Registration of reunion organisations	Information desk at events	Website[27]	Issuing the monthly magazine *Checkpoint*[30]
Management assistance for the Wounded Insignia Advisory Board	Financial support for activities	Social Media[27]	Providing free train tickets (veterans activities)
	(Mental) support during commemoration trips for veterans to former mission areas	Knowledge production	Facilitating discounts for activities, goods, etc.
		Research reports and factsheets[28]	Providing information
		Books	Access to healthcare 24/7
		Digital newsletter (monthly)	Case coordination for those who are helped by the National Veterans Healthcare System or Pension Fund
		Educational programme 'Veteran in the classroom'[29]	

veterans' policy and what the interests and needs of veterans are. Moreover, the Veterans Institute supports various organisations, initiatives or individuals both with financial support (e.g. supporting a research project, sponsoring a sports activity, financing a symposium) and more tangible support (e.g. providing for an information desk, performing a research project).

With the Veterans Law becoming effective, a new function has been added to the Veterans Institute, namely the Veterans Office (Veteranenloket). This office is the gateway for all who want services from the Veterans Institute. But this office is also the access point to care for veterans and their close relatives who are in need of care due to deployment. For this purpose, veterans and their relatives can contact the office, 24 hours a day, 7 days a week, by telephone, email or website. Part of the Veterans Office is case coordination for those who are helped by the National Veterans Healthcare System or by the Pension Fund for employees in the government, public and educations sectors (Algemeen Burgerlijk Pensioenfonds). This function will be explained in the next section of this chapter.

The National Veterans Healthcare System

The formation of the National Veterans Healthcare System was announced in 2005.[31] The reason for this was that the government saw it as its responsibility as a former employer to introduce a finely woven safety net of high-quality care institutions, both military and public, that would provide support and mental healthcare, especially tailored to the needs of veterans and easily accessible.[32] The system has been in place since 2007.

Figure 12.2 presents the organisations that are involved in the system. Left from the vertical dashed line are the organisations that are part of the system. The

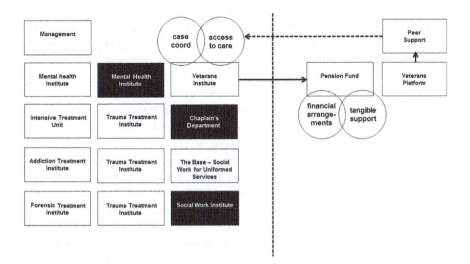

FIGURE 12.2 The Dutch National Veterans Healthcare System.

organisations that are located right from the vertical dashed line are not part of the system. However, these organisations closely cooperate with the National Veterans Healthcare System. The black boxes in the Figure are organisations that are part of the military organisation and the white boxes are public organisations. The public organisations – except for the Veterans Institute – provide for public care, and additionally, they provide for care which is specifically tailored to veterans' needs. The Base provides for social work for veterans and other ex-uniformed personnel such as police officers, firemen or ambulance personnel.

Most healthcare can be delivered in the vicinity of veterans, except for some specialised healthcare that is only available in some regions. A basic premise of the system is that it works following the stepped care model of healthcare delivery.[33] According to this model, 'the recommended treatment ... should be the least restrictive of those currently available, but still likely to provide significant health gain' (Bower and Gilbody, 2005: 11). 'More intensive treatments are generally reserved for [those] who do not benefit from simpler first-line treatments, or for those who can be accurately predicted not to benefit from such treatments' (Bower and Gilbody, 2005: 11). In that stepped care model, organisations work closely together.

What can be found in the system? First, the Veterans Institute. A part of its role has been mentioned already. In the National Veterans Healthcare System, it serves as the access point for the system. Veterans and their relatives can contact the Veterans Office 24/7 when in need of care. Additionally, the institute provides for case coordination. It is not uncommon that those who ask for help have problems that require the involvement of more than one institution. In most cases, the Pension Fund is also involved for financial arrangements, such as the application for a disability pension, or for tangible support, such as help in re-integrating to work. Case coordination must contribute to a smooth process in which aspects of care are geared to one another. Moreover, the person who receives help from multiple care providers has one point of contact: his case coordinator.

The chaplain's department provides for services related to giving meaning, ethics and religion, belief or the outlook on life. These services are provided by personnel with a Catholic, Protestant, Humanistic, Jewish, Hindu or Islamic education and training. This department provides for easy accessible care. Organisations for social work provide first-line support, whereas the two mental healthcare institutions and the three trauma treatment institutes provide for more intensive treatments. The three remaining institutes provide for highly specialised additional care, such as treatments for aggressive behaviour or addictions.

Finally, although not strictly part of the system but still worth mentioning, is the presence of peer support for veterans (nuldelijnshelpers). This peer support closely cooperates with the Veterans Office in that both know how to find each other when there is a notion that a veteran may be in need of care. Peer support is organised and coordinated by the Veterans Platform.[34] Via a digital social map for veterans,[35] those in need for peer support may contact one of the over 400 peer supporters – of whom about half of them are certified – who are nearby.[36] Besides digital availability, peer supporters may be present at veterans' cafés, veterans' homes[37] and activities where veterans meet each other, which makes this kind of support easily accessible for veterans.

Veterans free in their choice as to whether they are treated by a public or military care provider (in those cases that both provide the care which is needed, for example, social work). The care that is provided by the National Veterans Healthcare System is financed by compulsory health insurance and the general law on exceptional medical expenses (Algemene Wet Bijzondere Ziektekosten). Moreover, the Ministry of Defence funds those costs that are not covered by these insurances. At the end of 2014, there were 1,456 people registered with a case for help in the National Veterans Healthcare System. Moreover, 1,315 individuals were registered with a case for help at the Pension Fund.[38,39,40]

Conclusion

In 2014, the Veterans Law came into effect. With the advent of that law, the care for veterans and their relatives in the broadest sense was formally institutionalised. One of the aims of the law was to improve the current situation and to provide for a more coherent, more preventive, more proactive and more transparent veterans' policy.[41]

According to the law, the veterans' policy was evaluated by the government in 2016. Undoubtedly, this will imply changes to the wide array of services and the way in which they are delivered to veterans, their relatives and society. Several topics will be likely to affect the outcome of that evaluation and veterans' policy in due time. We will mention two of them; these are the changing veteran population and the scope of care.

First, the veteran population will change significantly in the near future. For example, today, nearly 25 per cent of the veterans are aged 80 or (much) older. This generation of veterans will, unfortunately, fade away in the coming years. At the same time, a large group of relatively young military personnel will be attaining the veteran status. Further, the percentage of women and veterans with different ethnic, cultural and religious backgrounds is increasing and, likewise, the percentage of veterans with multiple deployments will also increase.

The question is whether current support and care for veterans, in the broadest sense, is tailored to this new generation of veterans who are younger and more diverse. For example, there are questions whether care for female veterans matches their needs (Veteranennota 2014–2015, 2015).

Another question is how this new generation of veterans can best be reached to deliver support and care. For example, younger veterans are less inclined to unite in veterans' unions or to attend activities such as veterans' days, but are more likely to use social media as a platform to 'meet' each other than older veterans. This touches another aspect related to the accessibility of care. Despite the intention of the healthcare system to provide for easy accessible care, it appears that there are veterans who experience barriers to care (Duel *et al.*, 2015; Veteraneninstituut, 2015). It is hard to say what the scale of the problem is and what exactly the root of the problem is. Nevertheless, for organisations such as the Veterans Institute and

National Veterans Healthcare System, among others, this is a signal that additional measures may be necessary to reach those veterans who have deployment-related needs and who are – for whatever reason – not able or willing to find their way to care. This is especially important, as lately, a growing number of veterans who were deployed in the period 1979 to 1995 (Lebanon, Bosnia) accuse the Ministry of Defence of having been negligent in providing aftercare for their deployment-related needs. Despite their entitlement to a military disability pension and a debt of honour or damages arrangement (Ereschuld-en Schadeloosheidsregeling) they now claim additional compensation, for example, because of a damaged career or because of debts. In autumn 2015, the Dutch Administrative High Court (Centrale Raad van Beroep) declared a veteran's appeal for additional compensation well-founded and decided that the Ministry of Defence had previously failed in its duties in providing care for the veteran. As a consequence of this judgment, the Ministry of Defence may expect more claims with big financial consequences.[42]

The second topic that will be of importance in the near future is the scope of care. Several developments make this an important issue for the next few years. We will address three of these developments. First, special attention is needed to future multidisciplinary approaches of veterans' issues as veterans who need support and who increasingly face multiple problems simultaneously. For example, younger veterans may have psychological issues yet they are also still active on the labour market and in a phase of their lives where they might form a family or have responsibilities towards a partner and children. Problems on one domain of life due to the deployment may 'spill over' to other domains.

The second development concerns the significant budget cuts on public healthcare in recent years and a continuing strain on healthcare budgets for the years to come. The reasons for this strain are multiple, among them an increase in healthcare consumption per person and the delivery of better and costlier healthcare (Van der Horst et al., 2011). To keep the public healthcare system affordable, it is undergoing a major reform at present. A new development following this reform is that patients will be more responsible for managing their own help and will be more dependent on volunteer aid on certain domains of care. Moreover, certain types of healthcare delivery will no longer be paid for by insurance companies and those companies are prone to fund the care of a limited number of contracted care givers. It is unclear how all of these reforms will affect the availability, quality, and funding of healthcare delivery in the public domain in the near future and whether and how this will affect the demand for the healthcare delivery in the National Veterans Healthcare System.

The third development is a pressure towards those who are involved in providing healthcare for veterans to broaden their arsenal of care. Numerous private healthcare initiatives have emerged lately and the government and current organisations that are involved with providing healthcare are hard pressed to provide for funding of these initiatives. For example, the provision of service dogs for veterans with post-traumatic stress disorder. Besides the question whether all these initiatives provide evidence-based healthcare, there are – as mentioned earlier – limits to the budget that is available for veterans' care.

All those involved with the care for veterans are aware of these, and other, topics and developments. The question is, however, one of how far these issues imply adjustments of the veterans' policy and, if adjustments are needed, what those will be? At this moment, it is just too early to say.

We started this chapter with a citation from the Netherlands Defence Doctrine: 'We honour our dead, care for our wounded and support our veterans'. The overview presented in this chapter makes it clear that these are not hollow words. Veterans of older generations may have experienced otherwise when they returned from their missions. However, today, all veterans are supported by the government and within society there is ample acknowledgement and appreciation for their contributions. This has been firmly grounded in law, institutions, and services. Both the government and the many veterans' organisations exert themselves to attend to veterans' needs, to provide for the best care and to enhance public acknowledgement of, and appreciation for, veterans and their contributions in service of the country. Our veterans deserve nothing less.

Notes

1 This is the closing sentence of the Netherlands Defence Doctrine (2013: 111).
2 See Veteranenbesluit [Veterans Decree] (2014) and Veteranenwet [Veterans Law] (2012). So, contrary to other countries, such as the United Kingdom or the United States of America, military personnel will not attain veteran status if they have not been deployed to a war or peace operation. Another noteworthy aspect is that deployed military personnel do not have to leave the service to become a veteran. Military personnel who have been deployed and are on active duty are also veterans.
3 Veteranennota 2014–2015 (2015).
4 Concerning the Dutch situation, see, for example: Andres (2010); Bramsen *et al.* (2001); De Kloet (2007); De Vries *et al.* (2002); Dirkzwager (2002); Dirkzwager *et al.* (2005); Duel *et al.* 2015; Engelhard *et al.* (2007, 2015); Hoencamp *et al.* (2015); Klaassens *et al.* (2008); Mouthaan *et al.* (2005); Rietveld (2011); Schok (2009); Smid *et al.* (2013); Soetekouw (2000); Taal *et al.* (2014); Van Wingen *et al.* (2012); Van Zuiden (2012); Vermetten and De Loos (2003).
5 See Vermetten *et al.* (2014) for an overview of the mental healthcare system for military personnel.
6 The association was solely aimed at military war victims until 1977.
7 See: Commissie maatschappelijke erkenning veteranen (1991); De Swart and Thuijsman (2000); Elands (2000); Van der Mei (1989).
8 In 2015, 48 veterans' unions are member of the Veterans Platform. The Platform attends the interest of over 70,000 veterans. See http://veteranenplatform.nl/.
9 *Hoofdlijnen van het veteranenbeleid* [Outline of veterans' policy]. Letter from the Minister of Defence to the Chairman of the House of Representatives, 21490(2), 26 March 1990.
10 There are several criteria that discern whether a veteran qualifies for the Wounded Insignia. Among those criteria is that the veteran is, or was, wounded because of a hostile act.
11 For example, a debt of honour arrangement for veterans that are physically or mentally invalidated due to their deployment before 2007 and damages for those who are invalidated because of their deployment after 2007. Both measures are in addition to a regular military invalidity pension to compensate for (financial) damages that are not covered by that pension, such as loss of income.

12 See www.veteranendag.nl/.
13 The Veterans Registration System contains information (name, address, date of birth, gender, mission characteristics) of all veterans. This system makes it possible for the Ministry of Defence to get in contact with veterans for care related issues or other activities. See: Veteranenzorg [Care for Veterans] (2007).
14 See www.lzv-groep.nl/.
15 See www.government.nl/topics/health-insurance/contents/standard-health-insurance.
16 As mentioned earlier, in this chapter, we will focus on veterans when they have left the armed forces. Military personnel on active service can use the military healthcare system which is comparable to the public healthcare system in the kind of care that is available. When military personnel leave the armed forces, they are subjected to a compulsory medical examination. Moreover, there are provisions in the military so that military personnel who leave the armed forces receive support to find a new job (when applicable). So, in general, military personnel experiences a 'smooth transition' from the military into the civilian world.
17 Approximately 5 per cent of the veteran population is female. However, for reasons of brevity we will use 'he' to refer to all veterans.
18 Formally, the Minister of Defence determines which missions qualify for veteran status. In general, these are missions under conditions of war or peace support or peace enhancing missions.
19 This day was chosen as it is near the day the late Prince Bernhard of the Netherlands was born. Prince Bernhard, a Second World War veteran himself, is still popular among veterans, especially the older ones, for his (military) role in the Second World War and his post-war activities as Inspector General of the Armed Forces until 1976 and his involvement with the military and veterans until his death in 2004. Nowadays, the Inspector General of the Armed Forces is also the Inspector of Veterans affairs, who among their other tasks, acts as a mediator between veterans and institutions. Likewise, the National ombudsman also acts as Veterans ombudsman.
20 The Binnenhof (Inner Court) is a square in The Hague city centre. At its centre, one finds the Ridderzaal (Hall of Knights) and the square is lined by parliament buildings and government buildings. The square forms the very heart of Dutch government. See https://english.prodemos.nl/English/Visitor-Centre.
21 See www.4en5mei.nl/.
22 See www.4en5mei.nl/herinneren/oorlogsmonumenten/monumenten_zoeken/ oorlogs monument/2397.
23 See www.4en5mei.nl/herinneren/oorlogsmonumenten/over_oorlogsmonumenten.
24 In 2015, a large research project started that is, among other things, aimed at shedding a light on this discrepancy (De Reuver, 2015).
25 Officially, the Executive Department for Veterans Affairs, Reserve Personnel and Decorations (Uitvoeringsbedrijf Veteranen, Reservisten en Decoraties).
26 www.veteraneninstituut.nl/ and http://veteranenloket.nl/english/.
27 www.facebook.com/Veteraneninstituut.
28 www.veteraneninstituut.nl/overzicht-publicaties/.
29 www.facebook.com/veteraanindeklas.
30 www.veteraneninstituut.nl/diensten/checkpoint/archief-checkpoints/.
31 Veteranenzorg [Care for veterans] (2005).
32 Veteranenzorg [Care for veterans] (2008).
33 Landelijk Zorgsysteem voor Veteranen (2015).
34 For example, the recruitment and training of peer supporters.
35 See www.disk-veteranen.nl/.
36 Peer supporters who received a training at the Institute for Social Work, 'The Base', are certified.
37 There are over 70 veterans' cafés and about a couple of dozen veterans' homes in the Netherlands where veterans can meet each other. See www.veteraneninstituut.nl/ locaties_tax/veteranencafes/ and www.veteraneninstituut.nl/locaties_tax/ontmoeting-

scentra.

38 In 2014, most cases at the Pension Fund concerned the application of a (higher) Military Disability Pension, the application of tangible support, the support of a social worker, re-integration to work and debt repayment.

39 The figures are based on the Veteranennota 2014–2015 (2015). It is conceivable that a person has a case in the National Veterans Healthcare System and the Pension Fund at the same time.

40 There are no accurate numbers about the prevalence of deployment-related needs of care in the Netherlands. Therefore, the Ministry of Defence employs a rule of thumb on this topic based on several studies in the Netherlands and abroad. The rule of thumb implies that about 20 per cent of those deployed have (health) complaints following their deployment. Most complaints are light to moderate and will be solved within several months. For 10 per cent of those who have been deployed some kind of professional medical or psychosocial care is needed. For about 5 per cent, mental health complaints are severe which require a more intense treatment. For about 1 per cent to 2 per cent, the complaints will remain and long-term care is needed. See www.nrc.nl/nieuws/2012/08/21/1-op-de-20-veteranen-heeft-stress-syndroom-12356422-a231604 or http://www.veteraneninstituut.nl/zorg/.

41 Tweede Kamer der Staten-Generaal (2011).

42 Veteranenzorg [Care for Veterans] (2016).

Acknowledgements

We would like to thank Yvon M. de Reuver and Melanie Dirksen for their helpful comments on earlier drafts of this chapter.

References

Algra, G., Elands, M., Schoeman, J.R. (2007). The media and the public image of Dutch veterans from World War II to Srebrenica. *Armed Forces and Society*, 33, 396–413.

Andres, M.D. (2010). *Behind Family Lines. Family Members' Adaptations to Military-Induced Separations*. Breda: Uitgeverij Broese and Peereboom. Available online at https://pure.uvt.nl/portal/files/1183681/M.D._Andres_-_Behind_Family_Lines.pdf (accessed 20 January 2017).

Bower, P., Gilbody, S. (2005). Stepped care in psychological therapies: Access, effectiveness and efficiency. Narrative literature review. *British Journal of Psychiatry*, 186, 11–17.

Bramsen, I., Van der Ploeg, H.M., Dirkzwager, A.J.E., Van Esch, S.C.M. (2001). Veterans of old wars and recent conflicts in the Netherlands: Their long term psychological adjustment. *Occupational Medicine*, 51, 70–1.

Commissie Maatschappelijke Erkenning Veteranen (1991). *Veteranen. Een Nieuwe Dialoog met Overheid en Samenleving* [Veterans. A New Dialogue with the Government and Society]. Den Haag: Commissie Maatschappelijke Erkenning Veteranen.

De Kloet, C.S. (2007). *Afterwards: Neurobiological Alterations in Veterans With and Without Posttraumatic Stress Disorder*. Utrecht: Universiteit van Utrecht.

De Reuver, Y.M. (2015). *Collective Identity of Veterans and its Interrelation with the Experienced Acknowledgement and Appreciation by Society. The Beginning of a Theoretical Framework*. Paper presented at the 13th Biennial Conference of the European Research Group on Military and Society (ERGOMAS), Ra'anana, Israel.

De Swart, H.W., Thuijsman, C.J. (2000). Het Veteraneninstituut [The Veterans Institute]. *Militaire Spectator*, 169, 275–85. Available online at www.kvbk-cultureelerfgoed.nl/MS_PDF/2000/2000-0275-01-0070.PDF (accessed 20 January 2017).

De Vries, M., Soetekouw, P.M.M.B., Van der Meer, J.W., Bleijenberg, G. (2002). The role of post-traumatic stress disorder symptoms in fatigued Cambodia veterans. *Military Medicine*, 167, 790–4.

Dirkzwager, A.J.E. (2002). *Posttraumatic Stress Among Dutch Military Veterans: A Longitudinal Study*. Amsterdam: Vrije Universiteit Amsterdam.

Dirkzwager, A.J.E., Bramsen, I., Adler, H., Van der Ploeg, H.M. (2005). Secondary traumatization in partners and parents of Dutch peacekeeping soldiers. *Journal of Family Psychology*, 19, 217–26.

Duel, J. (2015). Hoe zien Nederlanders 'de veteraan'? [How does society looks at veterans?]. *Checkpoint*, January-February, 20–1.

Duel, J., De Reuver, Y.M. (2014). *Kerngegevens Veteranen 2014* [Basis facts about veterans 2014]. Doorn: Veteraneninstituut. Available online at www.veteraneninstituut.nl/wp-content/uploads/2015/07/duel-de-reuver-2014-kerngegevens-veteranen-2014.pdf (accessed 20 January 2017).

Duel, J., De Reuver, Y.M., Elands, M. (2015). *The Long-Term Consequences of Military Deployments for Veterans. The Relation Between Mission Factors and the Need for Deployment-Related Care of Veterans in Later Life*. Paper presented at the 13th Biennial Conference of the European Research Group on Military and Society (ERGOMAS), Ra'anana, Israel.

Elands, M. (2000). Oudere veteranen en de roep om maatschappelijke erkenning [Older veterans and their call for society's recognition]. *Militaire Spectator*, 169, 219–30. Available online at www.kvbk-cultureelerfgoed.nl/MS_PDF/2000/2000-0219-01-0064.PDF pdf (accessed 20 January 2017).

Engelhard, I.M., Van den Hout, M.A, Weerts, J.M.P., Arntz, A, Hox, J.J.C.M., McNally, R.J.M. (2007). Deployment-related stress and trauma in Dutch soldiers returning from Iraq. Prospective study. *British Journal of Psychiatry*, 191, 140–5.

Engelhard, I.M., Lommen, M.J., Sijbrandij, M. (2015). Changing for better or worse? Posttraumatic growth reported by soldier deployed to Iraq. *Clinical Psychological Science*, 3, 789–96.

Hoencamp, R., Idenburg, F.J., Van Dongen, T.T.C.F., De Kruijff, L.G.M., Huizinga, E.P., Plat, M.J., Hoencamp, E., Leenen, L.P.H., Hamming, J.F., Vermetten, E. (2015). Long-term impact of battle injuries; five year follow-up of injured Dutch servicemen in Afghanistan 2006-2010. *PLoS One*, 10, e0115119.

Hoofdlijnen van het veteranenbeleid [Outline of veterans' policy]. Letter from the Minister of Defence to the Chairman of the House of Representatives, 21490(2), 26 March 1990.

Klaassens, E. R., Van Veen, T., Weerts, J. M. P., Zitman, F. G. (2008). Mental health of Dutch peacekeeping veterans 10-25 years after deployment. *European Psychiatry*, 23, 486–90. Available online at https://openaccess.leidenuniv.nl/bitstream/handle/1887/16190/03.pdf?sequence=10 (accessed 20 January 2017).

Landelijk Zorgsysteem voor Veteranen (2015). *Meerjarenplan 2015–2018* [Multiannual review 2015–2018]. Doorn: Landelijk Zorgsysteem voor Veteranen.

Mouthaan, J., Dirkzwager, A.J.E., De Vries, M., Elands, M., Scagliola, S.I. & Weerts, J.M.P. (2005). *Libanon laat ons nooit helemaal los: Resultaten van onderzoek naar de gezondheid en het welzijn van UNIFIL'ers die in de periode 1979-1985 naar Libanon zijn uitgezonden* [The health and well-being of UNIFIL-veterans]. Doorn: Veteraneninstituut. Available online at www.veteraneninstituut.nl/wp-content/uploads/2015/07/mouthaan-et-al-2005-gehele-rapport-Libanon-laat-ons-nooit-helemaal-los.pdf (accessed 20 January 2017).

Netherlands Defence Doctrine (2013). Den Haag: Ministerie van Defensie. Available online at www.defensie.nl/binaries/defensie/documenten/publicaties/2013/11/20/defence-doctrine-en/defensie-doctrine_en.pdf (accessed 20 January 2017).

Rietveld, N. (2011). Deployment-related guilt and shame in Dutch veterans: Questions of conscience. In: Meijer, M., Rietveld, N. (eds.), *Military Leaders Facing Problematic Decision Making*. Conference Proceedings of the 13th International Military Mental Health Conference. Breda: Netherlands Defence Academy, Faculty of Military Science, pp. 99–108).

Scagliola, S. (2002). *Last van de oorlog. De Nederlandse oorlogsmisdaden in Indonesië en hun verwerking* [Troubled by the war. Dutch war crimes in Indonesia and how they were handled]. Amsterdam: Uitgeverij Balans.

Schok, M.L. (2009). *Meaning as a Mission: Making Sense of War and Peacekeeping*. Delft: Uitgeverij Eburon. Available online at http://dspace.library.uu.nl/handle/1874/35944 (accessed 20 January 2017).

Smid, G.E., Kleber, R.J., Rademaker, A.R., Van Zuiden, M., Vermetten, E. (2013). The role of stress sensitization in progression of posttraumatic distress following deployment. *Social Psychiatry and Psychiatric Epidemiology*, 48, 1743–54.

Soetekouw, P.M.M.B. (2000). *Symptomatic Cambodia veterans: Somatic aspects*. Nijmegen: Katholieke Universiteit Nijmegen.

Taal, E.L., Vermetten, E., Van Schaik, D.A., Leenstra, T. (2014). Do soldiers seek more mental health care after deployment? Analysis of mental health consultations in the Netherlands Armed Forces following deployment to Afghanistan. *European Journal of Psychotraumatology*, 5. doi:10.3402/ejpt.v5.23667.

Tweede Kamer der Staten-Generaal (2011). *Voorstel van wet van de leden Eijsink, Van Dijk, Hachchi, El Fassed, Voordewind, Ouwehand, Van der Staaij, Hernandez, Bruins Slot en Bosman tot vaststelling van regels omtrent de bijzondere zorgplicht voor veteranen (Veteranenwet). Memorie van toelichting zoals gewijzigd naar aanleiding van het advies van de raad van state. Kamerstuk 32414, nr. 7.* [Initiative from the House of Representatives for a law concerning the care for veterans; document 32414, nr 7].

Van den Berg, M.J., De Boer, D., Gijsen, R., Heijink, R., Limburg, L.C.M., Zwakhals, S.L.N. (2014). *Zorgbalans 2014. Op hoofdlijnen. De prestaties van de Nederlandse gezondheidszorg* [Health care balance 2014. Outline. The performance of the Dutch health care system]. Bilthoven: Rijksinstituut voor Volksgezondheid en Milieu. Available online at www.gezondheidszorgbalans.nl/dsresource?type=pdf&disposition=inline&objectid=r ivmp:259835 (accessed 20 January 2017).

Van der Horst, A., Van Erp, F., & De Jong, J. (2011). *Trends in gezondheid en zorg* [Trends in health and health care]. Den Haag: Centraal Planbureau. Available online at www.cpb.nl/ sites/default/files/publicaties/download/cpb-policy-brief-2011-11-trends-gezondheid-en-zorg.pdf (accessed 20 January 2017).

Van der Mei, D.F. (1989). *Dienstvervulling onder buitengewone en zeer moeilijke omstandigheden. De verantwoordelijkheid van de overheid voor de specifieke problematiek van oud-militairen Indiëgangers. Eindadvies van de Vertrouwensman Oud-militairen Indiëgangers* [Performing one's duty under extreme and very difficult circumstances. The responsibility from the government for the specific issues of former soldiers deployed to the Netherlands East Indies. Final advice from the trusted representative former soldiers deployed to the Netherlands East Indies]. Den Haag, February, 9–23.

Van Ewijk, C., Van der Horst, A., Besseling, P. (2013). *Gezondheid loont. Tussen keuze en solidariteit* [Health pays off. Between choice and solidarity]. Den Haag: Centraal Planbureau. Available online at www.cpb.nl/sites/default/files/publicaties/download/cpb-boek-7-toekomst-voor-de-zorg.pdf (accessed 20 January 2017).

Van Wingen, G.A., Geuze, E., Vermetten, E., Fernández, G. (2012). The neural consequences of combat stress: Long-term follow-up. *Molecular Psychiatry*, 17, 116–18.

Van Zuiden, M. (2012). *Predicting PTSD, Depression, and Fatigue After Military Deployment. Identification of Biological Vulnerability Factors*. Rotterdam: Optima Grafische Communicatie.

Available online at http://dspace.library.uu.nl/handle/1874/226254 (accessed 20 January 2017).

Vermetten, E., De Loos, W. (2003). *Medisch Onbegrepen Lichamelijke Klachten bij Veteranen; het Post-Deploymentsyndroom, diagnose en zorg in ontwikkeling* [Medically unexplained physical symptoms among veterans; the post-deployment syndrome, diagnosis en care developments]. In: W. Visser (red), *Hulpverlening aan Nederlandse Veteranen; Over Preventie, Signalering en Nazorg.* Utrecht: ICODO, pp. 51–63.

Vermetten, E., Greenberg, N., Boeschoten, M.A., Delahaije, R., Jetly, R., Castro, C.A., McFarlane, A.C. (2014). Deployment-related mental health support: comparative analysis of NATO and allied ISAF partners. *European Journal of Psychotraumatology,* 5, 23732.

Veteranenbesluit [Veterans Decree] (2014). *Staatsblad van het Koninkrijk der Nederlanden,* 221. Available online at https://zoek.officielebekendmakingen.nl/stb-2014-221.html (accessed 20 January 2017).

Veteraneninstituut (2014). *Factsheet: Veteranen en hun missies* [Factsheet: Veterans and their missions]. Doorn: Veteraneninstituut. Available online at www.veteraneninstituut.nl/wp-content/uploads/2014/11/FS5-Veteranen-en-hun-missies.pdf (accessed 20 January 2017).

Veteraneninstituut (2015). *Veteraan, hoe gaat het met u? Een onderzoek naar het welbevinden van de Nederlandse veteraan. Publiekssamenvatting* [A research into the wellbeing of Dutch veterans. Public summary]. Doorn: Veteraneninstituut in samenwerking met Trimbosinstituut en de Raad voor civiel-militaire Zorg en Onderzoek. Available online at www.veteraneninstituut.nl/wp-content/uploads/2015/11/Publiekssamenvatting-Veteraan-hoe-gaat-het-met-u-DEF.pdf (accessed 20 January 2017).

Veteranennota 2014–2015 [Veterans memorandum 2014–2015] (2015). Letter from the minister of Defence to the Chairman of the House of Representatives, 30139(148), 28 August 2015. Available online at https://zoek.officielebekendmakingen.nl/blg-521390 (accessed 20 January 2017).

Veteranenwet [Veterans Law] (2012). *Staatsblad van het Koninkrijk der Nederlanden,* 133. Available online at https://zoek.officielebekendmakingen.nl/stb-2012-133.html (accessed 20 January 2017).

Veteranenzorg [Care for Veterans] (2005). Letter from the Minister of Defence to the Chairman of the House of Representatives, 30139(2), 1 June 2005. Available online at https://zoek.officielebekendmakingen.nl/dossier/30139/kst-30139-2?resultIndex=247&sorttype=1&sortorder=4 (accessed 20 January 2017).

Veteranenzorg [Care for Veterans] (2007). Letter from the Minister of Defence to the Chairman of the House of Representatives, 30139(29), 8 June 2007. Available online at https://zoek.officielebekendmakingen.nl/dossier/30139/kst-30139-29?resultIndex=213&sorttype=1&sortorder=4 (accessed 20 January 2017).

Veteranenzorg [Care for Veterans] (2008). Letter from the Minister of Defence to the Chairman of the House of Representatives, 30139(53), 22 December 2008. Available online at https://zoek.officielebekendmakingen.nl/dossier/30139/kst-30139-53?resultIndex=180&sorttype=1&sortorder=4 (accessed 20 January 2017).

Veteranenzorg [Care for Veterans] (2016). Parliamentary report, 30139(164), 8 July 2016. Available online at https://zoek.officielebekendmakingen.nl/dossier/30139/kst-30139-164?resultIndex=0&sorttype=1&sortorder=4 (accessed 20 January 2017).

13

AN INTERNATIONAL PERSPECTIVE ON TRANSITION

Stephanie Hodson (Australia), Carl Castro (USA) and Alice Aiken (Canada)

Introduction

When the war ends for our soldiers, sailors and air personnel, there are issues that continue to arise. Most cope with the challenges of military service, including combat exposures, but all are changed. For some, the issues are a result of returning from the battlefield to their own private battlefield. Ultimately, all service members need to find a way to redefine their identity, in order to reintegrate into family and society. Often, family and society do not understand the full extent of the deployed members' experience, especially combatants, while the service members cannot fully explain their experience to those who were not part of it. Although Australia, Canada and the United States have different systems for selection, training and managing deployment experiences and when service members return they all return to different social structures, medical structures and expectations, there are elements of concern within mental health and social care that are common among many countries.

This chapter will present an 'integrative perspective' of issues that have come to the forefront, especially since the most recent conflict(s), from three countries that have been allies during these contemporary conflicts. We have selected topics that are unique and ones that the public does not usually think about, and we have focused on the similar challenges that each of our countries are faced with as well as on some strategies to address them. The topics that we have selected are:

- Transition – What are the unique mental and social care aspects of transition from military to civilian life?
- Disability and recovery – If you develop a disability how do you recover/reintegrate/come back from that, if possible?
- Stigma and barriers to care – What is the stigma associated with mental or social wounds, how is this impacted by transition from military service and how can it be addressed?

- Military and veteran families – Taking a culturally broad perspective of family, what are the issues for loved ones as a result of the member's service and what support should be available?
- Societal benefit – How does society benefit from the reintegration of service members?

Transition

For most, transition from military service is not just about leaving a job but leaving a way of life that includes very high standards of personal conduct and commitment. While most individuals do successfully transition, the strong sense of purpose and belonging that is often part of serving can be greatly missed when beginning a new chapter in life. For some, there can be a sense of losing direction or of no longer belonging. These feelings may be even stronger in those who leave the services involuntarily.

All transitions are inherently stressful. The transition from active duty military service back to civilian life is no exception. Recently, the United States (US) military have been assessing how to best prepare service members leaving active duty so that their integration back into society is as smooth as possible. To be sure, this has not been easy. No doubt the difficulty lies in the fact that the military does not know how to transition its service members back to civilian life. In the US, the military does not consider preparing its members to leave its responsibility.

Indeed, there is no federal agency in the US that has transitioning military service members back to society as its mission. The main mechanism that the military uses to facilitate the transition of it service members back to civilian life is the military transition programme (see www.dodtap.mil/). The military transition programme in the US, however, is relatively new. It was not mandated for all separating service members until ten years after the wars in Iraq and Afghanistan began. Furthermore, it was not an initiative created by the US Department of Defence. It was a programme expanded and mandated by the US Congress and led by the US Department of Labor. Thus, this programme is very heavy employment focused.

In Canada, the transition briefing for those leaving service is called the Second Career Assistance Network (SCAN) seminar. It is offered to all those releasing from the military, and spouses may attend, but attendance is not mandatory. More services are offered if someone is being released for medical reasons in Canada. A case manager will be appointed for the member, and this person will assist the member with all of their insurance and employment benefits. Additionally, in Canada, only those who were injured in service become clients of Veterans Affairs (VA), so the majority of Canadian veterans are not followed after release, unless they claim compensation for an injury through the VA.

As a result, the US and Canadian transition programmes, while focusing on the important topic of employment, often ignore other equally important transition issues, such as mental and physical health, housing, finance and legal issues and family matters. Invariably, these other non-employment related issues often play a role in a service member successfully transitioning from the military back to civilian life. In particular, research carried out with recent veterans shows that they continue to struggle to address mental and physical healthcare needs (Mahar *et al.*, 2016).

Australia has taken a holistic approach to transition. However, similar to the US experience, not all of the processes are mandatory. Service personnel have the opportunity to attend transition seminars, which are designed to address some of the mental and social care aspects, as well as important practical issues such as finances and legal issues before they transition (Commonwealth of Australia, 2016a). These seminars are coordinated by the regional Transitions Centres who manage the administrative process for all transitioning personnel, ensuring that personnel are linked to into other support services such as rehabilitation, compensation and training as required.

In a similar way as in Canada, not all Australian Defence Force (ADF) members who transition out of defence lodge a claim with VA. Currently, only one in five members with service after 2004 have a lodged a claim for compensation or applied for non-liability healthcare, making it difficult to track and understand issues within the veteran community. Australia is currently in the process of implementing initiatives to have a seamless handover from serving to veteran services (Commonwealth of Australia, 2015).

Additionally, in the area of mental and social health, the focus has been on developing resources that can be accessed by the whole veteran community. For example, the transition seminars include a lesson on 'Life SMART' or Self-Management Resilience Training (SMART Across Military and Civilian Life, 2015). This presentation builds on the continuum of resilience training conducted through a service member's career in the ADF (Cohn *et al.*, 2010), reinforcing that the skills learnt in the military are important life skills. Acknowledging that a single lesson is not enough to reinforce these skills, a supporting website and mobile application has been developed so that ex-serving members and their families can revisit the information when needed (see http://at-ease.dva.gov.au/highres).

All three nations are learning the importance of planning for transition. The point of actually transition is an inherently stress and busy period as the individual potentially navigates new housing, employment and medical services. While transition seminars or information at point of transition are important, the amount of information any individual can retain has to be considered. A holistic approach would see a focus on transition from point of entry to service, with recognition of competencies gained through military training including both employment and life skills.

Disability

Since the early 1990s, all three countries have seen an increased tempo of operations with difficult missions in the First Gulf War, Rwanda, Somalia, Sierra Leone, Serbia, Bosnia, Syria, Iraq, Afghanistan and many other areas. There has also been an increased use of troops used in aid of disaster assistance. For example, in Canada, this includes the Swiss Air Disaster, Haiti and more recently in Nepal. All of these missions have created the need for increased services from the VA for both physical and mental disabilities. With the increasing political instability around the world, this need will almost certainly not decrease in the near future.

In all three countries, there are two basic ways to receive disability services from the VA. A service member may receive a disability rating before they leave active duty or a veteran might receive a disability rating after they leave active duty. The veteran disability system in all three countries is a fluid process. A disability rating can change over time. In fact, in Canada, the VA reports that the average length of time following service that someone will claim an injury is ten years (Thompson *et al.*, 2013). This suggests that not all injuries are visible or acknowledged at the time of release but it is also suggested that veterans are likely to attribute injury or illness following service to their time in service.

While theoretically disability ratings can go up or down, in reality, in the US, disability ratings tend only to go up; they are generally never lowered. In fact, for some types of injuries, the US Congress has dictated the level of disability; further stipulating that the rating can never be lowered. This has led many in the US to call for major changes in how veteran disability ratings are determined and sustained. Indeed, the disability system in the US appears to encourage disability, and to discourage recovery from injury, although to be fair to veterans, rarely do many types of injuries, such as musculoskeletal injuries improve over time.

In the US, datum indicates that veterans from the Iraq and Afghanistan wars are more likely to receive a disability rating than from any other veteran era, including Vietnam veterans. This makes the current population of veterans the most disabled veterans of any era in the US. Further, the most likely disability diagnosis is for pain, followed by a mental health diagnosis. These pain diagnoses are usually due to musculoskeletal injuries which occurred while on active duty. These latter findings highlight the tremendous physical toll military service can place on the individual. And, in fairness to the veteran, it is indeed difficult to fully recover from musculoskeletal injuries. Indeed, rather than improving over time, musculoskeletal injuries tend to worsen (IOM, 2010, 2013).

In the area of mental health, as treatment outcomes improve and the focus is increasing on recovery not disability, issues of labelling ex-serving members as 'permanently incapacitated' or 'disabled' need to be addressed. A system is needed that encourages recovery, while recognising that, for some, military service can result in an enduring vulnerability that may require episodic care but that these veterans can lead meaningful lives and make a full contribution to the community.

Stigma and barriers to care

All three counties continue to monitor the levels of stigma seen amongst active duty personnel (McFarlane *et al.*, 2011; Zamorski, 2011). However, the challenge of stigma continues even after the service member leaves active duty. This is critical to understand, especially given the mental and physical health status of veterans.

In the active duty military, internal (self) and external (public) stigma is acknowledged and efforts have been put in place to overcome the impact (Dickstein *et al.*, 2010).

In fact, the Canadian military has been recognised as the leader in Canada for destigmatising mental health for a large group of predominantly male workers (Wang *et al.*, 2016). However, there are no such efforts to help veterans in the US or Canada ian VA systems, overcome the pervasiveness of stigma. Indeed, there is very little attention given to this problem. It is perhaps one of the reasons why the US veteran population are the most susceptible to die by suicide, and why Canadian Veterans, of all ages, are amongst the highest users of in-patient and out-patient mental health services in the healthcare system.

Often veterans, similar to their active duty counterparts, tend to prefer self-treatment of their injuries rather than seeking care through the military or veterans' healthcare systems. Often these self-treatment programmes include over-the-counter medications, which can lead to misuse, especially for the self-treatment of pain. Many service members and veterans also use alcohol to self-treat mental health issues. These findings serve to highlight the urgent need to address stigma associated with seeking physical mental healthcare in service members and veterans.

The VA in Australia, in comparison, has attempted to harness emerging technology to address the issue of stigma. Work with young men in Australia has shown that those with psychological distress are likely to research for information and resources late at night online (Burns *et al.*, 2013). An educational campaign, utilising resources such as YouTube videos with veterans talking about their experiences have been developed to direct veterans to the 'At Ease' portal (see http://at-ease.dva.gov.au/). The focus of the 'At Ease' portal is the provision of education and adaptive self-management tools that highlight care pathways where needed.

Furthermore, and to facilitate this access to care, personnel with one-day service can receive treatment for diagnosed post-traumatic stress disorder, anxiety, depression, alcohol or other substance use disorders without it needing to be service related and never needing to make an injury claim (Commonwealth of Australia, 2016b; Gill *et al.*, 2015; see www.dva.gov.au/health-and-wellbeing/treatment-your-health-conditions).

An emerging barrier to care of interest to all three countries is the issue of whether the ex-serving member recognises that they have a problem (Zamorski, 2011). In these cases, it is the family or friends of the individual that will ultimately convince them to seek care. Any programmes to reduce stigma and increase mental health literacy needs to not only focus on the veteran but also on their families and peers.

The military and veteran family

Families are fundamental in the support system for service members experiencing a physical or mental health injury. What is often less recognised is the effect that caring for these individuals can have on those around them. The carers not only have to deal with the pain of seeing a loved one suffer, they also need to deal with the impact of symptoms such as social isolation and anger. Research is emerging that demonstrates the impact that living with a serving or ex-serving member with an injury from military service has on the family, in particular, the impact on children and potential trans-generational impacts (Commonwealth of Australia, 2014). Families are a key source of support for the service member but they also experience the stressors of transition and where the service member has an injury, they may also be the primary carer while shouldering the bulk of house hold responsibility.

In the US, the military and veteran family occupy a unique population. While the active duty military family has many programmes and services specifically developed and designed for the military family, the VA in the US has no responsibility for the veteran family. This is a particularly alarming state of affairs given that recent research has shown that the veteran family, including both spouse and children, has a very difficult time during the transition process. Often it is non-profit organisations that step in to support the veteran family by providing them support that the VA is not allowed to provide for them.

In Canada, it is a similar situation. The military runs a robust programme of Military and Veteran Family Resource Centres (MFRCs) at each base in the country (see www.familyforce.ca/splash.aspx). MFRCs provide a broad range of services for the military families including day care, clubs and leisure services and even health and dental clinics in some areas. The range of programming is broad and tailored to each geographical area so it can fill needs for that particular group of military families. It was recognised that many military families rely heavily on the social and health supports offered by MFRCs, especially when they are posted from one region to another. However, once the serving member has left the military, these services were no longer available because, as in the US, the military has no responsibility for the veteran's family. In a pilot project launched this year, four of the MFRCs across Canada are providing services for Veterans families for the first two years after the service member releases (for details, visit www.familyforce.ca/splash.aspx) (Military Family Service Program, 2016). This represents the first government-sponsored transition service for the family.

A legacy of the Vietnam veterans' advocacy in the Australia content, was the creation of the Veterans and Veterans' Families Counselling Service (VVCS) (see www.vvcs.gov.au). The services provide free and confidential, nationwide counselling and support for war and service-related mental health conditions, such as post-traumatic stress disorder, anxiety, depression, sleep disturbance and anger for veterans and their families. Importantly, support is also available for relationship and family matters that can arise due to the unique nature of military service. The service is based on an episodic care model where care can be accessed through individual counselling or group programmes as required across the life span. This service in Australia has seen a steady increase in clients from contemporary deployments seeking support, half of which are presentations by family members (Commonwealth of Australia, 2015).

Ultimately, a successful transition is where both the military member and the family have fully integrated back into the civilian community. It important that the military member and family focus on opportunities in the future and not what they have lost. In developing programmes in this area, the focus needs to be not on building dependence but by reinforcing resilience and empowering individuals to find new support networks and interests. However, due to the impact on the family where an individual has suffered a disability or injury, there also needs to be access to specialist when required to help facilitate this process.

Benefits to society

When military veterans and their families have a successful transition then society benefits. Indeed, for US veterans of the Second World War, specifically through the creation of the G.I. Bill, along with the growth of unions, have been credited for creating the middle class in America (see Castro and Kintzle, 2014). Yet, it is unlikely, given the major economic changes that have occurred in the US over the past 50 years, that today's veterans are likely to match the achievements of their Second World War comrades. High-paying blue-collar jobs that were plentiful following the Second World War are relatively non-existent today, making the transition of today's veterans into civilian life much more difficult.

Certainly in the field of employment, employers in all three countries need to recognise the benefits of hiring veterans. The veterans, like any other employee, would have, in all cases, to satisfy the tangible requirements of the job. However, what Veterans bring to the work place that others do not, are their intangibles – their commitment to teamwork, their training in leadership, their sense of duty to the company for whom they work and their focus on the mission to be accomplished rather than a search for personal accolades. These qualities, that are inherent to those who have served, are invaluable to an employer in a worker, but also in someone who may have the potential to motivate their entire workforce. This was confirmed by recent research in the US that indicated veterans are most noted for their ability to work in a fast-paced, changing environment; as well as their leadership, teamwork, flexibility, dependability, integrity and loyalty (Hall *et al.*, 2014)

Conclusion

Service members deploy into high-risk situations as representatives of each of our three countries. Experiences on deployment, especially in combat zones, can help build maturity and resilience but also can result in injuries. Whether serving members experience a physical or mental health injury, transition from active service to civilian life can be difficult, not only for the veteran but also their family. It is essential that we support our veterans and their families through this process and that we have services that reduce stigma, promote recovery and build resilience. This chapter has highlighted some programmes that have started to address these issues, however, it is important that they are fully evaluated so the international military community can develop a strong evidence base for best practice in the area of transition. Ultimately, the goal is to support all transitioning personnel to re-integrate fully and, in turn, to lead meaningful lives and contribute fully to their community.

References

Burns, J.M., Davenport, T.A., Christensen, H., Luscombe, G.M., Mendoza, J.A., Bresnan, A., Blanchard, M.E., Hickie, I.B. (2013). *Game On: Exploring the Impact of Technologies on Young Men's Mental Health and Wellbeing. Findings from the first Young and Well National Survey.* Melbourne: Young and Well Cooperative Research Centre. Available online at www.youngandwellcrc.org.au (accessed 20 January 2017).

Castro, C.A., Kintzle, S. (2014). Suicides in the military: The post-modern combat veteran and the Hemingway effect. *Current Psychiatry Reports*, 16, 460–9.

Cohn, A., Hodson, S.E., Crane, M. (2010). Resilience training in the Australian Defence Force. *INPsych, Australian Psychology Society*, April. Available online at https://www.psychology.org.au/publications/inpsych/2010/april/cohn/ (accessed 20 January 2017).

Commonwealth of Australia (2014). *Vietnam Veterans Health Study. Volume 1, Introduction and Summary of the Studies of Vietnam Veterans Families.* Canberra: Department of Veterans' Affairs. Available online at dva.gov.au (accessed 27 September 2016).

Commonwealth of Australia (2015). *Annual Reports – 100th Anniversary of the Gallipoli Landings.* Canberra: Department of Veterans' Affairs. Available online at www.dva.gov.au/sites/default/files/files/about%20dva/annual_report/2014-2015/preliminaries.pdf (accessed 27 September 2016).

Commonwealth of Australia (2016a). *ADF Transition Handbook.* Canberra: Department of Defence. Available online at www.defence.gov.au/DCO/Transitions/ADF-Transition-Handbook.pdf (accessed 27 September 2016).

Commonwealth of Australia (2016b). *Factsheet HSV109 – Non-Liability Health Care.* Canberra: Department of Veterans' Affairs. Available online at www.dva/factsheet-hsv109-non-liability-health-care (Accessed 27 September 2016).

Dickstein, B.D., Vogt, D.S., Handa, S., Litz, B.T. (2010). Targeting self-stigma in returning military personnel and veterans: A review of intervention strategies. *Military Psychology*, 22, 224–36.

Gill, G.F., Bain, R., Seidl, I. (2015). Supporting Australia's new veterans. *Australian Family Physician*, 45, 102. Available online at www.racgp.org.au/afp/2016/march/supporting-australia%E2%80%99s-new-veterans/ (accessed 27 September 2016).

Hall, K., Harrell, M.C., Bicksler, B, Stewart, R., Fisher M.P. (2014). Veteran Employment: Lessons from the 100,000 Jobs Mission. Santa Monica: RAND Report. Available online at www.rand.org/pubs/research_reports/RR836.html (accessed 27 September 2016).

IOM (Institute of Medicine) (2010). *Returning Home from Iraq and Afghanistan: Preliminary Assessment of Readjustment Needs of Veterans, Service Members, and their Families.* Washington, DC: The National Academies Press.

IOM (Institute of Medicine) (2013). *Returning Home from Iraq and Afghanistan: Assessment of Readjustment Needs of Veterans, Service Members, and their Families.* Washington, DC: The National Academies Press.

McFarlane, A., Hodson, S.E., Van Hoof, M., Davies, C. (2011). *2010 ADF Mental Health and Prevalence and Wellbeing Study.* Canberra: Department of Defence.

Mahar A.L., Aiken A.B., Whitehead M, Groome P, Kurdyak P. (2016). Description of a longitudinal cohort to study the health of Canadian veterans living in Ontario. *Journal of Military, Veteran and Family Health*, 2, 33–42.

Military Family Services Program (2016). Ottawa: CFMWS. Available online at www.familyforce.ca/splash.aspx (accessed 10 August 2016).

SMART Across Military and Civilian Life (2015). Available online at http://at-ease.dva.gov.au/highres/understanding-smart/military-civilain-life (accessed 27 September 2016).

Thompson, J.M., Van Til, L., Poirier, A., Sweet, J., McKinnon, K., Sudom, K., Dursun, S., Pedlar, D. (2013). *Health and Well-being of Canadian Armed Forces Veterans: Findings from the 2013 Life After Service Survey.* Charlottetown: Veterans Affairs Canada, Research Directorate Technical Report, 3 July 2014.

Wang, C.J., Lam, R., Ho K., Attridge, M., Lashewicz, B., Patten, S., Marchand, A., Aiken, A., Schmitz, N., Gundu, S., Rewari, N., Hodgins, D., Bulloch, A., Merali, Z. (2016). Preferred features of e-mental health programs for prevention of major depression in male workers: Results from a national survey. *Journal of Medical Internet Research*, 18, e132.

Zamorski, M. (2011). *Towards a Broader Conceptualization of Need, Stigma, and Barriers to Mental Health Care in Military Organizations: Recent Research Findings from the Canadian Forces.* Ottawa: North Atlantic Treaty Organization. Available online at www.dtic.mil/get-tr-doc/pdf?AD=ADA582781 (accessed November 2015).

14

POSTSCRIPT

Jamie Hacker Hughes

The needs of British veterans (or ex-military or ex-service personnel) are diverse, as this book has shown. Veterans may be young or old, skilled or unskilled, injured or intact. It is hoped that this book will have given the reader an insight into issues faced by today's veterans and by the organisations that work with them. The book has also afforded the opportunity to showcase numerous examples of good practice in psychological healthcare and social care for veterans and their families, both from within the UK and from overseas. It has been a privilege to edit this book and to work with so many good colleagues and I hope that many will find sources of information, enlightenment and encouragement within these pages.

INDEX